College Majors

~ AND ~

Careers

*A Resource Guide
for Effective
Life Planning*

FIFTH EDITION

PAUL PHIFER

⊲ **W9-BUA-401**

Ferguson
An imprint of ☑®Facts On File

College Majors and Careers, Fifth Edition

Ferguson
An imprint of Facts On File, Inc.
132 West 31st Street
New York NY 10001

Library of Congress Cataloging-in-Publication Data

Phifer, Paul.
College majors and careers : a resource guide for effective life planning / by Paul Phifer.— 5th ed.
    p. cm.
Includes bibliographical references and index.
  ISBN 0-89434-378-5 (pbk. : alk. paper)
  1. Vocational guidance—United States. 2. Vocational interests-—United States. 3. College majors-—United States. 4. Professions—United States. I. Title.

HF5382.5.U5 P445 2002
331.7'02'0973--dc21   2002152068

Ferguson books are available at special discounts when purchased in bulk quantities for businesses, associations, institutions, or sales promotions. Please call our Special Sales Department in New York at (212) 967-8800 or (800) 322-8755.

You can find Ferguson on the World Wide Web at http://www.fergpubco.com

Cover design by Cathy Rincon

Printed in the United States of America

EB 10 9 8 7 6 5 4

This book is printed on acid-free paper.

About the Author

Paul Phifer has more than 30 years of experience as an educator at both the high school and college levels. He currently serves as the director of the Career Resource & Assessment Center at Grand Rapids Community College in Michigan. Phifer holds a master's degree in guidance and counseling from Western Michigan University and is a Licensed Professional Counselor (LPC), a National Certified Counselor (NCC), and a National Certified Career Counselor (NCCC). A father of four, Phifer has long been active in his community, first as a Big Brother and now as a Christian Career Development Facilitator for his church.

Acknowledgements

I would like to express my gratitude for the advice and support given to me by the Ferguson Publishing staff. In addition, I am grateful to the Grand Rapids Community College administration for their support of my various professional development requests over the years. I am also thankful for the many career writers from whose research and publications I was privileged to draw. Although not mentioned in bibliographical form, their works provided this resource with the degree of accuracy and quality required. But most importantly, I must acknowledge my Savior, Jesus Christ, whose indwelling spirit deserves all the credit for anything I might have included within these pages that may serve to enable the user to live a more directed and fulfilling life.

Dedication

To my wife, Margaret, for her continuing support of whatever I have endeavored to seriously pursue.

Contents

Introduction 1

I. Clusters of Majors 3

II. Who Will Be Helped by This Book? 5

III. How This Book Is Organized and How to Use It 7

IV. Choosing the Major That Best Reflects You 10

    Accounting 11
    Aerospace Engineering 14
    Agriculture 17
    Allied Health Assisting and Technology 20
    Allied Health Sciences 23
    Anthropology 26
    Architecture 29
    Art 32
    Astronomy 35
    Banking and Finance 38
    Biology 41
    Botany 44
    Business Administration and Management 47
    Chemical Engineering 50
    Chemistry 53
    Civil Engineering 56
    Communications 59
    Computer Science 62
    Construction 65
    Criminal Justice 68
    Culinary Arts 71
    Economics 74
    Education 77
    Electrical/Electronic Engineering 80
    Electrical/Electronics Technology 83
    English 86
    Food and Beverage Management/Service 89
    Foreign Language 92
    Forestry 95
    Geography 98
    Geology 101
    Health Administration, Management, and Related Services 104
    History 107

Home Economics..110
Horticulture 113
Hotel/Motel Management....................................116
Industrial Engineering..119
Industrial and Precision Production/Technology 122
Law 125
Legal and Protective Services 128
Library and Information Sciences 131
Marketing and Distribution 134
Mathematics..137
Mechanical Engineering.....................................140
Mechanics and Related Services..........................143
Medicine 146
Metallurgical and Mining Engineering...................149
Military Science..152
Nursing and Related Services..............................155
Performing Arts..158
Philosophy 161
Physics 164
Physiology...167
Political Science 170
Psychology 173
Recreation and Leisure......................................176
Rehabilitation Therapy and Related Services 179
Religion and Theology 182
Secretarial (Management and Information) Science.....185
Social Work..188
Sociology...191
Transportation..194
Zoology...197

V. Career-Related Questions and Answers...................201
  1 What does the word "career" mean? 201
  2 What is career decision-making?..................................201
  3 Is career development different for an older adult
      than for a younger person? 201
  4 What is career success? 202
  5 What is a career resource or information center?.............202
  6 Are career development and placement
      services the same? 202
  7 What are career development services?..........................203
  8 What are job placement services? 203
  9 What does a good career counselor do?.........................203
 10 What is a self-assessment?...204
 11 What is a college major? 204

12 What should I know before selecting a major? 205
13 How do I actually select a major? 206
14 What should I do if I want a college degree but
   don't know what to pick for my major? 207
15 What should I do if I only want to pursue a short-term
   program of a year or less? 207
16 I must register for a full load of classes tomorrow
   but don't know what to take—what should I do? 207
17 What is an MBA?...208
18 Should I go for an MBA? 208
19 Should I get a PhD?..209
20 What is an apprenticeship? 211
21 What is co-op education?...211
22 What are home study courses? 212
23 What is virtual education? 212
24 What is an internship? 213
25 What is mentoring?...213
26 What is networking and can it help me? 214
27 What are "high-tech" jobs?...215
28 How do I know if a program or institution is good?........215
29 What is a liberal arts major?...216
30 What are career tests?...216
31 Should the results of my career tests determine
   what I do in the future? 217
32 Should I accept career test results that point
   to a single field?...217
33 What does it mean when the results of my career testing
   show that I am interested in just about everything?.........218
34 Am I required to take a battery of tests to effectively
   plan my career? 218
35 What is the difference between an aptitude test and an
   interest inventory?..219
36 Should I "test out" of a required course?.........................220
37 Can occupational projections be trusted?.........................221
38 What are some common problems that often
   hamper career development? 221

Appendices

A. Self-Assessment Survey..223
B. Descriptions of Selected Occupations.............................239
C. Definitions of Selected Skill Statements.........................267
D. Definitions of Values and Personal Attributes...................269

Index of Occupations

Index of Occupations..272

Introduction

College Majors and Careers is designed to help students and prospective students of all ages with the critical decision of choosing a focus in a collegiate program. Whether you are just graduating from high school, preparing to enter a college or university, or planning a midlife career change, this book can help.

You will find descriptions of more than 60 college majors along with a list of careers each major commonly leads to, skills and personality traits best suited for those careers, degree requirements, ways to enhance your knowledge and skills outside the classroom, and resources for more information.

Why is there a need for a guide of this type? To answer this question requires a closer look at the society in which we live. It is a society that is changing at a phenomenal pace. In the last 30 years, computerization has transformed the United States from a primarily industrial nation to one with an overwhelming emphasis on information and services.

Such changes have brought unprecedented comforts, conveniences, and leisure time, but they also have created a more complex and stressful lifestyle for many Americans. The cost of living has skyrocketed. New concerns have arisen about crime, the quality of education, and the condition of our environment, and family structures have changed dramatically.

The job security enjoyed by previous generations is becoming a fading memory as companies downsize and make other short-term economic decisions in an increasingly competitive and global marketplace. The hiring of temporary workers and outsourcing have become routine, and job turnover rates are high.

These factors, combined with the unfulfilled personal needs experienced by many, are spurring increasing numbers of people to return to school or change careers. As a result, the business of career development services is booming.

In this environment, it is more important than ever to start early in determining a career path. This means not only choosing the college major that is right for you, but also recognizing that an occupation alone will not lead to a fulfilling life. In your educational pursuits, it is important to consider life's other major aspects, such as family, religion, and leisure activities. Today's society demands a comprehensive sense of direction, including a healthy balance of professional and personal activity.

This does not mean that you should make a mad rush to select the right curriculum or job. What it does mean is that you should become thoughtfully involved in the process of determining the educational, occupational, and leisure-time activities that most strongly support your basic values and bring the deepest meaning and purpose to your life. This is a lifelong process, and when approached correctly, it will reflect your unique personality configuration and lead to true fulfillment.

But the process of choosing a college major can be daunting. *College Majors and Careers* aims to motivate students to begin a realistic assessment of their lives and career goals. Its special mission is to help students who are saturated with information or experiencing apprehension from a lack of career awareness or direction. By linking the selection of a college major and associated occupations with your personality traits and preferences, the book should help you to narrow your focus and choose an academic and occupational direction that is likely to be most fulfilling for you.

Keep in mind that this book is intended as a starting point only. People are complex, and each individual has his or her own personality, needs, talents, and goals. Further research and a consultation with a career counselor is highly recommended. Additional career information can be found in career resource centers, counseling offices, libraries, and departmental offices.

May you have success on your journey!

Section I
Clusters of Majors

The majors are presented alphabetically, but each one may be viewed as a member of a family of related majors. History and political science, for example, are both in the social science field. Here's how the majors cluster in general fields:

Agriculture and Horticulture
Agriculture
Forestry
Horticulture

Architecture, Construction, and Technology
Architecture
Construction
Electrical/Electronics Technology
Industrial and Precision Technology
Mechanics and Related Services
Transportation

Business and Related Areas
Accounting
Banking and Finance
Business Administration and Management
Hotel/Motel Management
Marketing and Distribution
Secretarial (Management and Information) Science

Culinary Arts, Food Service, and Recreation
Culinary Arts
Food and Beverage Management/Service
Home Economics
Recreation and Leisure

Engineering
Aerospace
Chemical
Civil
Electrical/Electronic
Industrial
Mechanical
Metallurgical and Mining

Fine and Performing Arts
Art
Performing Arts

Government, Public Service, and Related Areas
Education
Law
Legal and Protective Services
Library and Information Sciences
Military Science
Religion and Theology
Social Work

Health Care, Medicine, and Nursing
Allied Health Assisting and Technology
Allied Health Sciences
Health Administration, Management, and Related Services
Medicine
Nursing and Related Services

Language Arts
Communications
English
Foreign Language
Philosophy

Life Sciences
Biology
Botany
Physiology
Zoology

Physical Sciences and Math
Astronomy
Chemistry
Computer Science
Geology
Mathematics
Physics

Social Sciences
Anthropology
Economics
Geography
History
Political Science
Psychology
Sociology

Section II

Who Will Be Helped by This Book?

College Majors and Careers is a valuable reference guide for:

Students
- Introduces them to a wide variety of college courses, giving them an overview of their content and how they relate to other fields of study.
- Emphasizes personal traits associated with success in each major and in careers that most logically follow that major.
- Lists leisure activities associated with various majors.
- Gives the approximate length and level of education required for employment in related occupations.
- Provides a sampling of preparatory high school courses for each major.
- Offers answers to many career-related questions and answers.
- Provides a summary description of each major field.
- Lists transferable skills useful in pursuing various academic programs.
- Serves as a springboard and motivation for more in-depth and focused career exploration.
- Cites resources and organizations that provide more information about each field.

Junior and Senior High School Counselors
- Augments existing data on college study and occupational life.
- Helps motivate students by clearly showing the relationships between study and later life.
- Serves as a resource for teacher in-service and counselor training sessions.
- Provides valuable information for assisting students with college major planning, helping to reduce curriculum, program, and course misplacement.
- Lists organizations and books for more background information.
- Offers a sampling of preparatory courses to help students plan an appropriate four-year program.
- Provides answers to career-related questions asked by many students as well as responses to concerns of students with special needs.

Parents
- Helps to clearly define the relationship between college study and work.
- Provides background for discussing college plans with children who are current or prospective college students.
- Cites references and resources for additional exploration.

Teachers

- Highlights the importance of career guidance. Makes it easier to motivate students by citing jobs related to their studies. Provides information useful in course orientation and introductions.
- Provides information to help suggest career options to students.
- Encourages use of the classroom as a laboratory for career exploration activities.
- Provides information that may help misplaced or misguided students.
- Encourages high school and college academic departments to become more aware of and sensitive to the career activities of their graduates.
- Provides a textbook for use in career education classes or as a referral source in libraries.
- Provides answers to many questions frequently asked by students.

College Counselors and Other Student Personnel Workers

- Offers valuable help in counseling, attracting, and recruiting students in the admissions process.
- Provides background for building closer links between the counseling staff and academic departments.
- Provides a base of knowledge useful in meeting student questions about educational programs and career options.
- Answers many questions frequently asked by students, including those with special needs.
- Suggests part-time and summer job options that may be closely related to students' academic training and potential career choices.
- Serves as a useful resource for counseling center clients as a part of their self-development research.
- Shows employers how various aspects of college support services help educate and prepare future employees.
- Provides information related to career direction suitability that should be useful for Upward Bound and Special Services personnel in meeting governmental guidelines.

Section III

How This Book Is Organized and How to Use It

Each of the college majors and career briefs featured contains information presented in a consistent format for easy reference. Each entry begins with a general definition of the major field, then continues with the sections described below.

High School Courses

Lists high school courses or areas that are closely related to the major or considered useful background for that field. Course titles and grade levels vary greatly among high schools. Courses cited are not all-inclusive and are intended to be used as a general guideline by students, parents, teachers, and counselors. Educators will need to exercise professional expertise and include local courses that may apply to a particular field but are not listed. It is strongly suggested that students consult with counselors concerning preparatory courses related to particular fields of study.

Related Occupations

Lists jobs appropriate for graduates with that major, followed by the average minimum level of education required. Some occupations listed in this section require additional, specialized academic training for licensure and/or full professional status. Interested students are encouraged to contact a career counselor or academic advisor about these requirements before making a decision.

Following is a key for the codes used in this section:

AA: Associate's degree (or two full years of college study after high school) is generally required or very helpful. In some cases, people enter the field after taking specialized courses that may not require two full years.

B: Bachelor's degree (four or more full years of college study after high school) generally required or helpful. This may be a BA (Bachelor of Arts) or BS (Bachelor of Science) degree.

C: Certificate, normally awarded following successful completion of one year or less of training and/or formal college education.

M: Master's degree is preferred for the field; usually requires one or two years of study after the bachelor's. This may be an MA (Master of Arts) or MS (Master of Science) degree.

P: First professional degree is required; usually after completion of bachelor's degree. Some professional degrees include the BD (Bachelor of Divinity), LLB (law school degree), MD (Doctor of Medicine), and DDS (Doctor of Dental Science).

D: Doctoral degree is preferred for full professional status in the field. These include the PhD (Doctor of Philosophy) and EdD (Doctor of Education), which usually take from three to five years after the bachelor's degree. However, interested students often enter their field as Research Assistants (RA) or Administrative Assistants (AA).

V: Requirements vary greatly and/or vocational training is generally required; may include a combination of academic and work experience.

Sometimes, two or more codes appear after an occupation, which means that employers may hire candidates with different levels of education for the same job. For example, under Communications, employers might hire a news photographer with either a two-year certificate or a four-year bachelor's degree, depending on the candidate's other characteristics and qualifications. Definitions for the least familiar of the cited occupations appear in Appendix B on page 239.

Leisure Activities

Identifies hobbies, interests, and activities related to the major as well as to many of the occupations cited. This list provides a clearer picture of how extracurricular activities are related to majors, occupations, and other life endeavors.

Skills

Presents a partial list of skills that may be related to success in the major or related occupations or are frequently used in either. Some are natural inborn traits (aptitudes); others are acquired through practice, study, or extra effort (abilities). Some of the skills may be developed or discovered while a student is advancing in a course of study or occupation. The list of skills also provides a valuable and time-saving stop-check for students who may be mistakenly moving in an unsuitable direction. Definitions of skill statements that may be unfamiliar or difficult to understand appear in Appendix C on page 267.

Values and Attributes

Lists some of the motivations and personal characteristics generally associated with the field of study. This is not to imply that other values are not present or that these values are held by everyone interested in the subject. The values listed should help students determine if the subject, and subjects related to it, will move them closer to what is really most important to them in life. Definitions of some of the values and attributes that may be unfamiliar or hard to interpret can be found in Appendix D on page 269.

Resources

Lists books and/or professional associations that can provide additional information related to the major. For names of other associations in the major field of interest, see the *Encyclopedia of Associations* (published by Gale Research Company) or *National Trade and Professional Associations of the United States* (published annually by Columbia Books). These should be available in the reference section of most public libraries. Readers should augment the resources cited in this book with references recommended by a local counselor or teacher. Obviously, some of the references cited are subject to change due to books going out of print, revisions and updates, and address changes. Information provided by the references cited does not necessarily reflect the viewpoints of the author or publisher.

Be aware that due to similarities in definition, the words major, college major, field of study, field, subject, and like terms are used interchangeably and all refer to a student's major area of study.

Career-Related Questions and Answers

Provides answers to key career-related questions either frequently asked by students or considered to be important for certain populations. As a career counselor, I have been asked the same or similar questions dozens of times by students, parents, and other professionals over the years. These are the most common questions along with their answers.

Choosing the Major That Best Reflects You

This section describes and offers pertinent information about 63 of the most popular college majors today.

Most of you will be able to acquire valuable insight by simply browsing through and identifying those majors that most interest you. However, it is suggested that you use this popular approach as a stop-check measurement only. To obtain a more accurate self-appraisal in terms of choosing a suitable major, it is recommended that you complete the Self-Assessment in Appendix A on page 223. Doing a self-assessment consists of identifying and summarizing your most pronounced personality attributes and most cherished life and work values. After completing the self-assessment, browse through this chapter and select the top two majors you believe most closely reflect the answers on your self-assessment summary page. Make sure to also consider your weaknesses. Finally, while the self-assessment activity will more than likely prove to be extremely beneficial, it is strongly recommended that you consult a qualified career counselor to confirm your findings.

Accounting

Accounting involves the examination, organization, management, and design of accurate recording and reporting procedures of financial and business transactions. The study of accounting helps you learn the various ways of maintaining accurate, up-to-date financial and business records. This includes methods of compilation, verification, supervision, revision, examination, efficiency recording, designing, and reporting of such practices for both individuals and businesses. Knowledge and implementation of good accounting procedures are required to achieve success in finance or business, whether it be for an individual, family, or corporation. Some of the major specializations include tax accounting, management accounting, environmental accounting, forensic accounting, government accounting, international accounting, and consulting.

High School Courses

Accounting

Banking

Bookkeeping

Business

Business Math

Computer Operations

Computer Programming

Consumer Math

Economics

Math

Statistics

Related Majors

Assurance Services

Auditing

Environmental Accounting

Forensic Accounting

Government Accounting

International Accounting

Management Accounting

Personal Financial Planning

Public Accounting

Tax Accounting

Related Occupations

See page 7 for detailed explanation of key.

Accountant—B

Actuary—B

Auditor—B

Bank Officer—AA/B

Bookkeeper—V/AA

Budget Accountant—B

Computer Systems Analyst—B

Controller—B/M

Cost Accountant—B

Internal Auditor—B

Internal Revenue Agent—B

International Accountant—B

Investment Banker—B

Management Accountant—B

Management Consultant—B/M

Market Research Analyst—B

Programmer—B

Public Accountant—B

Credit Manager—AA/B	Purchasing Agent—B
Economist—B	Statistician—B
Educator—B/M/D	Tax Accountant—AA/B
Financial Analyst—B	Tax Preparer—V/B
Financial Planner—B	Treasurer—B
Insurance Agent—V/B	Underwriter—B

Leisure Activities

- Working as a part-time or volunteer treasurer or income tax preparer
- Maintaining an accurate personal checkbook
- Joining a professional accounting organization
- Reading accounting-related publications
- Joining a financial advisory board
- Solving problems involving analytical and logical processes
- Attending accounting-related lectures, trade shows or conventions
- Working as a student aide in a high school or college accounting department
- Working with a personal computer

Skills

- Proficiency in written and oral communication
- Ability to organize, analyze, and interpret numerical data
- Aptitude for accuracy and detail
- Proficiency with computers
- Ability to work alone and concentrate for long periods of time
- Ability to make sound judgments and decisions and to solve quantitative problems
- Ability to explain complex financial data to others
- Intellectual capacity to do well in most undergraduate and graduate college programs
- Ability to lead, supervise, and direct others

Values and Attributes

- Achievement
- Tendency toward analytical and logical thinking
- Patience
- Intellectual growth
- Integrity
- Independence
- Capacity for precision, detail, and order
- Thoroughness
- Recognition and appreciation from others
- Ability to frame inquiry and respond objectively
- Resourcefulness
- Skill with numbers
- Imagination

Resources

- Rosenberg, Martin. *Opportunities in Accounting.* New York, NY: VGM Career Horizons, 1999.
- Ryder, Tim. *Accounting Jobs Worldwide: A Directory of International Opportunities.* Cincinnati, OH: Seven Hills Book, 1998.
- **American Accounting Association**
  5717 Bessie Drive
  Sarasota, FL 34233-2399
  941-921-7747
  http://accounting.rutgers.edu/raw/aaa
  (offers student membership, accreditation information, and a helpful list of links and organizations)
- **American Association of Latino Professionals in Accounting and Finance**
  510 West Sixth Street, Suite 400
  Los Angeles, CA 90014
  213-243-0004
  http://www.alpfa.org
  (provides information about career opportunities, scholarships, and student memberships)
- **American Institute of Certified Public Accountants**
  1211 Avenue of the Americas
  New York, NY 10036
  212-596-6200
  http://aicpa.org
  (publishes preparation information for CPA examinations, provides job posting services, career path and internship information; see the Web site sections on Students and Career Resources/Resume Match)
- **American Society of Women Accountants**
  1595 Spring Hill Road, Suite 330
  Vienna, VA 22182
  800-326-2163
  http://www.aswa.org
  (offers scholarships and employment opportunities)

Aerospace Engineering

Aerospace engineering is the practical application of physical science and mathematics in the research, design, development, testing, launching, and production of aircraft, spacecraft, navigational systems, and related equipment, systems, and processes in an efficient and economical manner. It involves the design and production of power units, vehicle structure, aerodynamics and guidance control as well as airplane, rocket, missile, and satellite launching. Specialties include aircraft design, guidance systems, instrumentation, fluid mechanics, thermodynamics, satellites, helicopters, rockets, and military aircraft.

High School Courses

Algebra	Math
Calculus	Mechanical Drawing
Chemistry	Mechanics
Computer Science	Physical Science
Computers	Physics
Drawing	Trigonometry
Geometry	

Related Majors

Agricultural Engineering	Environmental Engineering
Architectural Engineering	Manufacturing Engineering
Bioengineering	Marine Engineering
Biomedical Engineering	Mechanical Engineering
Chemical Engineering	Metallurgical Engineering
Civil Engineering	Nuclear Engineering
Computer Engineering	Petroleum Engineering
Electrical/Electronic Engineering	Systems Engineering

Related Occupations

See page 7 for detailed explanation of key.

Aerodynamist—B	Marine Engineer—B
Aeronautical Engineer—B/D	Mechanical Engineer—B
Aerospace Airplane Pilot—AA/B	Metallurgical Engineer—B
Aerospace Engineer—B/D	Nuclear Engineer—B/D
Astronomer—D	Petroleum Engineer—B
Astrophysicist—B/D	Physicist—B/D
Computer Programmer—B	Research Engineer—B/D
Computer Science Engineer—B	Safety Engineer—B

Consulting Engineer—B/M/D Systems Analyst—B
Electrical Engineer—B Systems Engineer—B
Environmental Engineer—B

Leisure Activities

- Reading publications related to flying or space
- Viewing aircraft or space-related documentaries and programs on TV or at the movies
- Browsing the Internet for aviation-related topics
- Developing hobbies or collections related to model airplanes, cars, mechanics, or electronic games and equipment
- Air travel
- Attending lectures or conferences related to aviation or engineering
- Visiting science museums and exhibits
- Belonging to a club or organization such as the American Institute of Aeronautics and Astronautics
- Solving analytic and logic problems

Skills

- High proficiency in mathematics and physical sciences
- Ability to analyze, organize, and interpret scientific data
- Ability to work well with others
- Ability to make keen observations and sound judgments
- Aptitude for accuracy and detail, spatial perception, and abstract reasoning
- Sensitivity to economic considerations and human needs
- Proficiency in an area of specialization and in current practices and trends
- Ability to conduct and clearly communicate results of scientific research
- Intellectual capacity to perform well in most undergraduate and graduate college programs
- Proficiency with computers

Values and Attributes

- Creativity
- Knowledge
- Achievement
- Desire to help others live better
- Strong interest in aviation and space
- Interest in seeing ideas developed into practical use
- Curiosity
- Imagination
- Perseverance
- Responsibility
- Capability

Resources

- Landis, Raymond B. *Studying Engineering: A Road Map to a Rewarding Career.* Los Angeles, CA: Discovery Press, 2000.

- **American Institute of Aeronautics and Astronautics**
  1801 Alexander Bell Drive, Suite 500
  Reston, VA 20191-4344
  703-264-7500
  http://www.aiaa.org
  (offers student membership)

- **Institute of Electrical and Electronics Engineers**
  1828 L Street NW, Suite 1202
  Washington, DC 20036-5104
  202-785-0017
  http://www.ieee.org
  (See the Career & Employment Resources link on the Web site)

- **Junior Engineering Technical Society**
  1420 King Street, Suite 405
  Alexandria, VA 22314
  703-548-5387
  http://www.jets.org
  (offers a helpful list of links, printed resources, accredited schools, and student-related information; see the publication on aerospace engineering)

- **Society of Flight Test Engineers**
  PO Box 4037
  Lancaster, CA 93539-4037
  661-538-9715
  http://www.sfte.org
  (offers job placement assistance and student membership)

- **Society of Women Engineers**
  230 East Ohio Street, Suite 400
  Chicago, IL 60611-3265
  312-569-5223
  http://www.swe.org
  (provides an array of helpful information; see the Web site's Career Guidance, Scholarships, and Student Activities sections)

Agriculture

Agriculture is the science of growing crops and raising livestock. It involves planting, cultivating, fertilizing, harvesting, processing, and distributing fruits, vegetables, and nursery stock. It also includes the raising, feeding, breeding, and marketing of livestock. In addition, agricultural study exposes you to the various by-products of livestock, such as dairy products, eggs, honey, and fur. Agricultural research related to increasing the yield and quality of products and by-products, sanitation, diseases, methods of efficiency, and other areas is another important part of the field.

High School Courses

Algebra
Biology
Chemistry
Earth Science
Food Science

Geometry
Landscape Gardening
Math
Trigonometry
Zoology

Related Majors

Agricultural Economics
Agricultural Engineering
Animal Science
Botany
Crop/Soil Sciences
Entomology

Fisheries and Wildlife
Food Science
Forestry
Horticulture
Natural Resources Management
Park and Recreation Administration

Related Occupations

See page 7 for detailed explanation of key.

Agricultural Engineer—B
Agronomist—B/D
Animal Scientist—B/D
Biochemist—B/D
Biologist—B/D
Botanist—B/D
Cattle Farmer—V/B
Chemical Lab Technician—AA
Cooperative Extension Agent—B
Dairy Farmer—V/B
Educator—B/D
Entomologist—B/D

Feed Store Operator—V
Fish Farmer—V/B
Florist—V
Food Scientist—B
Horticulturist—B/D
Laboratory Assistant—AA
Landscape Gardener—AA
Microbiologist—B/D
Nursery Manager—V
Parasitologist—B/D
Physiologist—D
Soil Conservationist—B/D

Farm Equipment Mechanic—AA/V   Soil Scientist—B/D
Farmer—V/B   Veterinarian—P

Leisure Activities

- Working part-time or as a volunteer on a farm, ranch, pet shop, garden center, or zoo
- Gardening
- Owning and caring for pets
- Belonging to the National FFA Organization or 4-H
- Scouting
- Attending farm shows and fairs
- Working as a student aide or volunteer in a school science or college agriculture department
- Attending clinics, lectures, and workshops related to agriculture
- Reading agriculture-related publications
- Developing hobbies and collections related to gardening, horses, or raising livestock

Skills

- Good understanding of and familiarity with agricultural techniques and applications
- Physical stamina, good vision, and manual dexterity
- Ability to recognize differences in shapes, shading, and color
- Proficiency in reading and writing
- Ability to make keen observations and sound judgments
- Ability to organize, analyze, and interpret scientific data
- Ability to make appropriate decisions and apply scientific methods to agricultural concerns
- Ability to manage and supervise others
- Ability to work both alone and with others
- General knowledge of farm supplies, equipment, services, and business/marketing practices
- Aptitude for science and mathematics

Values and Attributes

- Independence
- Desire to help people
- Achievement
- Strong interest in agriculture
- Fondness for outdoor activities
- Ability to adapt to frequent changes
- Patience
- Responsibility
- Perseverance
- Resourcefulness

Resources

- **American Farm Bureau Federation**

  225 Touhy Avenue

  Park Ridge, IL 60068

  847-684-8600

  http://www.fb.org

  (sponsors a Young Farmer's and Rancher's Program for ages 18 to 35; Web site also provides an extensive list of links to various agricultural sites)

- **American Society of Agronomy**

  677 South Segoe Road

  Madison, WI 53711

  608-273-8080

  http://www.agronomy.org

  (has a career resources booklet)

- **National Agri-Marketing Association**

  11020 King Street, Suite 205

  Overland Park, KS 66210

  913-491-6500

  http://www.nama.org

  (offers student membership and scholarships)

- **National FFA Organization**

  6060 FFA Drive

  PO Box 68960

  Indianapolis, IN 46268-0960

  317-802-6050

  http://www.ffa.org

  (features an excellent career center that includes internship information, a database of over 330 agriculture-related career fields, and a wealth of additional career information)

- **U.S. Department of Agriculture**

  Higher Education Program

  14th Street and Independence, SW

  Washington, DC 20250

  202-720-2791

  http://www.usda.gov

  (offers information on agriculture, conservation, food and nutrition, weather, and employment)

Allied Health Assisting and Technology

Allied health assisting and technology involves the study of areas of technological support and health-related assistance to physicians, dentists, and other health professionals. The skills and services in this field are considered essential to effective health care programs. Among the various specializations are dental assisting, hygiene, and technology; medical laboratory technology and assisting; radiography; dietetics and nutrition; and physical and occupational therapy.

High School Courses

Biology	Psychology
First Aid	Science
Health	Sociology

Related Majors

Cardiovascular Technology	Radiologic Technology
Health Information Technology	Respiratory Technology
Medical Assisting	Surgical Technology
Orthotic/Prosthetic Program	

Related Occupations

See page 7 for detailed explanation of key.

Biomedical Equipment Technician—AA	Occupational Therapy Assistant—AA
Cytotechnologist—AA/B	Operating Room Technician—AA
Dental Assistant—AA	Ophthalmic Medical Assistant—AA
Dental Hygienist—AA	Optician—AA
Dental Lab Technician—AA	Optometric Assistant—AA
Diagnostic Medical Sonographer—AA	Orthotics/Prosthetics Technician—AA
Dietetic Technician—AA	Perfusionist—V
EEG Technologist—AA	Physical Therapy Assistant—AA
EKG Technician—AA	Physician Assistant—AA/B
Emergency Medical Technician—AA	Podiatric Assistant—AA
Environmental Health Technician—AA	Radiological Technologist—AA
Medical Assistant—AA	Respiratory Therapy Technician—AA
Medical Lab Technician—AA	Surgical Technician—AA
Medical Records Technician—AA	Veterinary Technician—AA
Mental Health Technician—AA	X-Ray Technician—AA

Leisure Activities

- Attending science fairs
- Visiting science museums and exhibits
- Reading health-related publications
- Serving as an aide in a church or community health agency
- Working part-time in a hospital, medical center, or nursing home
- Attending lectures and workshops related to health care services
- Watching health-related documentaries, movies, or TV dramas
- Actively supporting health care expansion and medical research drives

Skills

- Ability to react quickly and maintain emotional and physical composure in stressful situations
- High proficiency for accuracy and detail
- Proficiency in interpersonal communication
- Proficiency in memorization and giving and receiving directions
- Physical stamina, good vision, and manual dexterity
- Ability to make keen observations, sound judgments, and appropriate decisions
- Ability to work cooperatively with people of differing backgrounds
- Good motor coordination

Values and Attributes

- Achievement
- Desire to help others
- Health
- Wisdom
- Interest in challenges and working directly with people
- Helpful and friendly attitude
- Sensitivity to the needs and pain of others
- Willingness to work irregular hours and on weekends
- Industriousness
- Capability
- Poise
- Dependability
- Resourcefulness

Resources

- Caldwell, Lynn Borders. *Guide To Careers in Health Professions.* New York, NY: The Princeton Review, 2001. (detailed information about 19 health fields and list of schools that offer programs)
- Metcalf, Zubie. *Career Planning Guide for the Allied Health Professions.* Philadelphia, PA: Lippincott Williams & Wilkins, 1998.
- **American Health Information Management Association**
  233 North Michigan Avenue, Suite 2150
  Chicago, IL 60601-5800
  312-233-1100
  http://www.ahima.org
  (see Web site's Careers link)
- **American Medical Technologists Association**
  710 Higgins Road
  Park Ridge, IL 60068
  847-823-5169
  http://www.amt1.com
  (offers information about certification exams for lab assistants, phlebotomists, and dental assistants)
- **American Society of Radiologic Technologists**
  15000 Central Avenue, SE
  Albuquerque, NM 87123
  800-444-2778
  http://www.asrt.org
  (offers student scholarships and job placement services)
- **Commission on Accreditation of Allied Health Education Programs**
  35 East Wacker Drive, Suite 1970
  Chicago, IL 60601-2208
  http://www.caahep.org/index.htm
  (highlights 17 accredited allied health programs)
- **U.S. Health Care Associations and Societies**
  http://www.jcaho.org/general+public/making+better+choices/health+care+links/us+health+care+associations+and+societies.htm
  (provides an extensive list of health care links)

Allied Health Sciences

Allied health sciences is the study of health science areas that are related to and supportive of medical services provided by physicians and dentists. You learn ways of supporting and maintaining health care and medical services for individuals and populations. In addition, you study scientific, educational, and social approaches to identification, evaluation, prevention and control of disease, sickness, disorders, and injury. Special areas of concentration include environmental health, occupational safety and health, dental and medical technology, research, health education, diet/nutrition, and rehabilitation.

High School Courses

Algebra

Biology

Chemistry

Geometry

Health

Physiology

Psychology

Science

Sociology

Trigonometry

Related Majors

Athletic Training

Biomedical Engineering

Dietary/Nutrition

Health Administration

Health Education

Medical Illustration

Medical Research

Medical Technology

Microbiology

Occupational Safety

Pharmacy

Physician Assistant

Technical Writing

Related Occupations

See page 7 for detailed explanation of key.

Athletic Trainer—B

Biomedical Engineer—B

Biostatistician—B/M

Blood Bank Specialist—B

Clinical Chemist—B

Cytologist—B

Dental Hygienist—AA/B

Dietitian—B

Health Care Administrator M/D

Health Educator—B/D

Hospital Administrator—M

Medical Engineer—B

Medical/Scientific Illustrator—B

Medical Technologist—B

Nuclear Medicine Technologist—B

Nutritionist—V

Pharmacist—B

Physician Assistant—AA/B

Radiation Therapy Technologist—AA

Radiologic Health Specialist—B

Health Microbiologist—B   Technical Writer—B
Histotechnologist—AA/B   Tissue Technologist—V

Leisure Activities

- Attending science fairs, health exhibits, and visiting museums
- Reading health science-related publications
- Doing lab experiments and researching health science-related topics
- Working part-time or as a volunteer for a health agency, hospital, or school health science department
- Writing reports and summaries
- Watching TV programs and documentaries related to the health sciences
- Attending health-related lectures and workshops
- Belonging to a health science club, health guild, or professional organization
- Actively supporting health care expansion and medical research drives

Skills

- Ability to concentrate for long periods of time
- Ability to conduct and clearly explain scientific research
- Ability to make keen observations and appropriate decisions
- Ability to work under pressure and meet deadlines
- High proficiency for accuracy and detail
- Proficiency in observing, collecting, and analyzing scientific data
- Proficiency in reading, writing, speaking, and memorization
- General knowledge of health sciences
- Physical stamina, good vision, and manual dexterity
- Intellectual capacity to perform well in most undergraduate and graduate college programs
- Proficiency with computers

Values and Attributes

- Intellectual growth
- Achievement
- Wisdom
- Health
- Desire to help others and make a contribution to humanity
- Interest in public health and safety
- Sensitivity to the needs and pain of others
- Scientific inquiry
- Patience
- Self-discipline
- Thoroughness

Resources

- Caldwell, Lynn Borders. *Guide To Careers in Health Professions.* New York, NY: The Princeton Review, 2001. (detailed information about 19 health fields and list of schools that offer programs)
- Damp, Dennis. *Health Care Job Explosion!: High Growth Health Care Careers and Job Locator.* 3rd Edition. Moon Township, PA: Bookhaven Press, 1998.

- **American Health Information Management Association**

  233 North Michigan Avenue, Suite 2150

  Chicago, IL 60601-5800

  312-233-1100

  http://www.ahima.org

  (see Web site's Careers link)

- **American Hospital Association**

  1 North Franklin

  Chicago, IL 60606

  312-422-3000

  http://www.aha.org

  (provides information on careers in medicine and health care)

- **American Medical Association**

  515 North State Street

  Chicago, IL 60610

  312-464-5000

  http://www.ama-assn.org

  (provides information on careers in medicine and health care)

- **Commission on Accreditation of Allied Health Education Programs**

  35 East Wacker Drive, Suite 1970

  Chicago, IL 60601-2208

  http://www.caahep.org/index.htm

  (highlights 17 accredited allied health programs)

- **U.S. Health Care Associations and Societies**

  http://www.jcaho.org/general+public/making+better+choices/health+care+links/us+health+care+associations+and+societies.htm

  (provides an extensive list of health care links)

Anthropology

Anthropology is the study of the origin and development of humans. It provides students with a better understanding of human physical differences, language systems, and the way cultures today compare with cultures of the past. Anthropology is sometimes considered a branch of archaeology. Specialties include cultural anthropology, physical anthropology, linguistic anthropology, and various ethnosciences.

High School Courses

Anatomy/Physiology
Anthropology
Computer Science
Foreign Languages
Geography

History
Psychology
Social Studies
Sociology
Statistics

Related Majors

Archaeology
Art History
Biological Anthropology
Foreign Language
Geography
Geology

History
Linguistics
Medical Anthropology
Museology
Psychology
Sociology

Related Occupations

See page 7 for detailed explanation of key.

Anthropologist—D
Archaeologist—M/D
Archivist—M/D
Art Conservator—B
Bibliographer—M
Cultural Anthropologist—D
Curator—M/D
Educator—B/M/D
Ethnologist—M/D
Genealogist—B/D

Geographer—B/D
Historian—M/D
Linguistic Anthropologist—D
Museum Worker—V
Paleontologist—B/D
Research Associate—B
Social Worker—M/D
Sociologist—D
Technical Writer—B

Leisure Activities

- Visiting libraries and museums
- Participating in historical preservation efforts
- Doing historical research
- Camping, backpacking, and exploring
- Participating in archaeological field experiences
- Reading publications related to anthropology
- Joining an organization such as the American Anthropological Association
- Collecting relics, antiquities, and artifacts
- Working part-time or as a volunteer in an antique shop, museum, or college anthropology department
- Serving as a graduate research assistant

Skills

- Background of general knowledge
- Aptitude for foreign language
- Intellectual capacity to perform well in most undergraduate and graduate college programs
- Proficiency in reading comprehension, writing, and public speaking
- Ability to conduct and explain scientific research clearly
- Good vision, spatial perception, and manual dexterity
- Proficiency with computers
- Ability to accurately interpret and evaluate events, information, and ideas related to the past
- Interpersonal communication skills

Values and Attributes

- Achievement
- Appreciation for and understanding of other cultures
- Desire for recognition and to influence humanity
- Desire to research and explore the human past
- Interest in learning about the similarities and differences between cultures
- Patience
- Alertness
- Curiosity
- Resourcefulness
- Integrity
- Imagination
- Analytical thought

Resources

- **American Anthropological Association**

  4350 North Fairfax Drive, Suite 640

  Arlington, VA 22203-1620

  703-528-1902

  http://www.aaanet.org

  (provides information on careers in anthropology, publishes a career brochure, and has produced a video entitled *Careers in Anthropology*)

- **Archaeological Institute of America**

  656 Beacon Street

  Boston, MA 02215-2006

  617-353-9361

  http://www.archaeological.org

  (offers information about careers in archaeology)

- **Society for American Archaeology**

  900 Second Street, NE, #12

  Washington, DC 20002-3557

  202-789-8200

  http://www.saa.org

  (provides a definition of archaeology and information about academic programs, careers, job opportunities, fieldwork, scholarships, and student membership; publishes several informative career booklets)

- **Society for Applied Anthropology**

  PO Box 2436

  Oklahoma City, OK 73101-2436

  405-843-5113

  http://www.sfaa.net

  (has career listings and publications that cover current topics in the social sciences)

Architecture

Architectural study includes design, construction, and development of both physical structures and elements of the natural environment. It exposes you to the combined skills of creative aesthetics and practical function. The field of architecture involves planning layout, drawing, research, design, making modifications, selecting materials and equipment, estimating time requirements and costs, determining specifications, supervising inspecting, and writing reports. The results of architectural design are evident in houses, churches, office buildings, hospitals, airports, bridges, highways, parkways, recreational facilities, and community developments. Landscape architecture, naval architecture, design theory, preservation, and health care facility design are a few of the major specialties in this area.

High School Courses

Algebra	Drafting
Architectural Drawing	Drawing
Art Interior	Geometry
Blueprint Reading	Math
Calculus	Sculpture
Decorating	Trigonometry

Related Majors

Cartography	Landscape Architecture
Civil Engineering	Naval Architecture
Environmental Design	Solar Design
Graphic Design	Structural Engineering
Industrial Design	Urban Planning
Interior Design	

Related Occupations

See page 7 for detailed explanation of key.

Aeronautical Drafters—AA	Educator—B/M/D
Architect—B/M	Graphic Designer—AA
Architectural Drafter—AA	Illustrator—V
Architectural Technician—AA	Industrial Designer—V
Building Contractor—V	Interior Designer—V
Cartographer—B	Landscape Architect—V
Civil Engineer—B	Model Maker—V
Civil Engineering Technician—AA	Structural Engineer—B
Commercial Artist—AA/B	Surveyor—AA

Computer Graphics Technician—AA	Technical Illustrator—AA
Contractor Administrator—B	Technical Photographer—AA/B
Design/Building Specialist—V	Technical Writer—B
Drafter—AA	Urban Planner—V/M

Leisure Activities

- Taking art classes
- Drawing and sketching
- Developing hobbies related to building models
- Working part-time or as a volunteer on a construction project or in an architectural firm
- Joining an architecture-related organization such as the American Institute of Architecture Students or the American Institute of Architects
- Reading architecture publications
- Doing jigsaw puzzles and playing games of strategy
- Designing house furniture and landscapes
- Taking elective courses in geometry, mechanical drawing, and blueprint reading
- Attending architecture-related lectures, workshops, trade shows, or conventions
- Serving as a student aide in a high school or college architecture department

Skills

- Aptitude for accuracy and detail
- Ability to apply complex mathematical and engineering concepts to practical, real-life problems
- Strong spatial and form perception
- Ability to work with others as well as alone for long periods of time
- Ability to make keen observations and appropriate decisions
- Aptitude for drawing and sketching
- Ability to recognize differences in shapes, shading, and color
- Intellectual capacity to perform well in most undergraduate or graduate college programs
- Ability to work under pressure and meet deadlines
- Aptitude for math
- Ability to communicate ideas both orally and in writing
- Ability to conduct and clearly explain scientific research
- Proficiency with computers

Values and Attributes

- Creativity
- Achievement
- Desire for recognition and appreciation from others
- Aesthetic awareness
- Ability to adapt to fluctuations and deadlines

- Ability to accept public scrutiny and criticism
- Analytical thought
- Imagination
- Artistic nature
- Practical mind
- Perseverance

Resources

- Piper, Robert, et al. *Opportunities in Architecture.* New York, NY: McGraw Hill, 2000.
- **American Institute of Architects**

  1735 New York Avenue, NW

  Washington, DC 20006

  202-626-7300

  http://www.aia.org

  (provides information about accredited schools, job placement service, internships, and career development)
- **American Institute of Architecture Students**

  1735 New York Avenue, NW

  Washington, DC 20006

  202-626-7472

  http://www.aiasnatl.org

  (offers a job center, hot topics, and a resume/portfolio online service)
- **Association of Collegiate Schools of Architecture**

  1735 New York Avenue, NW

  Washington, DC 20006

  202-785-2324

  http://www.acsa-arch.org

  (sponsors student design competitions; provides lists of architecture schools and information for prospective students)
- **National Architectural Accrediting Board**

  1735 New York Avenue, NW

  Washington, DC 20006

  202-783-2007

  http://www.naab.org/index.htm

  (provides list of accredited programs in the United States)

Art

Art is the study of the various creative visual ways to express human thoughts, interests, attitudes, emotions, and ideas. It includes both fine art and commercial art. Fine art includes painting and drawing, sculpture, photography, printmaking, and crafts, such as ceramics, weaving, textile design, fashion design, jewelry design, interior decorating, and metalsmithing. Commercial art includes advertising and publishing and includes design, illustration, film, videography, and TV and the making of murals, cards, and posters. Art history, art education, art therapy, journalism, and public relations are other key areas of concentration.

High School Courses

Art	Painting
Art History	Photography
Crafts	Pottery
Drawing	Sketching
Jewelry Design	Watercolors

Related Majors

Advertising	Graphic Design
Architecture	Industrial Design
Art Education	Interior Design
Art History	Medical Illustration
Art Therapy	Photography
Cinematography	Studio Art
Commercial Art	

Related Occupations

See page 7 for detailed explanation of key.

Antique Dealer—V	Film Producer—B
Architect—B/M	Florist—V
Archivist—B	Freelance Artist—AA
Art Appraiser—B	Graphic Designer—AA/B
Art Director—B	Industrial Designer—V
Art Therapist—B/M	Interior Decorator—AA
Cartoonist—AA/V	Jeweler—AA/V
Cinematographer—V/B	Medical/Scientific Illustrator—B
Computer Animator—AA	Model Maker—V
Copywriter—B	Motion Picture Photographer—V
Curator—M/D	Painter—V/B

Designer—V/B
Educator—B/M/D
Fashion Illustrator—AA
Film Editor—AA

Photojournalist—AA/B
Sculptor—V
Sign Painter—V
TV Director—V/B

Leisure Activities

- Entering art contests
- Working part-time or volunteering in an art studio, museum, or advertising agency
- Collecting art, jewelry, or crafts
- Working as a photographer or artist for a school newspaper
- Attending art shows, festivals, and art exhibits
- Collecting antiques
- Developing skills in weaving, sculpture, macramé, furniture restoration, or photography
- Freelance drawing and painting
- Sewing, knitting, and crocheting
- Making and editing movies
- Helping to develop advertising material for local community service organizations and other groups

Skills

- Proficiency for accuracy and detail
- Ability to concentrate intensely for long periods
- Ability to communicate ideas and emotions creatively
- Ability to recognize difference in shapes, shading, and color
- Familiarity with computer-aided design (CAD) techniques
- Aptitude for spatial relationships
- Ability to meet deadlines
- Good finger and manual dexterity
- Ability to make keen observations and appropriate decisions

Values and Attributes

- Aesthetic awareness
- Independence
- Self-expression and personal fulfillment
- Desire to influence others
- Creativity
- Feel for design and form
- Ability to adjust to creative ups and downs
- Ability to adjust to close public scrutiny and criticism
- Imagination
- Curiosity
- Patience
- Perseverance

- Dedication
- Flexibility
- Self-discipline

Resources

- Haubenstock, Susan, David Joselit, and Elise Rosen. *Career Opportunities in Art*. New York, NY: Facts On File, Inc., 2001.
- **American Institute of Graphic Arts**
  National Design Center
  164 Fifth Avenue
  New York, NY 10001
  212-807-1990
  http://www.aiga.org
  (offers information on careers in graphic design)
- **Americans for the Arts**
  1000 Vermont Avenue, NW, 12th Floor
  Washington, DC 20006
  202-371-2830
  http://www.artsusa.org/aboutus
  (serves as a clearinghouse; advocates for creating opportunities for every American to participate in and appreciate all forms of art)
- **Association for the Advancement of Arts**
  655 Eden Park Drive, Suite 730
  Cincinnati, OH 45202
  513-721-2223
  http://www.aaae.org
  (Web site has an extensive list of helpful art resource links)
- **National Art Education Association**
  1916 Association Drive
  Reston, VA 20191-1590
  703-860-8000
  http://www.naea-reston.org
  (offers general information on arts study)
- **Society of Illustrators**
  128 East 63rd Street
  New York, NY 10021-7303
  212-838-2560
  http://www.societyillustrators.org
  (offers student membership, scholarships, career tips, and other resources)

Astronomy

Astronomy, a branch of the physical sciences, is the study of our universe: its origin, its physical properties, its changes, and the distribution of its physical phenomena. An astronomer observes the planets, sun, solar system, and galaxies and then analyzes, interprets, and reports the findings. Astronomy is closely related to mathematics and is usually considered a subdivision of physics.

High School Courses

Algebra	Math
Calculus	Physical Science
Chemistry	Physics
Computer Science	Science
Earth Science	Trigonometry
Geometry	

Related Majors

Aeronautical Engineering	Electrical/Electronic Engineering
Aerospace Engineering	Geology
Astrophysics	Geophysics
Chemistry	Meteorology
Computer Science	Physical Science
Earth Science	Physics

Related Occupations

See page 7 for detailed explanation of key.

Acoustical Engineer—V	Geologist—V
Acoustical Physicist—B	Geophysicist—B/D
Aerospace Engineer—B/D	Mathematician—B/D
Aerospace Engineering Technician—AA	Metallurgical Engineer—B
Astronomer—D	Meteorologist—V/D
Astrophysicist—B/D	Mineralogist—B/D
Biophysicist—B/D	Oceanographer—B/D
Cartographer—B	Optical Physicist—B
Computer Programmer—B	Radiographer—V
Educator—B/M/D	Research Technician—AA
Electrical/Electronics Engineer—B	Seismologist—V
	Systems Analyst—B

Leisure Activities

- Visiting planetariums, observatories, and science museums
- Involvement in outdoor activities
- Attending science fairs and exhibits
- Joining a photography club, the American Association of Amateur Astronomers, The Webb Society, or other astronomy club
- Watching TV programs on natural science
- Doing lab experiments and projects
- Reading astronomy or science publications
- Working part-time or as a volunteer in a planetarium, observatory, campus astronomy department, or weather station
- Operating a ham radio
- Computer programming
- Repairing radios/TVs

Skills

- Ability to analyze and solve quantitative problems and make appropriate decisions
- Proficiency in reading, writing, speaking, and memorization
- Ability to concentrate for long periods of time
- Aptitude for accuracy and detail
- Acute spatial and form perception
- Proficiency in mathematics
- Intellectual capacity to perform well in most undergraduate and graduate college programs
- Ability to conduct and clearly explain scientific research
- Good vision, finger dexterity, and mechanical ability
- Proficiency with computers
- Ability to make keen observations

Values and Attributes

- Achievement
- Independence
- Intellectual growth
- Recognition
- Analytical and logical thinking
- Intellectual curiosity about the atmosphere, space, and universal phenomena
- Fondness for physics and mathematics
- Imagination
- Self-discipline
- Perseverance
- Patience
- Precision

Resources

- **American Association of Amateur Astronomers**
  PO Box 7981
  Dallas, TX 75209-0981
  http://www.corvus.com
  (see the Web site's FAQ section to read the online article, "Career Profile: Astronomy."

- **American Astronomical Society**
  2000 Florida Avenue, Suite 400
  Washington, DC 20009-1231
  202-328-2010
  http://www.aas.org
  (maintains job register, has a resume posting service, and publishes a career brochure)

- **American Meteor Society**
  Robert Lunsford
  161 Vance Street
  Chula Vista, CA 91910-4828
  http://www.amsmeteors.org
  (geared to those interested in learning surveillance techniques related to meteor astronomy activity; for both amateurs and professionals)

- **Astronomical League**
  http://www.astroleague.org
  (composed of 250 amateur astronomical societies; encourages amateur astronomy)

- **The Webb Society**
  http://www.webbsociety.freeserve.co.uk
  (has publications, handbooks and observing guides, and links to other astronomy sites)

Banking and Finance

Banking and finance is a major field in business that involves the study of how money is stored, protected, received, distributed, and generally managed. Banking and finance is a broad area and overlaps with a number of more specialized fields, such as securities and insurance. Study in this area focuses on methods of deposits and withdrawals, checking and savings accounts, loans, interest rates, credit, trusts, investments, accounting procedures, budgets and financing, and securities. Areas of specialization are numerous and include savings and loans, checking, customer service, clerical, accounting, credit cards, computer systems, research, budget, expenditures and cost analysis, supervision and administration, trust services, and securities.

High School Courses

Accounting	Consumer Math
Bookkeeping	Economics
Business Math	Math
Computer Programming	

Related Majors

Accounting	Economics
Actuarial Science	Financial Planning
Business	Insurance and Risk Management
Business Economics	International Business
Business Management	Management Information Systems
Computer Programming	Mathematics
Computer Science	Statistics

Related Occupations

See page 7 for detailed explanation of key.

Accountant—B	Educator—B/M/D
Account Executive—B	Financial Aid Officer—B
Actuary—B	Financial Analyst—B
Advertising Manager—V	Financial Planner—B
Appraiser/Assessor—B	Insurance Agent—V/B
Bank Economist—B/D	Internal Auditor—B
Bank Teller—V	International Banking Officer—B
Branch Manager—B	Investment Banker—B
Budget Accountant—B	Loan Officer—B
Computer Programmer—B	Securities Clerk—AA/V
Controller-Accountant—B	Statistician—B

Correspondent Banking Officer—B Stockbroker—B
Cost Accountant—B Systems Analyst—B
Credit Analyst—AA/B Treasurer—B
Credit Manager—AA/B Trust Administrator—V

Leisure Activities

- Working as a part-time or volunteer treasurer or tax preparer
- Sitting on a financial advisory board
- Reading publications related to banking and finance
- Attending finance-related lectures, workshops, or conventions
- Participating in investment activities (real or virtual)
- Solving problems involving analytical and logical processes
- Joining a professional organization such as the American Bankers Association
- Working part-time in a bank, savings and loan agency, or credit union
- Serving as a student aide in an accounting or business department

Skills

- Ability to organize, analyze, and interpret numerical data
- Aptitude for accuracy and detail
- Ability to make sound judgments and decisions and to solve quantitative problems
- Ability to explain complex financial transactions and data to others
- Proficiency with computers
- Proficiency in written and oral communication
- Ability to communicate and get along with people of different personalities and backgrounds
- Knowledge of financial and economic history, practices, and trends

Values and Attributes

- Wealth
- Recognition and appreciation from others
- Achievement
- Good eyesight and emotional well-being
- Tendency to be organized, confident, and businesslike
- Ability to handle money
- Interest in working with both people and data
- Integrity
- Alertness
- Ambition
- Discretion
- Trustworthiness

Resources

- Paradis, Adrian A. *Banking Careers*. New York, NY: NTC/Contemporary Publishing Company, 2000.
- VGM Books, ed. *Resumes For Banking and Financial Careers*. New York, NY: NTC/Contemporary Publishing Company, 2001.
- **American Bankers Association**
  1120 Connecticut Avenue, NW
  Washington, DC 20036
  800-226-5377
  http://www.aba.com
  (sponsors job resume bank and online courses)
- **Association for Financial Professionals**
  7315 Wisconsin Avenue, Suite 600 West
  Bethesda, MD 20814
  301-907-2862
  http://www.afponline.org
  (has information on careers, certification, and industry news)
- **Center for Futures Education**
  PO Box 309
  Grove City, PA 16127
  724-458-5860
  http://www.thectr.com
  (provides information on workshops, home study courses, educational materials, and publications for futures and securities professionals; publishes "How to Become a Futures Broker," an informative 24-page booklet [cost: $3])
- **Credit Union National Association**
  PO Box 431
  Madison, WI 53701-0431
  800-356-9655
  http://www.cuna.org
  (offers training assistance; see Youth Programs & Resources in the Products and Services section of the Web site)
- **Financial Women International**
  200 North Glebe Road, Suite 820
  Arlington, VA 22203-3728
  703-807-2007
  http://www.fwi.org
  (offers career support for women in finance and has a job bank)

Biology

Biology is the study of life, from the simplest forms of plants and animals (including one-celled animals and algae) to the highly complex structure of the human being. It includes the study of how organisms are structured as well as how they function and relate to each other. Among the major branches of biology are human anatomy and physiology, botany (the study of plants), microbiology (the study of microscopic organisms), zoology (the study of animals), and ecology (the study of the relationship between organisms and the environment). You may elect to concentrate in one or more of the subdivisions.

High School Courses

Biology	Physiology
Chemistry	Science
Earth Science	Zoology
Health	

Related Majors

Agriculture	Genetics
Biochemistry	Horticulture
Biophysics	Marine Biology
Botany	Medicine
Chemistry	Microbiology
Environmental Science	Molecular Biology
Forestry	Zoology

Related Occupations

See page 7 for detailed explanation of key.

Biochemist—B/D	Microbiologist—B/D
Biologist—B/D	Mycologist—D
Botanist—B/D	Nutritionist—B
Dietitian—B	Occupational Therapist—B
Ecologist—B/D	Paramedic—AA
Educator—B/M/D	Parasitologist—B/D
Florist—V	Physical Therapist—B
Food Scientist—B	Physician—P
Forester—B	Physiologist—D
Funeral Director—AA/B	Public Health Director—B
Geneticist—B/D	Research Assistant—B/M
Horticulturist—B/D	Respiratory Therapist—AA

Medical/Scientific Illustrator—B   Taxonomist—B

Medical Lab Technician—AA   Veterinarian—P

Medical Librarian—M/D   Zoologist—B/D

Leisure Activities

- Attending science exhibits, county and state fairs, and 4-H shows
- Participating in Camp Fire Girls, Bluebirds, or Scouts
- Belonging to an environmental group, the Humane Society, a health club, or a community social group
- Browsing in floral shops or nature centers
- Working part-time or as a volunteer in a greenhouse or nursery
- YMCA/YWCA involvement
- Hiking, fishing, trapping, backpacking, or gardening
- Visiting zoos or museums
- Owning or caring for pets
- Reading science magazines, books, and other related publications
- Performing lab experiments
- Taking nature walks
- Bird-watching
- Developing hobbies or collections related to leaves, butterflies, trees, flowers, or other natural items

Skills

- Ability to concentrate for long periods of time
- Ability to make keen observations and appropriate decisions
- Proficiency in reading, writing, thinking, questioning, analyzing, and problem solving
- Ability to operate scientific equipment
- Intellectual capacity to perform well in most undergraduate and graduate college programs
- Proficiency for accuracy and detail
- Ability to organize and maintain accurate records
- Proficiency in speaking and memorization
- Ability to conduct and clearly explain scientific research
- Good vision and manual dexterity
- Thorough knowledge of basic biological theories and practices

Values and Attributes

- Achievement
- Creativity
- Desire to help humanity
- Intellectual growth
- Precision
- Enthusiasm for exploring
- Spirit of scientific inquiry

- Strong interest in living organisms
- Diligence
- Endurance
- Interest in challenges
- Patience
- Perseverance

Resources

- Belikoff, Kathleen. *Opportunities in Biological Sciences.* New York, NY: NTC/Contemporary Publishing Company, 1999.
- Miller, Louise. *Careers for Nature Lovers and Other Outdoor Types.* New York, NY: NTC/Contemporary Publishing Company, 2001.
- **American Institute of Biological Sciences**
  Communications Office
  1444 Eye Street, NW, Suite 200
  Washington, DC 20005
  202-628-1500
  http://www.aibs.org
  (publishes various brochures and a book entitled, *Guide to Non-Traditional Careers in Science*)
- **American Society for Biochemistry and Molecular Biology**
  Education Information
  9650 Rockville Pike
  Bethesda, MD 20814-3996
  301-530-7145
  http://www.asbmb.org
  (offers career information, a list of schools, and information on PhD standards)
- **American Society for Microbiology**
  1752 N Street, NW
  Washington, DC 20036
  http://www.asmusa.org
  (offers summer career prep institute and special programs for minorities; publishes *Careers in Biology*)
- **Ecological Society of America**
  1707 H Street, NW, Suite 400
  Washington, DC 20006
  202-833-8773
  http://esa.org
  (offers a wide variety of publications, including *Careers in Ecology* and the journal *Issues in Ecology*)

Botany

Botany is a major branch of the biological sciences and involves the study of plants. Plant groups typically included are bacteria, algae, fungi, lichens, mosses, ferns, conifers, and flowering plants. Botany focuses on plant growth, structure, function, classification, distribution, and reproduction. Within the field of botany are a number of specialized areas, including morphology (microscopic and macroscopic plant structure), horticulture (the cultivation of ornamental plants and fruit and vegetable crops), and forestry. Plant habitat and the relationship of plants to humans and to our general environment are other important areas of botanical study.

High School Courses

Biology	Landscape Gardening
Chemistry	Physiology
Earth Science	Science

Related Majors

Agriculture	Economic Botany
Agronomy	Food Science and Technology
Biochemistry	Forestry
Biology	Horticulture
Biophysics	Landscape Architecture
Biotechnology	Molecular Biology
Chemistry	Plant Science

Related Occupations

See page 7 for detailed explanation of key.

Agronomist—B/D	Groundskeeper—V
Bacteriologist—B/D	Horticulturist—B/D
Biochemist—B/D	Landscape Gardener—AA
Botanist—B/D	Mycologist—D
Cooperative Extension Worker—B	Nursery Manager—V
Curator—M/D	Nutritionist—V
Cytologist—B/D	Phycologist—M/D
Dietitian—B	Plant Breeder—V
Ecologist—B/D	Range Manager—AA/B
Educator—B/M/D	Seed Analyst—B
Farmer—V/B	Silviculturist—V
Farm/Ranch Manager—B/V	Soil Conservationist—B/D
Florist—V	Taxonomist—B

Food Scientist—B

Forester—B

Geneticist—B/D

Virologist—M/D

Wood Technologist—B

Leisure Activities

- Visiting nature centers, botanical gardens, conservatories, farms, parks, and museums
- Attending flower shows and fairs
- Browsing through floral shops, 4-H exhibits, and science displays
- Hiking, exploring, camping, sightseeing, and nature photography
- Gardening, canning, and freezing foods
- Sailing, canoeing, and swimming
- Developing hobbies and collections related to flowers, leaves, house plants, or floral design
- Working part-time or as a volunteer in a greenhouse, nursery, state park, or camp
- Joining a science club, orchid club, or conservation group
- Reading science publications
- Supporting or participating in natural resource preservation efforts
- Undertaking nature studies or rural expeditions

Skills

- Proficiency in observing, collecting, and analyzing data
- Physical stamina, good vision, and manual dexterity
- Ability to concentrate for long periods of time
- Proficiency in reading, writing, speaking, and memorization
- Ability to conduct and clearly explain scientific research
- Proficiency for accuracy and detail
- Intellectual ability to perform well in most undergraduate or graduate college programs
- Proficiency in problem solving and decision making
- Thorough knowledge of general biology

Values and Attributes

- Aesthetic awareness
- Independence
- Intellectual growth
- Interest in public health and safety
- Fondness for outdoor activities
- Deep appreciation for nature
- Green thumb
- Thoroughness
- Perseverance
- Patience
- Curiosity

Resources

- Miller, Louise. *Careers for Nature Lovers and Other Outdoor Types.* New York, NY: NTC/Contemporary Publishing Company, 2001.
- **American Society for Horticultural Science**
  113 South West Street, Suite 200
  Alexandria, VA 22314-2851
  703-836-4606
  http://www.ashs.org
  (offers student membership and sponsors college horticultural clubs)
- **American Society of Agronomy**
  677 Segoe Road
  Madison, WI 53711
  608-273-8080
  http://www.agronomy.org
  (offers online career development and placement service and publishes a career booklet entitled "Exploring Careers in Agronomy")
- **Botanical Society of America**
  Attn: Business Manager
  1735 Neil Avenue
  Columbus, OH 43210-1293
  614-292-3519
  http://www.botany.org
  (offers an excellent online pamphlet entitled, "Careers in Botany," publishes *Botany for the Next Millennium,* and provides an extensive list of resources)
- **The Nature Conservancy**
  4245 North Fairfax Drive, Suite 100
  Arlington, VA 22203-1606
  800-628-6860
  http://nature.org
  (offers internship opportunities with state chapters or at its headquarters)

Business Administration and Management

The field of business administration and management involves the coordination, implementation, promotion, supervision, and direction of the activities of individuals, organizations, and businesses. Effective techniques of business management constitute the backbone of strong economic, political, and social systems at all levels. Study in this major exposes you to methods of operation, coordination, sales and marketing, finance and budget, personnel, property and equipment management/maintenance, and security. Other key areas of concentration are organization, leadership, planning, interpersonal communications, delegating, supervising community resources, employee organizations, and policy making/implementation.

High School Courses

Accounting	Management
Business	Psychology
Business Law	Sociology
Economics	Speech

Related Majors

Accounting	International Business
Business Communications	Labor/Personnel Relations
Business Education	Management Information
Entrepreneurship	Marketing
Finance and Banking	Operations Management and Supervision
Human Resources Management	

Related Occupations

See page 7 for detailed explanation of key.

Accountant—B	Hotel/Motel Manager—V/B
Advertising Executive—B	Human Resources Manager—B
Airport Manager—B	Production Superintendent—B
Chamber of Commerce President—B	Public Relations Specialist—B
Chief Executive Officer—B	Recreation Director—B
City Manager—B	Restaurant Manager—AA/V

College Dean—M/D	Sales Manager—V
Comptroller—B/M	School Administrator—M/D
Consultant—B/D	Traffic Manager—V
Convention Manager—B	TV Director—V
Database Manager—B	Warehouse Manager—AA/V
Department Store Manager—B	Wholesaler—B
Director of Career Placement—B/M	YMCA/YWCA Director—B
Director of Food Services—B	

Leisure Activities

- Working part-time in a local business establishment
- Participating in oratory contests
- Planning, starting, or managing a part-time business endeavor
- Assisting in the planning of a civic or social event
- Playing games of strategy, competition, or achievement
- Attending lectures, workshops, and conferences related to business management
- Serving as a student aide in a college business department
- Participating in a management training program
- Serving as a volunteer in a social agency
- Belonging to a Junior Achievement Club or a professional business organization

Skills

- Ability to clearly communicate ideas and concepts to others
- Proficiency in reading, writing, and speaking
- Ability to solve problems and make appropriate decisions
- Strong background in business, marketing, and human relations
- Proficiency in organizing, planning, coordinating, and directing activities
- Ability to inspire productivity and exact loyalty from others
- Ability to respond spontaneously and work well under pressure
- Intellectual capacity to perform well in most undergraduate and graduate college programs
- Aptitude for leadership
- Proficiency in interpersonal communication
- Proficiency with computers

Values and Attributes

- Achievement
- Wealth
- Prestige
- Willingness to work beyond expectations
- Tendency to be responsible, show initiative, and exercise patience
- Leadership
- Decisiveness

- Resourcefulness
- Diplomacy
- Integrity
- Ambition

Resources

- **American Business Women's Association**

  9100 Ward Parkway

  PO Box 8728

  Kansas City, MO 64114-0728

  800-228-0007

  http://www.abwahq.org

  (has information on educational programs and career resources)

- **American Management Association**

  1601 Broadway

  New York, NY 10019

  212-586-8100

  http://www.amanet.org

  (provides job postings, online employment application, internships, and a career book)

- **Careers in Business**

  http://www.careers-in-business.com

  (Web site covers a variety of business career areas and other business information)

- **Junior Achievement**

  One Education Way

  Colorado Springs, CO 80906

  719-540-8000

  http://www.ja.org

  (nonprofit organization that teaches young people about business, free enterprise, and the workforce)

- **U.S. Small Business Administration**

  409 Third Street, SW

  Washington, DC 20416

  800-U-ASK-SBA

  http://www.sbaonline.sba.gov

  (Web site has small business statistics and other relevant information)

Chemical Engineering

Chemical engineering is the the practical application of science and mathematics in the process, manufacture, equipment design, and development related to raw and synthetic substances and energy in an economical and efficient manner. It contributes to the development of products that affect nearly every aspect of life, including foods, fuels, drugs, plastics, glass, soaps, paints, paper, and much more. Areas of special concentration include plastics, petroleum, research and development, environmental control, food, energy, pharmaceuticals, and education.

High School Courses

Algebra	Math
Calculus	Physical Science
Chemistry	Physics
Computer Science	Science
Earth Science	Trigonometry
Geometry	

Related Majors

Agronomy	Material Engineering
Chemistry	Mathematics
Electrical Engineering	Metallurgical Engineering
Engineering Physics	Mining/Mineral Engineering
Environmental Engineering	Petroleum Engineering
Food Science	Pharmacy

Related Occupations

See page 7 for detailed explanation of key.

Agricultural Engineer—B	Food Scientist—B
Agronomist—B	Geological Engineer—B
Biochemist—B/D	Materials Handling Engineer—B
Ceramic Engineer—B	Metallurgical Engineer—B
Chemical Engineer—B	Metallurgist—B
Chemical Engineering Technician—AA	Nuclear Engineer—B/D
Chemical Research Engineer—B/D	Petroleum Engineer—B
Chemist—B/D	Pharmacist—B
Computer Science Engineer—B	Pharmacologist—D
Consulting Engineer—B/M/D	Plastics Engineer—B
Electrical Engineer—B	Safety Engineer—B

Environmental Engineer—B   Textile Engineer—B
Fire Protection Engineer—V   Toxicologist—B/D

Leisure Activities

- Performing lab experiments and doing science projects
- Attending science fairs, exhibits, and demonstrations
- Reading publications related to chemistry or engineering
- Working part-time or as a volunteer in a hospital, chemistry lab, engineering firm, science department, or pharmaceutical firm
- Joining a chemistry or engineering club or organization

Skills

- High proficiency in mathematics and physical sciences
- Ability to analyze, organize, and interpret scientific data
- Ability to work well with others
- Ability to make keen observations and sound judgments
- Aptitude for accuracy and detail, spatial perception, and abstract reasoning
- Sensitivity to economic considerations and human needs
- Proficiency in an area of specialization and knowledgeable of current practices and trends
- Ability to conduct and clearly communicate scientific research
- Intellectual capacity to perform well in most undergraduate and graduate college programs
- Proficiency with computers

Values and Attributes

- Creativity
- Achievement
- Knowledge
- Desire to help others live better
- Sensitivity to the health and safety of others
- Desire to see ideas developed into practical use
- Curiosity
- Integrity
- Perseverance
- Responsibility
- Imagination

Resources

- Friary, Richard J. *Jobs in the Drug Industry: A Career Guide for Chemists.* San Diego, CA: Academic Press Limited, 2000.
- Woodburn, John. *Opportunities in Chemistry Careers.* New York, NY: VGM Career Horizons, 1997.
- **American Chemical Society**
  1155 16th Street, NW
  Washington, DC 20036
  800-227-5558
  http://www.acs.org
  (offers career guidance, counseling, and employment help; see the Career Services link on the Web site)
- **American Institute of Chemical Engineers**
  3 Park Avenue
  New York, NY 10016-5991
  800-242-4363
  http://www.aiche.org
  (offers student membership, internships, career-related information, and related links)
- **International Chemistry Society**
  Chemsoc, Royal Society of Chemistry
  Burlington House
  Piccadilly, London
  WIJ 0BA UK
  http://www.chemsoc.org
  (Careers and Job Centre section of the Web site provides reviews of chemistry career information, job service, career fairs, and personal profiles)
- **Junior Engineering Technical Society**
  1420 King Street, Suite 405
  Alexandria, VA 22314
  703-548-5387
  http://www.jets.org
  (sponsors activities geared to assist students to determine engineering readiness, special outreach to minorities, information about careers, helpful links, etc.)

Chemistry

Chemistry is a major branch of the physical sciences and involves the study of substances and energy. It focuses on their composition, characteristics, changes, reactions, uses, and benefits and dangers to humanity. Major sub-branches within chemistry include inorganic and organic chemistry, analytical chemistry, applied chemistry, biochemistry, and physical chemistry. Chemistry is used to produce food, clothing, furniture, drugs, plastics, glass, paper, and electronic devices. Knowledge of chemistry is crucial to environmental protection efforts and human health and safety.

High School Courses

Algebra

Chemistry

Cooking

Earth Science

Foods

Geometry

Math

Physical Science

Science

Trigonometry

Related Majors

Agriculture

Biochemistry

Chemical Engineering

Chemistry Education

Dietetics

Food Science

Mathematics

Medicine

Pharmacy

Toxicology

Related Occupations

See page 7 for detailed explanation of key.

Agronomist—B/D

Anesthesiologist—B

Biochemist—B/D

Ceramic Engineer—B

Chemical Engineer—B

Chemist—B/D

Consumer Protection Specialist—B

Dietitian—B

Educator—B/M/D

Food and Drug Analyst—B

Food Scientist—B

Geneticist—B/D

Geologist—B

Industrial Health Engineer—B

Internist—P

Laboratory Analyst—B

Metallurgist—B

Nuclear Scientist—B/D

Nutritionist—B

Patent Examiner—B/P

Pharmacist—B

Pharmacologist—D

Pharmaceutical Sales Representative—B

Physicist—B/D

Science Technician—AA

Technical Writer—B

Toxicologist—B/D

Wood Scientist—D

Leisure Activities

- Performing lab experiments and doing science projects
- Attending science fairs, exhibits, and demonstrations
- Reading chemistry and science journals
- Cooking
- Watching scientific TV programs
- Working part-time or as a volunteer in a hospital, chemistry lab, or pharmaceutical firm
- Joining a chemistry or science club

Skills

- Good vision and manual dexterity
- Ability to conduct and clearly explain scientific research
- Aptitude for accuracy and detail
- Ability to organize, analyze, and interpret scientific data
- Proficiency in reading, writing, speaking, and memorization
- Ability to make keen observations and appropriate decisions
- Strong mathematical background
- Intellectual capacity to perform well in most undergraduate and graduate college programs
- Proficiency with computers

Values and Attributes

- Achievement
- Intellectual growth
- Public recognition
- Desire to help humanity
- Willingness to take risks
- Pleasure in learning new skills
- Sensitivity to the health and safety of others
- Patience
- Curiosity
- Integrity
- Flexibility
- Responsibility

Resources

- Friary, Richard J. *Jobs in the Drug Industry: A Career Guide for Chemists.* San Diego, CA: Academic Press Limited, 2000.
- Woodburn, John. *Opportunities in Chemistry Careers.* New York, NY: VGM Career Horizons, 1997.
- **American Chemical Society**
  1155 16th Street, NW
  Washington, DC 20036
  800-227-5558
  http://www.acs.org
  (offers career guidance, counseling, and employment help; see the Career Services section of the Web site)
- **American Institute of Chemical Engineers**
  3 Park Avenue
  New York, NY 10016-5991
  800-242-4363
  http://www.aiche.org
  (offers student membership, internships, career-related information, and helpful links)
- **International Chemistry Society**
  Chemsoc, Royal Society of Chemistry
  Burlington House
  Piccadilly, London
  WlJ 0BA UK
  http://www.chemsoc.org
  (Careers and Job Centre section of the Web site provides review of chemistry career information, job service, career fairs, and personal profiles)

Civil Engineering

Civil engineering is the practical, economic, and efficient application of mathematical and scientific knowledge, experience, and theory in the use of material and natural resources to design and supervise the building of structures and facilities. Studies include the techniques of constructing bridges, dams, roads, railways, airports, water disposal systems, buildings, pipelines, and more. The four main areas of civil engineering are structures, transportation, sanitation, and soils. Specialties include geotechnical, environmental, transportation, hydraulic, structural, and pipeline engineering.

High School Courses

Algebra	Geometry
Architectural Drawing	Industrial Arts
Blueprint Reading	Math
Calculus	Physical Science
Chemistry	Physics
Drafting	Science
Drawing	Trigonometry
Earth Science	

Related Majors

Architecture	Geological Engineering
Architectural Engineering	Mining and Mineral Engineering
Construction Engineering	Petroleum Engineering
Electrical Engineering	Structural Engineering
Engineering Physics	Surveying
Environmental Engineering	Transportation and Material Moving

Related Occupations

See page 7 for detailed explanation of key.

Architect—B/M	Industrial Engineer—B
Architectural Engineer—B	Mechanical Engineer—B
Civil Engineer—B	Mining Engineer—B
Civil Engineering Technician—AA	Petroleum Engineer—B
Construction Engineer—B	Photogrammetrist—B
Consulting Engineer—B/M/D	Pipeline Engineer—B
Ecologist—B	Public Works Engineer—B
Environmental Engineer—B	Research Engineer—B/D
Geological Engineer—B	Safety Engineer—B

Geologist—B

Geotechnical Engineer—B

Highway Engineer—B

Hydraulics Engineer—B

Hydrologist—B

Sanitary Engineer—B

Structural Engineer—B

Transportation Engineer—B

Urban Planner—B/M

Leisure Activities

- Participating in clubs or organizations that require you to make oral presentations and write reports
- Doing jigsaw puzzles and playing games of strategy
- Solving analytic and logic problems
- Reading publications related to civil engineering
- Becoming a member of a student or professional engineering organization
- Attending engineering-related lectures, workshops, or conferences
- Engaging in hobbies related to building and designing structures
- Working part-time or as a volunteer with an engineering or construction firm or in a college engineering department

Skills

- Ability to analyze, organize, and interpret scientific data
- Ability to work well with others
- Ability to make appropriate decisions and solve problems
- Ability to make keen observations and sound judgments
- Aptitude for accuracy and detail
- Proficiency in mathematics and science
- Proficiency in spatial perception and abstract reasoning
- Sensitivity to economic considerations and human needs
- Proficiency in an area of specialization and knowledge of current practices and trends
- Proficiency in written and oral communication
- Ability to conduct and clearly communicate scientific research
- Intellectual capacity to perform well in most undergraduate and graduate college programs
- Proficiency with computers

Values and Attributes

- Creativity
- Knowledge
- Desire to help others live better
- Achievement
- Ability to work on a team
- Enjoyment of challenges and the outdoors
- Interest in seeing ideas developed into practical uses
- Interest in moving from place to place
- Curiosity

- Alertness
- Flexibility
- Patience
- Responsibility
- Imagination

Resources

- Hagerty, Joseph, and Louis Cohn. *Opportunities in Civil Engineering Careers.* New York, NY: VGM Career Horizons, 1997.
- **American Society of Civil Engineers**
  1801 Alexander Bell Drive
  Reston, VA 20191-4400
  800-548-2723
  http://www.asce.org
  (offers student career development service and student membership and publishes *Engineering Your Future* by Stuart G. Walesh)
- **Junior Engineering Technical Society**
  1420 King Street, Suite 405
  Alexandria, VA 22314
  703-548-5387
  http://www.jets.org
  (sponsors activities geared to assist students to determine engineering readiness, special outreach to minorities, information about careers, helpful links, etc.)

Communications

Communications is the branch of language arts that focuses on the comprehensive expression of sound and visual, oral, and written symbols. Study in communications is geared toward understanding the many ways human beings develop, collect, disseminate, and transfer information through symbols, particularly via the mass media. Also included are the various ways that communication informs, persuades, entertains, and controls. Communication is involved in almost everything we do and ranges from the simplest non-verbal communication efforts to the complex electronic messages of computers. Major areas of specialization include print and broadcast journalism, film, graphic design, television and radio production, multimedia design, and advertising.

High School Courses

Debate	Speech
Drama	Technical English
English	Theater
Journalism	Writing

Related Majors

Advertising	Journalism
Art	Photographic Technologies
Broadcast Journalism	Public Relations
Communications Technologies	Radio and Television Broadcasting
Computer Graphics	Speech Communications
English	Telecommunications
Film	Writing

Related Occupations

See page 7 for detailed explanation of key.

Account Executive—B	Lecturer—B
Actor/Actress—V/B	Lobbyist—B
Advertising Worker—B	Media Specialist—V/B
Announcer—AA/B	Music Director—B
Arbitrator—B	News Photographer—AA/B
Auctioneer—V	Online Content Developer—B
Broadcast Technician—AA	Producer (Film, TV)—B
Columnist—B	Proofreader—V
Commentator—B	Public Relations Specialist—B
Copy Editor—B	Publisher—B

Copywriter—B	Reporter—B
Disc Jockey—V	Research Library Technician—AA
Editor—B	Speech Writer—B
Educator—B/M/D	Technical Writer—B
Foreign Correspondent—B	TV Director—B
Journalist—B	Video Engineer—V/B

Leisure Activities

- Participating in local theater productions
- Attending movies, stage productions, lectures, or readings
- Working part-time or as a volunteer for a radio or TV station, printing or publishing firm, department store, or advertising agency
- Participating on a debate or forensic team
- Serving as an editor of a small newspaper, magazine, or newsletter
- Joining a yearbook staff or broadcasting or drama club
- Visiting libraries
- Competing in writing or oratory contests
- Fund-raising
- Reading professional publications
- Participating in election campaigns
- Working as a student assistant in a language arts or communications department
- Freelance writing
- Working or spending a significant amount of time communicating via the computer

Skills

- Ability to analyze, interpret, and appropriately convey physical and social events and behaviors to others
- Ability to meet deadlines and work under pressure
- Ability to read accurately and analytically
- Ability to relate to people of varying backgrounds
- Ability to respond quickly to unexpected circumstances
- Ability to solve problems and make decisions
- Background of general knowledge
- Good listening, clarifying, questioning, and responding skills
- Comprehensive command of grammar
- High proficiency in written and oral communication
- Proficiency in the use of computers

Values and Attributes

- Creativity
- Desire for recognition and to influence others
- Independence
- Intellectual growth

- Poise and composure under close public scrutiny and criticism
- Appreciation for clear and stimulating communication
- Pleasant and friendly attitude
- Imagination
- Integrity
- Self-confidence
- Tactfulness
- Versatility

Resources

- Henry, Millsum, David R. Olsen, and Nancy Torrance. *IT in the Social Sciences: A Student's Guide to the Information and Communication Technologies.* Malden, MA: Blackwell Publishers, 2001.
- Mogel, Leonard. *Careers in Communication and Entertainment.* New York, NY: Kaplan, 2000.
- Sequin, James. *Media Career Guide: Preparing for Jobs in the 21st Century.* New York, NY: Bedford/St. Martin's, 2000.
- **American Advertising Federation**

  1101 Vermont Avenue, NW, Suite 500

  Washington, DC 20005-6306

  202-898-0089

  http://www.aaf.org

  (provides information on college chapters, competitions, and internships)
- **Association for Women in Communications**

  780 Ritchie Highway, Suite 28-S

  Severna Park, MD 21146

  410-544-7442

  http://www.womcom.org

  (provides career information, student chapters, and helpful links of particular interest to women)
- **Broadcast Education Association**

  1771 N Street, NW

  Washington, DC 20036-2891

  202-429-5354

  http://www.beaweb.org

  (provides scholarship information, a list of schools offering degrees in broadcasting, and a free monthly email newsletter that contains useful information about broadcast education and the broadcasting industry)
- **Dow Jones Newspaper Fund**

  PO Box 300

  Princeton, NJ 08543-0300

  609-452-2820

  http://djnewspaperfund.dowjones.com/fund

  (provides information about internships and the newspaper business)

Computer Science

Computer study focuses on the design, manufacture, application, and effectiveness of computers, computer materials, and computer equipment. It includes the management, analysis, and dissemination of information via computer. From tiny hand-held electronic devices to huge multiterminal computer networks, computers pervade our culture and affect nearly every aspect of our daily lives.

High School Courses

Algebra	Geometry
Computer Programming	Statistics
Computer Science	Trigonometry
English	Word Processing

Related Majors

Computer Education	Computer Technology
Computer Engineering	Consulting
Computer Graphics	Data Processing
Computer Management	Mathematics
Computer Programming	Software Engineering

Related Occupations

See page 7 for detailed explanation of key.

Chief Information Officer—B	Hardware Service Person—AA/B
Computer-Aided Designer—AA/B	Operations Manager—AA/B
Computer Animator—AA	Robotics Technician—AA
Computer Applications Engineer—B	Software Engineer—B
Computer Operator—AA/B	Software Package Developer—B
Computer Programmer—B	Software Package Marketer—B
Computer Science Engineer—B/M/D	Software Salesperson—AA/B
Computer Security Specialist—B	Statistician—B
Computer Service Technician—AA	Systems Analyst—B
Database Analyst—B	Systems Consultant—B
Database Manager—B	Systems Manager—B
Data-Entry Equipment Operator—AA	Technical Support Technician—V
Data Processing Manager—B	Technical Writer—B
Educator—B/M/D	Webmaster—V
Electronic Data Processing Auditor—B	Word Processor—AA
Hardware Salesperson—AA/B	

Leisure Activities

- Working with a personal computer
- Working part-time or as a volunteer in a computer store, computer firm, or computer science department
- Repairing electronic appliances and other mechanical gadgetry
- Writing, score-keeping, or practicing electronics as a hobby
- Doing puzzles and playing games of strategy
- Browsing the Internet
- Solving analytic and logic problems
- Joining a computer club or organization
- Reading computer publications

Skills

- Ability to cope with constant change
- Ability to analyze, make appropriate decisions, and solve problems
- Ability to think logically
- Ability to organize
- Proficiency in writing and speaking
- Aptitude for abstract reasoning, keen observation, and intense concentration
- Ability to work with others
- High proficiency in the understanding and use of computers
- Proficiency for accuracy and detail
- Computational ability (using algebra for technician areas and using calculus for computer science areas)
- Ability to work under pressure
- Ability to understand and practically apply information derived from technical manuals and related materials

Values and Attributes

- Achievement
- Continuous intellectual growth
- Curiosity and enthusiasm for gadgetry
- Sense of responsibility
- Sensitivity to multiple perspectives
- Objectivity
- Perseverance
- Creativity
- Patience
- Thoroughness

sources

- Bird, Drew. *Information Technology Careers—The Hottest Jobs for the New Millennium*. Coriolis Group, 2000.
- Kahn, Jetty. *Computer Technician Career Starter: Finding and Getting a Great Job*. 2nd Edition. Ayer, MA: Learning Express, 2001.
- **American Computer Scientists Association**
  908-272-0066
  http://www.acsa2000.net
  (offers job placement assistance and student programs)
- **Association for Computing Machinery**
  1515 Broadway
  New York, NY 10036-5701
  212-869-7440
  http://www.acm.org
  (provides information on internships, student membership, and the ACM student magazine, *Crossroads*)
- **IEEE Computer Society**
  1730 Massachusetts Avenue, NW
  Washington, DC 20036
  202-371-0101
  http://www.computer.org
  (provides information on scholarships, student membership, and the student newsletter, *looking.forward*)
- **Information Technology Association of America**
  1401 Wilson Boulevard, Suite 1100
  Arlington, VA 22209
  703-522-5055
  http://www.itaa.org
  (has information on jobs and issues in information technology)

Construction

Construction study concentrates on the building trades industry and involves learning about the structural, technical, and finishing aspects of construction, renovation, and maintenance on buildings, highways, industrial structures, systems, and utilities installations. Construction is a vast area and includes many specialties. A few of these are masonry, carpentry, heavy equipment operation, plumbing, electricity, bricklaying, contracting, roofing, painting, and insulation.

High School Courses

Algebra

Applied Math

Architectural Drawing

Blueprint Reading

Drafting

Geometry

Health

Industrial Arts

Math

Physical Education

Woodworking

Related Majors

Air Conditioning/Refrigeration

Brick Masonry

Carpentry

Construction Engineering

Construction Technology

Electricity

Heavy Equipment Operating

Insulation Work

Iron Work

Painting

Plastering

Plumbing

Safety Engineering

Sheet Metal

Stone Masonry

Welding

Related Occupations

See page 7 for detailed explanation of key.

Bricklayer—V

Building Manager—AA/V

Carpenter—V

Carpet Installer—V

Concrete Mason—V

Construction Engineer—V/B

Drywall Applicator—V

Electrician—V

Estimator—AA/B

General Contractor—B/V

General Superintendent—B/V

Marblesetter—V

Operating Engineer—V

Painter—V

Paperhanger—V

Pipefitter—V

Plasterer—V

Plumber—V

Project Manager—V/B

Rigger—V

Roofer—V

Safety Engineer—B

Glazier—V

Insulation Worker—V

Ironworker—V

Job Superintendent—V/B

Sheet Metal Worker—V

Stone Mason—V

Terrazzo Worker—V

Tilesetter—V

Leisure Activities

- Working part-time or as a volunteer worker with a construction firm, landscape gardening center, on a farm, or in various outdoor physical activities
- Building and repairing items as a hobby
- Reading manuals and books related to construction
- Engaging in outdoor sports and games that involve physical stamina, strength, and endurance
- Renovating and decorating your own home or yard
- Becoming a member of an organization such as the Scouts or 4-H

Skills

- Ability to work in awkward positions and at times in dangerous situations
- Physical stamina and good health, vision, and motor coordination
- Mechanical aptitude
- Finger dexterity
- Aptitude for accuracy and detail
- Proficiency in math
- Ability to read and interpret blueprints, specifications, diagrams, and schematic drawings
- Ability to meet deadlines
- Ability to make sound judgments, appropriate decisions, and solve problems
- Ability to follow direction and work alone as well as with others
- General knowledge of building trade organizations, practices, and trends
- Thorough knowledge and ability in an area of specialization

Values and Attributes

- Security
- Accomplishment
- Desire to make a contribution to society
- Willingness to work outdoors and in uncomfortable weather
- Ability to adjust to hazardous environments
- Enjoyment of hands-on activities
- Thoroughness
- Patience
- Precision
- Courage
- Resourcefulness
- Carefulness

Resources

- **Associated General Contractors of America**
  333 John Carlyle Street, Suite 200
  Alexandria, VA 22314
  703-548-3118
  http://www.agc.org
  (offers information on careers and training)

- **Construction Specifications Institute**
  99 Canal Center Plaza, Suite 300
  Alexandria VA 22314
  800-689-2900
  http://www.csinet.org
  (has information on college student memberships, scholarships, certification, and education programs)

- **Mechanical Contractors Association of America**
  1385 Piccard Drive
  Rockville, MD 20850
  301-869-5800
  http://www.mcaa.org
  (provides employment opportunities, sponsors student chapters, internships and more)

- **National Association of Home Builders**
  1201 15th Street, NW
  Washington, DC 20005
  800-368-5242
  http://www.nahb.com
  (exposes interested students to emerging housing technologies)

- **Sheet Metal and Air Conditioning Contractor's National Association**
  4201 Lafayette Center Drive
  Chantilly, VA 20151-1209
  703-803-2980
  http://www.smacna.org

Criminal Justice

Criminal justice concerns public safety and law enforcement. Studies include basic criminal justice theories as well as practices, systems, strategies, functions, and problems (particularly crime and its many affects on society). Major criminal justice areas are law enforcement, criminal courts, and corrections. Many disciplines overlap criminal justice, including sociology, psychology, political science, medicine, law, history, philosophy, economics, and computer science. You may elect to specialize in law enforcement, investigations, court administration, criminal law, juvenile and family services, safety and security, forensics, organized crime, corrections, violence, civil disobedience, white-collar crime, applied research, and management.

High School Courses

Civics	Physical Education
Economics	Psychology
Government	ROTC
Health	Social Studies
History	Sociology

Related Majors

Computer Science	Psychology
Corrections	Public Administration
Criminology	Social Work
Law	Sociology
Military Science	Urban Studies
Political Science	

Related Occupations

See page 7 for detailed explanation of key.

Academic Teacher—B	FBI Agent—B
Attorney—P	Fire Chief—B/M
Chaplain—V	Foreign Service Officer—B
Child Welfare Worker—B	Forensics Psychologist—P
CIA Agent—B/M	Judge—P
Corrections Facilities	Military Officer—B
Manager—AA/B	Police Supervisor—B/M
Coroner—B/M	Politician—B
Court Administrator—B/P	Sheriff—B
Criminal Investigator—AA/B	Social Worker—M
Criminologist—M/D	Secret Service Agent—B

Detective

District Attorney—P

Drug Enforcement Agent—B

Substance Abuse Counselor—M

Warden—B/M

Leisure Activities

- Working part-time or as a volunteer in a law office, as a security guard, or in a court house, police station, prison, or juvenile delinquency agency
- Watching police and/or law-related dramas on TV or at the movies
- Reading and/or writing about criminal justice or social issues
- Participating in a related internship or co-op program
- Military experience
- Belonging to a debate or forensic team
- Serving as a leader in a school or community organization

Skills

- Possess good oral and written communication skills
- Sensitivity to and tolerance of people of differing genders, ages, and ethnicities
- Ability to work well under pressure
- Aptitude for leadership
- Good understanding of crime and its affect on society
- Ability to conduct scientific research and conduct effective interviewing
- Possess strong ethical and moral values
- Ability to make decisions and solve complex social problems
- Broad background in the liberal arts

Values and Attributes

- Have a knack for scientific inquiry and research
- Analytical and logical thinking
- Place a high priority on safety and protection of citizens
- Genuine desire to help people
- Appreciation for law and order
- Justice
- Integrity
- Trustworthiness

Resources

- Morgan, Marilyn. *Careers in Criminology.* New York, NY: NTC/Contemporary Publishing Company, 2000.
- **American Bar Association**
  541 North Fairbanks Court
  Chicago, IL 60611
  312-988-5522
  http://www.abanet.org
  (has general information on law schools and other student services)
- **American Bar Association Guide to Criminal Justice**
  http://www.abanet.org/crimjust
- **Association of American Law Schools**
  1201 North Connecticut Avenue, NW, Suite 800
  Washington, DC 20036-2605
  202-296-8851
  http://www.aals.org
  (offers general information about law schools)
- **National Association of Blacks in Criminal Justice**
  North Carolina Central University
  PO Box 19788
  Durham, NC 27707
  919-683-1801
  http://www.nabcj.org
- **National Criminal Justice Association**
  720 7th Street, NW, 3rd Floor
  Washington, DC 20001-3716
  202-628-8550
  http://www.ncja.org
  (seeks to promote justice systems, enhance public safety, and prevent or reduce the harmful effects of crime; offers student membership, internships, and a list of related links)
- **Professional Associations in Criminal Justice**
  http://courses.smsu.edu/mkc096f/advisenet/PROFESSIONAL%
  2QASSOCIATIONS/prof.html

Culinary Arts

Culinary arts include the art, science, and business of cooking, baking, and preparing foods and beverages of all types for public and private institutions, agencies, and eating establishments. It exposes you to the practices and techniques of quantity and fine food preparation as well as presentation, food storage, customer service, budgeting, purchasing, equipment use, recipe/menu development and use, sanitation, employee supervision, management, and governmental regulations. A few of the major specialties are baking, buffet catering, meat cookery, cold meat and seafood preparation, soups and stocks, salads, vegetables, fish and shellfish, and sauces.

High School Courses

Baking	Foods
Chemistry	Health
Cooking	Home Economics

Related Majors

Baking and Pastry Arts	Home Economics
Culinary Arts Management	Hospitality
Dietetics	Hotel/Motel Management
Entrepreneurship	Nutrition
Food Science	Restaurant and Resort Management

Related Occupations

See page 7 for detailed explanation of key.

Baker—AA/V	Food Service Supervisor—V/B
Broiler Cook—V	Kitchen Manager—V
Butcher—V	Meatcutter—V
Caterer—V	Nutritionist—B
Chef—V	Pastry Chef—V
Coffee Maker—V	Restaurant Owner—V/B
Cook—V	Salad Maker—V
Dietitian—B	Sandwich Maker—V
Executive Chef—V	Sous Chef—V
Food Scientist—B	Technical Writer—B

Leisure Activities

- Attending lectures, clinics, and workshops related to food preparation
- Working part-time or as a volunteer in a school or community cafeteria or restaurant
- Baking and/or cooking for church or at home
- Reading publications related to culinary arts
- Joining an organization such as the American Culinary Federation
- Entering baking or food contests
- Attending conventions, trade shows, or fairs that highlight culinary interests

Skills

- Good motor skills, manual dexterity, and eye-hand coordination
- Good health and vision
- Ability to read and interpret recipes and menus
- Ability to meet deadlines and work well under pressure
- Ability to clearly communicate and understand others
- Ability to see and feel differences among shapes, shading, colors, and textures
- Ability to work well alone and with others
- Ability to adapt well to extreme temperature, noise, and odor variations
- Proficiency for accuracy and detail
- Ability to stand or sit in uncomfortable positions for extended periods of time
- Ability to cope with frequent change and variety
- Good mental and emotional well-being
- Keen sense of taste, smell, and touch
- Ability to organize and coordinate activities

Values and Attributes

- Desire for recognition and appreciation from others
- Achievement
- Creativity
- Strong interest in cooking and baking
- Tendency to maintain good health habits
- Willingness to work long and irregular hours and on weekends
- Dedication
- Perseverance
- Resourcefulness
- Flexibility
- Tactfulness
- Cleanliness

Resources

- Masi, Mary. *Culinary Arts Career Starter.* Ayer, MA: Learning Express, 1999.
- **American Culinary Federation**

  10 San Bartola Drive

  St. Augustine, FL 32086

  904-824-4468

  http://www.acfchefs.org

  (sponsors apprenticeship programs, provides information about certification, a job bank, and accreditation)
- **American Institute of Baking**

  PO Box 3999

  Manhattan, KS 66505-3999

  785-537-4750

  http://www.aibonline.org

  (has information on education and research in the science of baking, bakery management, equipment, ingredients, cereal science, nutrition, food safety and hygiene, occupational safety and maintenance engineering)
- **International Council on Hotel, Restaurant and Institutional Education**

  2613 North Parham Road, 2nd Floor

  Richmond, VA 23294

  804-346-4800

  http://chrie.org

  (lists schools with programs in hotel and restaurant management, food service management, and the culinary arts)
- **National Restaurant Association Educational Foundation**

  175 West Jackson Boulevard, Suite 1500

  Chicago, IL 60604-2702

  800-765-2122

  http://www.edfound.org

  (offers information about scholarships, career assistance, training, and student membership)

Economics

Economics is the study of the production, consumption, and distribution of goods and services. Economics study attempts to clarify how the use of natural, technological, and financial resources affect the lives of human beings. Economic concerns can range from how a poor Appalachian family survives financially to the complex international trade laws between nations. Topics of specialization include the energy costs, business cycles, employment and unemployment, housing, health care, money policies, taxation, labor contracts, agriculture, and international trade.

High School Courses

Accounting

Bookkeeping

Business Math

Consumer Math

Economics

Math

Related Majors

Accounting

Banking

Economic Education

Economic History

Finance

Home Economics

Insurance

Market Research

Mathematics

Political Science

Urban Planning

Related Occupations

See page 7 for detailed explanation of key.

Account Executive—B

Actuary—B

Appraiser/Assessor—V

Auditor—B

Bank Officer—AA/B

Buyer—B

Controller—B

Cost Accountant—B

Credit and Loan Worker—AA

Economist—B/D

Educator—B/M/D

Financial Planner—B

Foreign Service Officer—B

Home Economist—B

Insurance Agent—V/B

Internal Revenue Agent—B

Labor Relations Specialist—B

Manpower Director—B

Market Research Analyst—B

Real Estate Agent—V

Sales Manager—B

Sales Representative—AA

Securities Analyst—B

Statistician—B

Stockbroker—B

Tax Preparer—B

Technical Writer—B

Trust Administrator—B

Urban Planner—B

Leisure Activities

- Working as a part-time or volunteer cashier, treasurer, pollster, or salesperson
- Joining an international club or Junior Achievement Club
- Participating in fund-raising events
- Joining a professional economics organization
- Reading economics-related publications
- Joining an investment club
- Solving budgetary problems
- Bartering
- Writing reports or serving as a research assistant or student aide in an economics department
- Running a part-time business
- Joining a financial advisory board

Skills

- Ability to conduct and clearly explain scientific research
- High proficiency in written and oral communication
- Strong background in economic theory and econometrics
- Ability to explain complex concepts and theories to others
- Thorough knowledge of statistical procedures
- Ability to collect and organize data
- Ability for accuracy and detail
- Ability to make keen observations and appropriate decisions
- Ability to solve problems and make sound predictions
- Intellectual capacity to do well in most undergraduate and graduate college programs
- Proficiency with computers

Values and Attributes

- Achievement
- Intellectual growth
- Security
- Ability to adjust to frequent changes
- Fondness for research and detail
- Interest in economic and fiscal trends
- Dependability
- Patience
- Objectivity
- Resourcefulness
- Perseverance
- Curiosity

Resources

- **American Economic Association**

  2014 Broadway, Suite 305

  Nashville, TN 37203

  615-322-2595

  http://www.aeaweb.org

  (offers several journals, publications, and Internet resources for economists)

- **American Marketing Association**

  311 South Wacker Drive, Suite 5800

  Chicago, IL 60606

  800-AMA-1150

  http://www.ama.org

  (provides job placement service and sponsors student chapters)

- **Economic History Association**

  Department of Economics

  213 Summerfield Hall

  University of Kansas

  Lawrence, KS 66045

  785-864-2847

  http://cs.muohio.edu/EHA

  (offers student membership and a newsletter and publishes *Journal of Economic History*)

- **Junior Achievement**

  One Education Way

  Colorado Springs, CO 80906

  719-540-8000

  http://www.ja.org

  (nonprofit organization that teaches young people about business, free enterprise, and the workforce)

- **National Association of Business Economists**

  1233 20th Street, NW, Suite 505

  Washington, DC 20036

  202-463-6223

  http://www.nabe.com

  (publishes a booklet entitled "Careers in Business Economics" and a salary survey and offers a ranking of economic departments)

Education

Education is the study of how human beings teach, learn, and develop values, skills, and character qualities. The survival and success of societies, groups, and individuals hinges on effective education. Education takes place formally or informally from the time you are born until the moment you die. Study in this field is almost unlimited and includes infant care; child psychology and adolescent education; preschool, elementary, and secondary education; adult and parent education; education of the elderly; education of people who have disabilities; education of the disadvantaged; military and employee education; and so on. A few of the major specializations are preschool, elementary, secondary, higher, adult and continuing, and special education; educational administration and supervision, guidance and counseling; testing and evaluation; business, industrial arts, and vocational/technical training.

High School Courses

Economics
English
History
Interpersonal Communications
Management
Math
Philosophy

Psychology
Public Speaking
Religious Studies
Science
Social Studies
Sociology

Related Majors

Adult Education
Art Education
Business Education
Educational Administration
Educational Consulting
Elementary Education
Guidance and Counseling
Health Education
Higher Education

Library and Information Science
Music Education
Physical Education
Preschool Education
Religious Education
Secondary Education
Special Education
Teacher Education
Vocational Education

Related Occupations

See page 7 for detailed explanation of key.

Adult and Vocational Education
   Teacher—B

4-H Agent—B
Librarian—M

Assistant Principal—M
Christian Education Worker—B/P
College Dean—D
College Professor—M/D
Counselor—B/M
Director of Admissions—M
Director of Career Placement—M/D
Director of Guidance—M/D
Director of Student Affairs—B
Education Consultant—M/D
Elementary School Teacher—B
Financial Aid Director—M
Personnel Director—B

Preschool Teacher—B
Principal—B
Registrar—M
School Psychologist—M/D
School Superintendent—M/D
Secondary School Teacher—B
Social Worker—M
Special Education Teacher—B/M
Teacher (ESL)—B
Teacher Aide—AA
Tutor—B
Vocational Rehabilitation Counselor—M

Leisure Activities

- Working part-time or as a volunteer in a preschool, nursery, elementary, or secondary school
- Participating on a debate or forensic team, in oratory contests, or in a student organization
- Playing team sports or participating in community service organizations
- Serving as a religious school, children's church, or vacation Bible school teacher
- Reading educational publications
- Attending lectures, workshops, or conventions related to education
- Helping to organize and plan social or political events
- Working part-time or as a volunteer peer counselor, tutor, 4-H leader, or Scout leader

Skills

- Ability to persuade and influence others
- Proficiency in interpersonal communications
- Intellectual capacity to perform well in most undergraduate and graduate college programs
- Broad background of knowledge
- Ability to organize and maintain accurate records
- Proficiency in one or more specialized areas
- Ability to solve problems and make appropriate decisions
- Aptitude for leadership
- Ability to maintain composure in stressful situations
- Understanding of educational theories and practices
- Ability to communicate ideas, facts, and abstract concepts to others
- Ability to relate to and interact with people of different personalities and backgrounds

Values and Attributes

- Desire to help others to learn and succeed
- Achievement
- Recognition and appreciation from others
- Intellectual growth
- Enjoyment of working and being with people
- Fondness for and dedication to human potential
- Sensitive, warm, friendly attitude
- Thirst for knowledge and understanding
- Patience
- Endurance
- Integrity
- Tactfulness
- Objectivity

Resources

- Eberts, Majorie, et al. *Opportunities in Education.* New York, NY: VGM Career Horizons, 2000.
- Echgoie-McDavid, Susan. *Career Opportunities in Education.* New York, NY: Facts on File's Career Opportunities Series, Checkmark Books, 2000.
- **American Federation of Teachers, AFL-CIO**
  555 New Jersey Avenue, NW
  Washington, DC 20001
  http://www.aft.org
  (provides information about paraprofessionals, preschool, and higher education)
- **Association for Career and Technical Education**
  1410 King Street
  Alexandria, VA 22314
  800-826-9972
  http://www.acteonline.org
  (offers job bank and publishes *Career Tech Update*)
- **National Council for Accreditation of Teacher Education**
  2010 Massachusetts Avenue, NW, Suite 500
  Washington, DC 20036-1023
  202-466-7496
  http://www.ncate.org
  (promotes and evaluates quality standards for educators on all levels and publishes a list of accredited schools)
- **National Education Association**
  1201 16th Street, NW
  Washington, DC 20056
  202-833-4000
  http://www.nea.org
  (provides list of average teacher salaries and employment services; see the Web site's Tomorrow's Teachers link)

Electrical/Electronic Engineering

Electrical/electronic engineering is the practical application of mathematics and science in the production, control, distribution, and uses of electricity as well as the research, design, development, testing, and supervision of the manufacture of electronic equipment. Electrical/electronic engineering is an extremely large branch of engineering and ranges from the design of tiny electrical circuits to the construction of large electrical power plants. The four major branches of electrical engineering are communications, control systems, electronics, and power. Students may concentrate in the area of electronic controls, radio, electromechanics, machine design, or construction.

High School Courses

Algebra	Geometry
Blueprint Reading	Math
Calculus	Physics
Chemistry	Radio/TV Repair
Computer Science	Science
Electricity	Statistics
Electronics	Trigonometry

Related Majors

Aeronautical/Aerospace Engineering	Electrician
Biomedical Engineering	Engineering Education
Civil Engineering	Engineering Mechanics
Computer and Information Science	Mathematics
Computer Science Engineering	Nuclear Engineering
Electrical/Electronic Technology	Petroleum Engineering

Related Occupations

See page 7 for detailed explanation of key.

Acoustical Engineer—B/D	Environmental Engineer—B
Aeronautical Engineer—B/D	Field Service Engineer—B
Biomedical Engineer—B/D	Fire Protection Engineer—B
Circuit Engineer—B	Illuminating Engineer—B
Communications Engineer—B	Mechanical Engineer—B
Computer Science Engineer—B	Nuclear Engineer—B
Consulting Engineer—B/M/D	Physicist—B/D

Control Engineer—B
Electrical Engineer—B
Electrical Engineering
  Technician—AA
Electrician—V
Electronics Instructor—B

Radio Engineer—B
Safety Engineer—B
Technical Writer—B
Transmissions Engineer—B
Video Recording Engineer—V

Leisure Activities

- Reading publications related to electricity and engineering
- Attending lectures and conferences related to engineering
- Repairing electrical items around the house
- Developing hobbies and interests related to electronic games and equipment
- Building models
- Belonging to a club or organization related to electrical engineering
- Working part-time or as a volunteer in an electronics shop, electrical firm, radio/TV repair shop, or college engineering department
- Participating in clubs or organizations that require you to make oral presentations and write reports

Skills

- Proficiency with computers
- Proficiency in mathematics and physical sciences
- Ability to analyze, organize, and interpret scientific data
- Ability to work well with others
- Ability to make keen observations and sound judgments
- Aptitude for accuracy and detail, spatial perception, and abstract reasoning
- Sensitivity to economic considerations and human needs
- Proficiency in an area of specialization and knowledge of current practices and trends
- Ability to conduct and clearly communicate scientific research
- Intellectual capacity to perform well in most undergraduate and graduate college programs

Values and Attributes

- Achievement
- Creativity
- Knowledge
- Desire to help others live better
- Interest in challenges
- Enthusiasm for developing ideas and concepts in a practical way
- Imagination
- Dependability
- Patience
- Perseverance
- Conscientiousness

Resources

- **American Society for Engineering Education**
  1818 N Street, NW, Suite 600
  Washington, DC 20036
  202-331-3500
  http://www.asee.org
  (offers student membership and publishes the ASEE *Directory of Engineering Colleges*)

- **Institute of Electrical and Electronic Engineers**
  1828 L Street, NW, Suite 1202
  Washington, DC 20036-5104
  202-785-0017
  http://www.ieee.org
  (offers student memberships, career books, videotapes, and scholarships)

- **Junior Engineering Technical Society**
  1420 King Street, Suite 405
  Alexandria, VA 22314
  703-548-5387
  http://www.jets.org
  (sponsors activities to help students determine engineering readiness and offers special outreach to minority students and information about careers)

- **National Society of Professional Engineers**
  1420 King Street
  Alexandria, VA 22314-2794
  703-684-2800
  http://www.nspe.org
  (offers career information)

Electrical/Electronic Technology

Electrical and electronics technology is the application of scientific theories and principles in the design, production, installation, testing, service, use, and control of electrical and electronic parts, equipment, and systems. Study includes theory and history, applied mathematics, testing measurement, circuitry, construction, currents and voltage, safety, pneumatics and electronic instruments, instrumentation, maintenance and repair, and much more. Specialties in this area include instrumentation, construction electricity, robotics, broadcast communications, industrial electronics, radio/TV, radar, automated equipment, and digital technology.

High School Courses

Algebra	Math
Applied Math	Physical Science
Blueprint Reading	Radio/TV Repair
Electricity	Science
Electronics	Small Engine Repair
Geometry	Trigonometry

Related Majors

Automotive Technology	Electrical Engineering Technology
Automated Manufacturing Technology	Heating and Air Conditioning
Communications Technology	Industrial Maintenance Technology
Computer Service and Repair	Instrumentation
Data Processing Technology	Machine Tool Technology
Diesel Mechanics	Radio and Television Repair
Electrical Engineering	Robotics

Related Occupations

See page 7 for detailed explanation of key.

Aircraft Electronics Technician—AA	Industrial Electronics Maintenance Worker—AA
Audio and Sound Specialist—AA	
Automated Equipment Technician—AA	Instrumentation Technician—AA
Biomedical Equipment Technician—AA	Marine Electronics Specialist—AA
Broadcast Technician—AA	Photo-Optics Technician—AA
Electrical Appliance Repairer—V	Quality Control Technician—AA

Electrical Engineering
  Technician—AA
Electrical Technician—AA
Electronic Equipment
  Salesperson—V
Electronic Systems Tester—AA
Electronics Technician—AA/V

Radar Technician—AA
Radio and Electrical Inspector—B
Radio Repairer—V
Robotics Technician—AA
Technical Writer—B
TV Technician—AA

Leisure Activities

- Reading publications related to electricity or electronics
- Repairing electrical items around the house
- Developing hobbies and interests involving electronic games and equipment
- Building models
- Belonging to an electronics club or related organization
- Working part-time or as a volunteer in an electronics shop, electrical firm, or radio/TV repair shop

Skills

- Ability to understand and apply scientific theories and principles
- Ability to read, interpret, and follow directions, schematic drawings, diagrams, and blueprints
- Eye-hand coordination
- Aptitude for accuracy and detail
- Ability to concentrate intensely and work alone for long periods of time
- Ability to make keen observations and solve problems
- Spatial perception and proficiency in color coordination
- Finger and manual dexterity
- Aptitude for working with electronics and mechanics
- Proficiency in mathematics and physical science
- Ability to analyze, make sound judgments, and make appropriate decisions

Values and Attributes

- Independence
- Wisdom
- Achievement
- Enjoyment of hands-on work related to electrical gadgetry
- Enthusiasm for learning and applying new methods and techniques
- Patience
- Resourcefulness
- Conscientiousness
- Competence
- Thoroughness
- Dependability

Resources

- Serby, Michael. *Careers in Television and Radio.* London, UK: Kogan Page, 2000.

- **Electronics Technicians Association**

  ETA-1

  5 Depot Street

  Greencastle, IN 46135

  800-288-3824

  http://www.eta-sda.com

  (publishes career brochures and offers student membership, accreditation information, and helpful links)

- **International Society of Certified Electronics Technicians**

  3608 Pershing Avenue

  Fort Worth, TX 76107-4527

  817-921-9101

  http://www.iscet.org

  (offers training and testing programs for certified electronics technicians)

- **Junior Engineering Technical Society**

  1420 King Street, Suite 405

  Alexandria, VA 22314

  703-548-5387

  http://www.jets.org

  (sponsors activities to help students determine engineering readiness and offers special outreach to minority students and information about careers)

English

English is a major branch of the language arts and its main focus is on the written word. However, a broader, more commonly accepted definition would include the study of literature, speech, and writing in all forms. The study of English orients you to the discipline of thinking. You learn to critically evaluate your own speaking and writing, as well as the speaking and writing of others, and to express your thoughts and feelings coherently. You also learn how to edit your work and write for different audiences. The appropriate use and understanding of English is considered basic to everyday life and reflects a person's level of educational achievement. A few of the specialized areas within English are writing, literature, reading, and speech.

High School Courses

Business English	Poetry
Debate	Public Speaking
Drama	Speech
English	Speed Reading
Forensics	Technical English
Literature	Writing

Related Majors

American Literature	Journalism
Communications	Linguistics
Comparative Literature	Publishing
Creative Writing	Speech
English Language	Technical and Business English
English Literature	Theater Arts
Foreign Language	

Related Occupations

See page 7 for detailed explanation of key.

Actor/Actress—B/V	Library Technical Assistant—AA
Author—B	Linguist—M
Bibliographer—B	Lobbyist—B
Book Store Manager—B	Media Specialist—B
Columnist—B	Playwright——V/B
Copy Editor—B	Proofreader—V
Disc Jockey—AA	Publisher—B
Editor—B	Reading Specialist/Consultant—B
Educator—B/M/D	Reporter—B

Freelance Writer—V
Interpreter/Translator—B
Journalist—B
Librarian—M

Secretary—AA
Speech Writer—B
Technical Writer—B

Leisure Activities

- Participating in local theater productions
- Attending movies, plays, lectures, or readings
- Freelance writing
- Providing a typing, tutoring, resume, or editing service
- Writing reports, papers, or poems
- Conversing with others
- Participating on a debate or forensics team or in practical politics
- Editing or reporting for a small newspaper or newsletter
- Joining a yearbook staff
- Participating in a book club
- Visiting libraries
- Working part-time or as a volunteer for a high school or college radio or TV station
- Competing in writing or oratory contests
- Reading essays, articles, novels, short stories, plays, poetry, and professional journals

Skills

- Background of general knowledge
- High proficiency in reading, writing, and speaking
- Comprehensive command of grammar and vocabulary
- Good listening, clarifying, questioning, and responding skills
- Ability to conduct and clearly explain research results
- Ability to read analytically
- Capacity to work well under pressure
- Ability to make keen observations and appropriate decisions
- Ability to concentrate for long periods of time

Values and Attributes

- Intellectual growth
- Independence
- Creativity
- Desire for recognition and to influence others
- Willingness to work toward a deadline
- Fondness for writing and/or speaking
- Self-discipline
- Tactfulness
- Integrity
- Imagination

Resources

- Ward, Ben. *Careers In English Language Teaching.* Los Angeles, CA: American Language Press, 2001.
- Degalan, Julie, and Stephen E. Lambert. *Great Jobs For English Majors.* New York, NY: NTC/Contemporary Publishing Company, 2000.
- Ferguson, Donald, Jim Patten, and Morley Safer. *Opportunities in Journalism Careers.* New York, NY: NTC/Contemporary Publishing Company, 2001.
- Guiley, Ellen, and Janet Frick, eds. *Career Opportunities for Writers.* 4th Edition. New York, NY: Career Opportunities Series, 2000.

- **Association of American Publishers (AAP)**
  71 Fifth Avenue
  New York, NY 10003-3004
  212-255-0200
  http://www.publishers.org
  (has general information about the book publishing and marketing business)

- **Dow Jones Newspaper Fund**
  PO Box 300
  Princeton, NJ 08543-0300
  609-452-2820
  http://djnewspaperfund.dowjones.com/fund
  (sponsors various internships and job placement assistance)

- **Magazine Publishers of America**
  919 Third Avenue, 22nd Floor
  New York, NY 10022
  212-872-3700
  http://www.magazine.org
  (has information about magazine internships)

- **Society for Technical Communication**
  901 North Stuart Street, Suite 904
  Arlington, VA 22203-1822
  703-522-4114
  http://stc.org
  (publishes a salary survey and offers internships and student memberships)

Food and Beverage Management/Service

Food and beverage management/service is the art and business of managing and providing food services of all types for public and private institutions, agencies, and eating establishments. It includes the study of food-service techniques in hospitality, hotel and restaurant maintenance, facilities, food purchasing and cost, food preparation and service, and front office operations. Other areas of focus are marketing, sanitation and safety, menu and nutrition, catering, and financial record keeping.

High School Courses

Bookkeeping
Business Management
Cooking
Food Service
Foods
Health

Home Economics
Psychology
Sales
Sociology
Speech

Related Majors

Bookkeeping
Culinary Arts
Customer and Personal Services
Food Service
Home Economics
Hospitality Management

Hotel/Motel Management
Marketing and Tourism Management
Nutrition
Pastry Arts
Restaurant Management
Senior Services Management

Related Occupations

See page 7 for detailed explanation of key.

Assistant Restaurant Manager—AA/V
Banquet Manager—AA/V
Cafeteria Manager—AA/V
Chef—AA/V
Dietitian—B
Dining Room Attendant—V
Director of Recipe—V
Executive Housekeeper—B
Fast Food Worker—V
Food and Beverage Director—V

Home Economist—B
Host/Hostess—V
Hotel/Motel Manager—B
Maitre d'Hotel—V
Merchandising Supervisor—V
Nutritionist—B
Purchasing Agent—B
Restaurant Manager—AA/B
Sanitation/Maintenance Worker—AA
Steward/Stewardess—V

Food Production Manager—V   Storeroom Supervisor—V

Food Service Manager—V/B

Leisure Activities

- Joining an organization such as the National Restaurant Association
- Working part-time or as a volunteer in a restaurant or hotel
- Planning or organizing community events that involve eating and/or serving
- Engaging in your own part-time food business endeavor
- Helping to organize, plan, and implement church or school picnics
- Reading publications related to food service or management
- Working part-time as a store cashier or manager
- Attending workshops, lectures, or conferences related to food service
- Hosting social events

Skills

- Ability to solve problems and make appropriate decisions
- Aptitude for accuracy and detail
- Ability to follow directions and read and interpret menus
- Ability to work under pressure, maintain composure, and react spontaneously
- Ability to organize and coordinate activities
- Proficiency in interpersonal communication
- Ability to accept public scrutiny and criticism
- Ability to interact with people of different backgrounds and personalities
- Good health and vision
- Ability to work well with others
- Good motor skills, manual dexterity, and eye-hand coordination
- Familiarity with laws related to alcoholic beverages and minors

Values and Attributes

- Recognition and appreciation from others
- Desire to help others
- Creativity
- Achievement
- Pleasant and friendly personality
- Desire to serve and please others
- Willingness to work long and irregular hours and on weekends
- Sensitivity, poise, and integrity
- Persuasiveness
- Neatness
- Diplomacy
- Cleanliness
- Leadership
- Industriousness

Resources

- **American Culinary Federation**

  10 San Bartola Drive

  St. Augustine, FL 32086

  904-824-4468

  http://www.acfchefs.org

  (sponsors an apprenticeship program and provides information about certification and accreditation, which includes how to become a certified chef)

- **American Personal Chef Association**

  4572 Delaware Street

  San Diego, CA 92116

  800-644-8389

  http://www.personalchef.com/association.htm

  (committed to training and supporting those interested in starting a chef business)

- **International Council on Hotel, Restaurant and Institutional Education**

  2613 North Parham Road, 2nd Floor

  Richmond, VA 23294

  804-346-4800

  http://chrie.org

  (has a list of schools with programs in hotel and restaurant management, food service management, and the culinary arts)

- **National Restaurant Association Educational Foundation**

  175 West Jackson Boulevard, Suite 1500

  Chicago, IL 60604-2702

  800-765-2122

  http://www.edfound.org

  (offers information about scholarships, career assistance, training, and student membership; see Careers and Education link)

Foreign Language

Foreign language is a branch of the language arts that involves the study of languages other than your native tongue. Studies in a foreign language improve your ability to communicate, help you to develop cultural awareness and sensitivity, and expand your general knowledge. Proficiency in more than one language has become a valuable asset and enhances your occupational possibilities as well as enjoyment of overseas travel. Foreign language courses are offered in most schools, colleges, and universities in the United States.

High School Courses

Anthropology
English
Foreign Language
History
Latin
Sociology
Speech

Related Majors

Anthropology
Arabic
Chinese
Classics
English
French
German
Greek
Hebrew
Humanities
International Relations
International Studies
Italian
Japanese
Linguistics
Portuguese
Russian
Spanish

Related Occupations

See page 7 for detailed explanation of key.

Actor/Actress—V/B
Announcer—B
Anthropologist—B/D
Bilingual Educator—B/M
Civil Service Worker—B
Copy Editor—B
Customs Inspector—AA
Diplomat—B/M
FBI/CIA Agent—B/D
Film Editor—AA
Flight Attendant—AA
Foreign Correspondent—B
Hotel Information Clerk—V
Hotel Manager—AA/B
Import/Export Clerk—V
Interpreter/Translator—B
Journalist—B
Linguist—M
Maitre d'Hotel—AA/V
Missionary—B
Proofreader—V
Speech Pathologist—B/M
Technical Writer—B
Translator—B

Foreign Service Officer—B   Peace Corps/VISTA Volunteer—B
Historian—B/D   Travel Agent—AA

Leisure Activities

- Traveling abroad
- Attending movies or participating in stage productions
- Visiting libraries
- Attending lectures and readings
- Working part-time or as a volunteer for Peace Corps, VISTA, or Red Cross International
- Joining a foreign language club
- Participating in oratory contests, student exchanges, or pen-pal experiences
- Working part-time or as a volunteer news announcer for a local radio or TV station, in a foreign language department, or in an ethnic restaurant
- Joining an international service organization such as the American Friends Service Committee or World Vision

Skills

- Ability to make analogies
- Ability to adjust to new environments
- Ability to organize and memorize detailed information
- Background of general knowledge
- Comprehensive command of grammar and vocabulary
- Good listening, clarifying, and responding skills
- High proficiency in reading, speaking, and writing
- Proficiency in phonetics and ability to imitate sounds
- Tendency toward logical thinking

Values and Attributes

- Intellectual growth
- Appreciation for the culture and lifestyles of others
- Desire for peace and harmony
- Linguistic ability
- Adaptability
- Alertness
- Creativity
- Patience
- Self-discipline

Resources

- Ward, Ben. *Careers In English Language Teaching.* Los Angeles, CA: American Language Press, 2001.
- **American Institute for Foreign Study**
  River Plaza, 9 West Broad Street
  Stamford, CT 06902-3788
  800-727-AIFS
  http://www.aifs.com
  (sponsors exchange and study-abroad programs, internships, and scholarships and seeks to promote international understanding)
- **American Translators Association**
  225 Reinekers Lane, Suite 590
  Alexandria, VA 22314
  703-683-6100
  http://www.atanet.org
  (has information on the translating and interpreting professions, including information on accreditation)
- **Linguistic Society of America**
  1325 18th Street, NW, Suite 211
  Washington, DC 20036
  202-835-1717
  http://www.lsadc.org
  (has information about linguistic programs at colleges and universities)
- **Modern Language Association**
  26 Broadway, 3rd Floor
  New York, NY 10004-1789
  646-576-5000
  http://www.mla.org
  (promotes study and teaching of language and literature, offers job placement assistance, and publishes a brochure entitled "Knowing Other Languages Brings Opportunities")

Forestry

Forestry is concerned with the management, development, and use of forests and related areas. It involves the application of scientific methods as well as creative imagination. Forestry covers a broad spectrum and includes the care and maintenance of rangelands, grasslands, and brushlands. Study in this field includes wood science, forestry management, economics, conservation, fire protection and disease control, scaling, surveying, recreational use, research, and a number of other areas. Forestry overlaps with a number of fields including biology, physics, chemistry, and engineering. Among the many specializations are tree planting/harvesting, watershed management, wildlife management, forestry management, public recreation, fire control, disease and pest control, conservation, and wood science.

High School Courses

Algebra	Math
Biology	Physical Science
Chemistry	Physics
Earth Science	Science
Geometry	Trigonometry

Related Majors

Agriculture	Forestry Engineering
Biology	Horticulture
Botany	Natural Resources
Conservation	Rangeland Ecology and Management
Fire Protection/Safety Technology	Recreation Parks and Tourism Management
Forest Resource Management	Wildlife and Fisheries Resources
Forestry Education	

Related Occupations

See page 7 for detailed explanation of key.

Agricultural Extension Worker—B	Rancher—V
Agronomist—B	Range Manager—AA/B
Botanist—B	Seed Analyst—B
Ecologist—B	Silviculturist—B
Educator—B/M/D	Smoke Jumper—V
Farm/Ranch Manager—B/V	Soil Conservationist—B
Forester—B	Surveyor—AA
Forestry Technician—AA	Taxonomist—B

Mycologist—D	Tree Nursery Manager—V
Naturalist—B	Tree Surgeon—V
Park Police—AA/V	Virologist—B
Park Ranger—B	Wildlife Manager—B
Plant Geneticist—B	Wood Technologist—B

Leisure Activities

- Visiting nature centers, botanical gardens, state and national parks, conservatories, camps, and museums
- Hiking, exploring, camping, sightseeing, backpacking, and collecting items related to nature
- Joining a professional organization such as the Society of American Foresters
- Subscribing to a science publication such as the *Journal of Forestry*
- Joining a forestry club or conservation group
- Supporting or participating in natural resource preservation efforts
- Undertaking nature studies or rural expeditions
- Working part-time as a park aide, forest aide, nursery worker, or nature tour guide

Skills

- Physical stamina, good vision, and manual dexterity
- Ability to work alone and with little supervision
- Ability to conduct and clearly explain scientific research
- Ability to communicate well with others
- Proficiency in reading, writing, speaking, and memorization
- Ability to supervise and manage people and activities
- Intellectual ability to perform well in most undergraduate and graduate college programs
- Thorough knowledge of forestry and related areas
- Proficiency in problem solving and decision making

Values and Attributes

- Independence
- Aesthetic awareness
- Desire to help humanity
- Intellectual growth
- Creativity
- Fondness for outdoor activities
- Desire to conserve and protect the natural environment
- Ability to endure sometimes challenging physical conditions
- Appreciation of nature
- Perseverance
- Desire for challenges
- Curiosity
- Responsibility

Resources

- Fasulo, Michael, and Paul Walker. *Careers in the Environment.* New York, NY: NTC/Contemporary Publishing Company, 2000.
- Miller, Louise. *Careers for Nature Lovers and Other Outdoor Types.* New York, NY: NTC/Contemporary Publishing Company, 2001.

- **American Forests**

  PO Box 2000

  Washington, DC 20013

  202-955-4500

  http://www.americanforests.org

  (promotes conservation and publishes *American Forests* magazine; has information on a wide variety of forest-related activities)

- **Society of American Foresters**

  5400 Grosvenor Lane

  Bethesda, MD 20814-2198

  301-897-8720

  http://www.safnet.org/index.shtml

  (provides forestry facts and information; see the Web site's About Forestry link)

- **USDA Forest Service**

  PO Box 96090

  Washington, DC 20090-6090

  202-205-8333

  http://www.fs.fed.us

  (has information about government careers in forestry as well as information on national forests across the country)

Geography

Geography is the study of the interrelationships between the earth and its people. It is considered both a social and natural science. Geography focuses on climate, land, water, space, mineral resources, population density, changes in environment, and how people adapt to them. Geographical study encompasses human geography, economic geography, physical geography, political geography, medical geography, regional geography, and educational geography.

High School Courses

Civics
Earth Science
Economics
Geography
Government
Physical Geography
Social Studies
Sociology
World History

Related Majors

Anthropology
Archaeology
Cartography
Economic Geography
Economics
Educational Geography
Environmental Studies
Geology
Global Studies
History
Human Geography
Physical Geography
Sociology
Urban Planning

Related Occupations

See page 7 for detailed explanation of key.

Anthropologist—D
Cartographer—B
Cartographic Technician—AA
Climatologist—B
Computer Mapper—B
Ecologist—B
Educator—B/M/D
Environmental Scientist—B
Environmental Technician—AA
Geographer—B/D
Geologist—B
Geomorphologist—B/D
Geophysicist—B/D
Landscape Architect—B
Market Research Analyst—B
Meteorologist—B
Oceanographer—B
Petrologist—B
Photogrammetric Technician—AA
Photogrammetrist—B
Photographer—B
Research Assistant—B/M
Seismologist—B
Sociologist—D
Soil Conservationist—B
Surveyor—AA/V

Historian—B/D   Urban Planner—M/D
International Economist—B

Leisure Activities

- Visiting natural science museums
- Involvement in outdoor activities
- Attending geographical seminars and conferences
- Watching TV shows related to the natural habitat
- Exploring and traveling
- Hiking, camping, and backpacking
- Reading or subscribing to professional publications
- Solving analytical and logical problems
- Joining organizations such as the American Geographical Society or the National Council for Geographic Education
- Working part-time or as a volunteer in an architectural firm, school geography department, or at an archaeological site

Skills

- Proficiency in the use of computers
- Ability to understand and interpret maps, graphs, and charts
- Acute spatial and form perception
- Good vision and finger dexterity
- Thorough understanding of geographical principles and statistical techniques
- Proficiency in reading, writing, and speaking
- Ability to analyze, make appropriate decisions, and solve quantitative problems
- Ability to conduct and clearly explain scientific research
- Aptitude for accuracy and detail
- Intellectual capacity to perform well in most undergraduate and graduate college programs

Values and Attributes

- Achievement
- Intellectual growth
- Independence
- Desire to help and influence humanity
- Desire to help people understand and adapt to their environment
- Keen interest in both the natural and social sciences
- Spirit of scientific inquiry
- Curiosity
- Patience
- Persistence
- Resourcefulness

Resources

- **American Geographical Society**
  120 Wall Street, Suite 100
  New York, NY 10005-3904
  212-422-5456
  http://www.amergeog.org
  (provides information about college programs and career pathways; offers scholarships and internships)
- **Association of American Geographers**
  1710 16th Street, NW
  Washington, DC 20009-3198
  202-234-1450
  http://www.aag.org
  (See the Web site's Careers in Geography section)
- **National Council for Geographic Education**
  Jacksonville State University
  206A Martin Hall
  Jacksonville, AL 36265-1602
  256-782-5293
  http://www.ncge.org
  (offers geography events, workshops, publications, and career information and sponsors the National Geography Olympiad)
- **National Geographic Society**
  PO Box 98199
  Washington, DC 20090-8199
  800-647-5463
  http://www.nationalgeographic.com/main.html
  (provides a wealth of information for geography lovers and publishes an outstanding periodical)
- **Portland State University Web Site**
  http://www.career.pdx.edu/majorgeography.htm
  (provides a rich array of career information and geography links)

Geology

Geology is a major branch of the physical sciences that involves the study of the earth. Geology is divided into two main fields: physical geology (the study of earth matter and influencing forces) and historical geology (the history of the earth). Geology includes the study of rocks, soils, mountains, rivers, oceans, and caves. Study in geology also encompasses the exploration and production of mineral and energy resources. Sub-branches of geology include meteorology, climatology, oceanography, geophysics, petrology, sedimentology, stratigraphy, paleontology, mineralogy, and geochemistry.

High School Courses

Algebra
Chemistry
Earth Science
Geography
Geometry
Math
Physical Science
Physics
Science
Trigonometry

Related Majors

Astronomy
Astrophysics
Earth and Planetary Science
Environmental Science
Geography
Geochemistry
Geological Engineering
Geophysical Engineering
Geophysics and Seismology
Hydrology
Metallurgy
Meteorology
Mineralogy
Oceanography

Related Occupations

See page 7 for detailed explanation of key.

Astronomer—D
Cartographer—B
Chemist—B
Environmental Scientist—B
Geodesist—B
Geographer—B/D
Geologist—B
Geophysicist—B/D
Hydrographer—B
Hydrologist—B
Laboratory Technician—AA
Metallurgical Engineer—B
Mineralogist—B/D
Mining Engineer—B
Nuclear Engineer—B/D
Oceanographer—B/D
Paleontologist—B/D
Petroleum Engineer—B
Petrologist—B
Pharmacist—B
Photogrammetrist—B
Physicist—B/D
Seismologist—B
Stratigrapher—B

Metallurgist—B   Surveyor—AA
Meteorological Technician—AA   Technical Writer—B

Leisure Activities

- Visiting science museums
- Participating in outdoor activities
- Attending science fairs and exhibits
- Watching TV shows related to the natural habitat
- Exploring and traveling
- Hiking, mountain climbing, camping, and backpacking
- Doing jigsaw puzzles and playing games of strategy
- Joining a geology or archeological club
- Developing hobbies and collections related to soils, rocks, coins, jewelry, or other artifacts
- Reading science magazines

Skills

- Intellectual capacity to perform well in most undergraduate and graduate college programs
- Ability to work with people of varied backgrounds
- Acute spatial and form perception
- Ability to make appropriate decisions and to solve quantitative problems
- Aptitude for accuracy and detail
- Proficiency in reading, writing, speaking, and memorization
- Ability to conduct and clearly explain scientific research
- Physical stamina, good vision, and manual dexterity
- Thorough knowledge of geological principles and mathematics
- Proficiency with computers

Values and Attributes

- Independence
- Intellectual growth
- Achievement
- Enthusiasm for exploration, travel, and outdoor work
- Spirit of scientific inquiry
- Resourcefulness
- Imagination
- Patience
- Determination
- Dedication

Resources

■ **American Geological Institute**

4220 King Street

Alexandria, VA 22302-1502

703-379-2480

http://www.agiweb.org

(provides information about scholarships and careers, including career statistics and profiles of geoscientists; see the Web site's Geosciences section)

■ **American Geophysical Union**

2000 Florida Avenue, NW

Washington, DC 20009-1277

202-462-6900

http://www.agu.org

(has information on local meetings, publications, job opportunities, and science news)

■ **Association of Engineering Geologists**

Department of Geology and Geophysics

Texas A&M University

TAMU 3115

College Station, TX 77843-3115

979-845-0142

http://aegweb.org

(has student chapters)

■ **Geological Society of America**

PO Box 9140

3300 Penrose Place

Boulder, CO 80301-9140

303-447-2020

http://www.geosociety.org

(distributes information about careers in geoscience and offers employment service, internships, and a helpful list of links)

■ **Society of Exploration Geophysicists**

PO Box 702740

Tulsa, OK 74170-2740

918-497-5500

http://www.seg.org

(has information on student chapters at colleges and universities and services for high school students)

Health Administration, Management, and Related Services

Health administration, management, and related services are concerned with the effective and efficient delivery of health care services to community residents. It involves the coordination and management of public and private hospitals, nursing homes, assisted-living facilities, medical centers, clinics, mental health organizations, community health programs, and more. Study in this area concentrates on the business practices, leadership skills, and support services employed by health care administrators and managers in their effort to identify, treat, prevent, and control disease, sickness, and injury. Students are exposed to the various strategies used to ensure a high quality of patient care service in a cost-effective manner. A few of the concentrations within this field are patient care, publicity, budget and finance, maintenance, housekeeping, personnel, food service and nutrition, employee relations, facilities and equipment, governmental regulations, benefits, and record keeping.

High School Courses

Accounting	Economics
Bookkeeping	Health
Business Management	Psychology
Business Math	Sociology
Computer Science	Speech
Consumer Math	

Related Majors

Business	Marketing Management
Business Administration	Public Administration
Business Economics	Public Health
Business Education	Public Relations

Related Occupations

See page 7 for detailed explanation of key.

Activities Supervisor—B

Chief Dietitian—B

Coordinator of Rehabilitation
Services—B/M

Director of Volunteer Services—B

Emergency Medical Services
Coordinator—B

Executive Housekeeper—B

Health Consultant—B/D

Health Information Specialist—B

Health Services Administrator—M

Hospital Comptroller—B

Hospital Food Service Manager—B

Hospital Personnel Director—B

Hospital Records Administrator—B

Information Specialist—B/M

Medical Engineer—B

Medical Records Administrator—B

Nursing Home Director—M

Occupational Safety and Health
Inspector—B

Psychiatric Social Worker—M

Public Health Educator—B

Public Health Service Officer—B

Public Health Statistician—B

Public Relations Specialist—B

Leisure Activities

- Reading publications related to health care services and management
- Attending lectures, workshops, and conferences related to health concerns
- Belonging to a health club or professional health organization
- Working part-time or as a volunteer in a hospital or nursing home, health agency, or business establishment
- Actively supporting health endeavors
- Joining a health advisory board
- Serving as a club or program officer

Skills

- Ability to clearly communicate ideas and concepts to others
- Ability to inspire productivity and exact loyalty from others
- Aptitude for leadership
- Proficiency in interpersonal communications
- Proficiency in reading, writing, and speaking
- Knowledge of health care services, policies, and trends
- Intellectual capacity to perform well in most undergraduate and graduate college programs
- Ability to solve problems and make appropriate decisions
- Proficiency in organizing, planning, coordinating, and directing activities
- Ability to meet deadlines and work well under pressure
- Proficiency in the use of computers

Values and Attributes

- Desire to help others and make a contribution to humanity
- Health
- Achievement
- Prestige
- Willingness to work beyond expectations
- Strong interest in health care services
- Initiative
- Resourcefulness
- Decisiveness
- Diplomacy
- Integrity
- Responsibility

Resources

- Kouner, Anthony R. *Health Care Management in Mind—Eight Careers.* New York, NY: Springer-Verlag, 2000.
- Swanson, Barbara M. *Careers in Health Care.* New York, NY: NTC/Contemporary Publishing Company, 2000.
- **American Association of Healthcare Administrative Management**
  11240 Waples Mill Road, Suite 200
  Fairfax, VA 22030
  703-281-4043
  http://www.aaham.org
  (offers certification programs, employment service, and scholarships)
- **American College of Health Care Administrators**
  300 North Lee Street, Suite 301
  Alexandria, VA 22314
  703-739-7900
  http://www.achca.org
  (offers student membership and college chapters)
- **American College of Healthcare Executives**
  One North Franklin Street, Suite 1700
  Chicago, IL 60606-3491
  312-424-2800
  http://www.ache.org
  (offers scholarships, student workshops and membership, career information, minority student internships, and publishes a number of career-related books)
- **Pam Pohly's Net Guide: Health Professional Associations, Academies and Organizations**
  http://www.pohly.com/assoc2.shtml
  (a comprehensive compilation of health care association resource links)

History

History is the study of major social, political, cultural, and economic events of the past. Applying the results of historical study is important for the preservation and future growth of nations and institutions. Knowledge of the past enables people to develop pride and appreciation for the accomplishments of others. In addition, a thorough understanding of past problems and the strategies used to resolve them can help people to plan their present and future lives more effectively. Historical study is usually divided into ancient, medieval, and modern periods.

High School Courses

Anthropology
Civics
Government
History

Social Studies
Sociology
World History

Related Majors

African American History
Anthropology
Archaeology
Art History
Genealogy

History Education
Humanities
Library and Information Science
Music History
Political Science

Related Occupations

See page 7 for detailed explanation of key.

Anthropologist—D
Archaeologist—D
Archivist—B
Curator—B
Economist—B
Educator—B/M/D
FBI/CIA Agent—B
Foreign Correspondent—B
Foreign Service Officer—B/M
Freelance Writer—B
Genealogist—B/D
Gerontologist—B

Historian—B/D
Lawyer—P
Librarian—M
Market Research Analyst—B
News Reporter—B
Peace Corps/VISTA Volunteer—B
Political Scientist—B/D
Public Administrator—B
Research Assistant—B
Technical Writer—B
Writer—V

Leisure Activities

- Traveling
- Visiting libraries and museums
- Collecting relics, stamps, antiques, or coins
- Working part-time or as a volunteer in a library, museum, historical society, or history department
- Maintaining a diary
- Viewing historical dramas or documentaries on TV or at a theater
- Joining a historical association or supporting historical preservation efforts
- Visiting book stores, antique shops, or flea markets
- Reading history-related publications
- Attending auctions or antique shows
- Participating in activities that involve research

Skills

- Ability to accurately identify and evaluate records of past events, ideas, and facts
- Intellectual capacity to perform well in most undergraduate and graduate college programs
- Proficiency in reading comprehension, writing, and speaking
- Ability to conduct and clearly explain scientific research
- Ability to collect and organize important historical data
- Ability to concentrate for long periods of time
- Broad background of general knowledge
- Ability to make keen observations, solve problems, and make appropriate decisions
- Proficiency for accuracy and detail

Values and Attributes

- Appreciation for past events and accomplishments
- Independence
- Intellectual growth
- Recognition
- Strong interest in reading and writing
- Continuous desire to study and research the past
- Analytical mind
- Objectivity
- Curiosity
- Resourcefulness
- Reflective nature
- Integrity
- Patience

Resources

- Degalan, Julie, and Stephen E. Lambert. *Great Jobs For History Majors.* New York, NY: NTC/Contemporary Publishing Company, 2001.
- **American Association for State and Local History**
  1717 Church Street
  Nashville, TN 37203-2991
  615-320-3203
  http://www.aaslh.org
  (publishes a free leaflet entitled, "The Gift of History," which helps explain what history is and why it matters)
- **American Historical Association**
  400 A Street, SE
  Washington, DC 20003-3889
  202-544-2422
  http://www.theaha.org
  (offers job placement assistance and online career-related articles)
- **Society of American Archivists**
  527 South Wells, 5th Floor
  Chicago, IL 60607-3922
  312-922-0140
  http://www.archivists.org
  (sponsors student chapters; offers career information and a list of helpful related associations)

Home Economics

Home economics is concerned with the quality and efficiency of family life and home care. Study in this area covers a broad spectrum and overlaps with a number of related fields. The four major divisions of home economics are food and nutrition; family life and child care; clothing and textiles; and home management, decorating, and equipment. Key areas of concentration include consumer management, budget, education, recreation, housing, health, nutrition, and transportation.

High School Courses

Child Care

Clothing Design

Consumer Math

Cooking

Family Living

Food Service

Foods

Health

Home Economics

Sewing

Related Majors

Child Care

Clothing, Apparel, and Textile Studies

Family/Community Studies

Family Resource Management Studies

Food and Nutrition Studies

Health Education

Home Economics Education

Home Furnishing

Individual and Family Development

Interior Design

Vocational Home Economics

Related Occupations

See page 7 for detailed explanation of key.

Buyer—B

Child Care Worker—AA

Child Welfare Worker—B

Clothing Designer—B

Cook/Chef—AA/V

Cooperative Extension Worker—B

Day Care Director—AA/B

Dietitian—B

Director of Food Service—B

Dressmaker—V

Economist—B

Executive Housekeeper—B

Fashion Designer—B

Food and Drug Inspector—B

Food Scientist—B

Food Service Manager—V/B

Home Economist—B

Home Health Aide—V/C

Hotel/Motel Manager—B

Interior Decorator—B

Market Researcher—B

Merchandise Displayer—B

Nutritionist—B

Purchasing Agent—B

Sales Manager—B

Social Service Aide—AA

Social Worker—B/M

Tailor—V

Leisure Activities

- Participating in charitable outreach endeavors
- Working part-time or as a volunteer in a day care center, hotel, hospital, or community service agency
- Reading publications related to homemaking
- Joining an organization such as 4-H or Family, Career and Community Leaders of America, Inc.
- Attending lectures, workshops, or conferences related to home economics
- Cooking
- Sewing
- Working part-time in a food, clothing, furniture, appliance, or hardware store
- Working as a student aide in a home economics department

Skills

- Ability to organize, conduct, and clearly explain scientific research
- Ability to persuade and influence others
- Knowledge of community resources
- Proficiency in interpersonal communications
- Ability to communicate and interact with people of different backgrounds and personalities
- General knowledge in many areas
- Proficiency in speaking, writing, and listening
- Ability to analyze and think practically
- Ability to make keen observations, evaluations, and appropriate decisions
- A good understanding of human nature
- Ability to solve problems

Values and Attributes

- Helpfulness
- Achievement
- Creativity
- Desire to work closely with people
- Strong interest in improving the quality of home life
- Sensitivity to the practical needs of people
- Resourcefulness
- Dependability
- Organization
- Patience
- Tactfulness

Resources

- **American Association of Family and Consumer Sciences**

  1555 King Street

  Alexandria, VA 22314

  703-706-4600

  http://www.aafcs.org

  (offers student membership, mentorships, networking opportunities, information about accreditation, a job bank, and an extensive list of helpful resource links)

- **American Dietetic Association**

  216 West Jackson Boulevard, Suite 800

  Chicago, IL 60606-6995

  312-899-0040

  http://www.eatright.org

  (offers information about accreditation, educational programs, and careers in dietetics)

  Family, Career and community Leaders of America, Inc.

  1910 Association Drive

  Reston, VA 20191-1584

  703-476-4900

  http://www.fcclainc.org

  (offers meetings, programs, and publications for young people in family and consumer sciences)

- **National Child Care Association**

  1016 Rosser Street

  Conyers, GA 30012

  800-543-7161

  http://www.nccanet.org

  (provides information regarding quality child care; offers student membership and helpful related links)

Horticulture

Horticulture is the branch of agriculture that involves the production and use of fruits, vegetables, and ornamental plants. It includes the study of trees, flowers, shrubs, vines, and grasses. Horticulture sites, such as greenhouses, garden centers, and nurseries, play an important role in home gardening and landscaping pursuits. Specialties include fruits, vegetables, flowers; food handling, processing, and storage; landscaping, arboriculture, turf and range management, nursery management, and plant breeding.

High School Courses

Biology

Chemistry

Earth Science

Floral Arranging

Gardening

Landscape Gardening

Science

Related Majors

Agriculture

Agronomy

Biology

Botany

Floriculture

Food Science

Forestry

Greenhouse Technology

Land Management

Landscape Design

Plant Sciences

Turf Management

Related Occupations

See page 7 for detailed explanation of key.

Agronomist—B

Biochemist—B

Botanist—B

Dietitian—B

Educator—B/M/D

Entomologist—B

Florist—V

Food Scientist—B

Forester—B

Grounds Manager—V

Horticultural Therapist—B

Horticulturist—B

Landscape Architect—B

Landscape Gardener—V

Nutritionist—B

Park Ranger—V

Plant Breeder—B

Plant Geneticist—B/D

Seed Analyst—B

Silviculturist—B

Soil Conservationist—B

Technical Writer—B

Tree Surgeon—V

Leisure Activities

- Working part-time in a garden center, nursery, fruit orchard, or greenhouse
- Reading publications related to horticulture
- Visiting botanical gardens, state and national parks, conservatories, and arboretums
- Attending flower shows and state fairs
- Gardening, canning, and freezing fruits and vegetables
- Developing hobbies and collections around flowers, leaves, house plants, or floral design
- Joining a science club, 4-H club, orchid club, or a conservation group
- Supporting or participating in natural resource preservation efforts
- Belonging to a professional organization such as the American Society for Horticultural Science
- Attending clinics, lectures, and workshops related to horticulture
- Working as a student aide in a high school or college greenhouse

Skills

- A good understanding of and familiarity with all types of plants
- Physical stamina, good vision, and manual dexterity
- Ability to recognize differences in shapes, shading, and color
- Ability to work alone as well as with others
- Ability to make keen observations and sound judgments
- Proficiency in reading and writing
- General knowledge of horticulture supplies, equipment, services, and business/marketing practices
- Proficiency for accuracy and detail
- Ability to manage and supervise others
- Ability to apply scientific methods to horticultural concerns

Values and Attributes

- Creativity
- Aesthetic awareness
- Desire to help humanity
- Independence
- Green thumb
- Strong interest in plants
- Fondness for outdoor activities
- Perseverance
- Industriousness
- Curiosity
- Imagination
- Cooperation
- Friendliness

Resources

- **American Horticultural Society**
  7931 East Boulevard Drive
  Alexandria, VA 22308
  703-768-5700
  http://www.ahs.org
  (offers employment assistance, educational brochures, and programs)
- **American Horticultural Therapy Association**
  909 York Street
  Denver, CO 80206
  303-370-8087
  http://www.ahta.org
  (encourages development of horticultural activities for therapeutic and rehabilitative purposes)
- **American Society for Horticultural Science**
  113 South West Street, Suite 200
  Alexandria, VA 22314-2851
  703-836-4606
  http://www.ashs.org
  (offers career placement assistance and student membership and sponsors college horticultural clubs)
- **Botanical Society of America**
  1735 Neil Avenue
  Columbus, OH 43210-1293
  614-292-3519
  http://www.botany.org
  (offers the booklets entitled "Careers in Botany" and "Botany for the Next Millennium")
- **Associated Landscape Contractors of America**
  150 Elden Street, Suite 270
  Herndon, VA 20170
  800-395-2522
  http://www.alca.org
  (has information about certification, careers, scholarships, and internships in landscaping and horticultural services; see the Student page on the Web site)

Hotel/Motel Management

Hotel/motel management is concerned with the efficient, profitable management and operation of hotels, motels, and other hospitality-oriented institutions. Study in this area focuses on customer service, public relations, marketing, sales, maintenance, housekeeping, supervision, hotel and restaurant management and service, sanitation and safety, budgeting, conventions, and personnel. Specializations include executive housekeeping, maintenance engineering, front office operations, food and beverage management, budget, sales, advertising, recreation, purchasing, accounting, personnel training, conventions, restaurant management, reservations, sanitation and safety, and security.

High School Courses

Accounting	Foods
Business	Math
Business Management	Psychology
Economics	Sociology
Food Service	Speech

Related Majors

Business Management	Recreation and Leisure
Hospitality and Restaurant Management	Resort and Condominium Management
	Senior Services Management
Professional Golf Management	Tourism/Travel Management

Related Occupations

See page 7 for detailed explanation of key.

Airport Manager—B	Front Office Manager—V
Assistant Housekeeper—V	General Manager—B
Assistant Manager—AA	Mall Manager—B
Building Engineer—AA/V	Managing Director—B
Building Manager—V	Marketing Manager—B
Cafeteria Manager—AA/V	Office Manager—AA
Club Manager—B	Personnel Director—B
Director of Sales—V/B	Purchasing Agent—B
Executive Housekeeper—B	Tour Planner—V
Food and Beverage Director—AA/V	Resident Manager—B

Food Production Manager—V Resort Manager—B

Food Service Manager—V YMCA/YWCA Director—B

Leisure Activities

- Working part-time as a bellhop, desk clerk, or hotel restaurant employee
- Organizing get-togethers, parties, or community events
- Leading a student group
- Participating on a debate or forensic team
- Participating in writing or oratory contests
- Reading publications related to management
- Attending lectures, workshops, and conferences related to hotel/motel management
- Joining a related professional organization
- Managing or helping others to manage apartments on a part-time basis

Skills

- Proficiency in interpersonal communication
- Proficiency in reading, writing, and speaking
- Ability to solve problems and make appropriate decisions
- Ability to interact with people of different backgrounds and personalities
- Aptitude for accuracy and detail
- Ability to maintain composure under pressure and react spontaneously
- Good physical stamina, vision, and health
- Ability to accept public scrutiny and criticism
- Ability to supervise and coordinate the activities of others
- General knowledge of the hospitality industry
- Familiarity with business, finance, and marketing techniques
- Ability to persuade and influence others

Values and Attributes

- Recognition and appreciation from others
- Skill with people
- Achievement
- Desire to help others
- Willingness to go the extra mile
- Desire to work with and please others
- Willingness to work long and irregular hours and on weekends
- Pleasant and friendly personality
- Diplomacy
- Helpfulness
- Ability to adapt to frequent relocation
- Attentiveness
- Leadership
- Imagination
- Knowledge

Resources

- Henkin, Shepard, et al. *Opportunities in Hotel and Motel Management Careers.* New York, NY: NTC/Contemporary Publishing Company, 2000.
- **American Hotel and Lodging Association**
  Human Resources Department
  1201 New York Avenue, NW, Suite 600
  Washington, DC 20005-3931
  202-289-3100
  http://www.ahma.com
  (offers student membership)
- **International Council on Hotel, Restaurant and Institutional Education**
  2613 North Parham Road, 2nd Floor
  Richmond, VA 23294
  804-346-4800
  http://chrie.org
  (publishes a career self-development magazine, *HOSTEU,* as well as *Guide to College Programs in Hospitality and Tourism*)
- **National Restaurant Association Educational Foundation**
  175 West Jackson Boulevard, Suite 1500
  Chicago, IL 60604-2702
  800-765-2122
  http://www.edfound.org
  (offers information about scholarships, career assistance, training, and student membership; see Careers and Education link)

Industrial Engineering

Industrial engineering uses the principles of science, mathematics, and engineering to efficiently and economically integrate people, machines, equipment, materials, and energy in order to maximize production. In this major you learn techniques for efficient production, time-and-motion study, data processing design, management control, quality control, plant layout, safety procedures and conditions, and environmental control. Specialties include operations research, management, ergonomics, environmental controls, plant layout and design, production planning and control, and computer processing.

High School Courses

Algebra
Blueprint Reading
Business Management
Calculus
Chemistry
Drafting
Economics

Geometry
Industrial Arts
Math
Mechanical Drawing
Physical Science
Trigonometry

Related Majors

Computer Engineering
Computer Systems Analysis
Electrical/Electronics Engineering
Engineering Technology
Environmental Health Engineering

Industrial Production Technology
Materials Engineering
Mechanical/Manufacturing Engineering
Quality Control/Safety Technology
Welding Engineering

Related Occupations

See page 7 for detailed explanation of key.

Automotive Engineer—B
Consulting Engineer—B/M
Electrical Engineer—B
Educator—M/D
Environmental Engineer—B
Fire Protection Engineer—B
Human Resources Manager—B
Industrial Engineer—B
Manufacturing Engineer—B
Materials Handling Engineer—B

Mechanical Engineer—B
Operating Engineer—B
Plant Engineer—B
Plastics Engineer—B
Process Engineer—B
Quality Control Engineer—B
Research Engineer—B/D
Safety Engineer—B
Systems Analyst—B
Systems Engineer—B

Leisure Activities

- Participating in fund-raising or social events that involve organization and planning
- Working part-time or as a volunteer in a supervisory position in a factory or a school industrial arts department
- Solving analytic, logic, and budgetary problems
- Reading publications related to engineering
- Attending engineering-related lectures and workshops
- Participating in clubs or organizations that require you to make oral presentations and write reports
- Working part-time as a research assistant

Skills

- Ability to synthesize and integrate various factors of production
- Proficiency in mathematics and science
- Ability to make keen observations and sound judgments
- Proficiency in written and oral communication
- Ability to conduct and clearly communicate scientific research
- Knowledge of work measurements and standards
- Intellectual capacity to perform well in most undergraduate and graduate college programs
- Aptitude for leadership
- Ability to analyze, organize, and interpret scientific data
- Knowledge of basic manufacturing and assembly processes
- Good interpersonal skills and ability to work effectively with others

Values and Attributes

- Creativity
- Knowledge
- Achievement
- Desire to help others live better
- Enjoyment of challenges
- Interest in seeing ideas developed into practical use
- Initiative
- Perseverance
- Flexibility
- Organization
- Imagination
- Curiosity

Resources

- **The Institute of Industrial Engineers**

  3577 Parkway Lane, Suite 200

  Norcross, GA 30092

  770-449-0460

  http://www.iienet.org

  (provides job placement service and offers student membership; see the Web site's Career Center section)

- **Junior Engineering Technical Society**

  1420 King Street, Suite 405

  Alexandria, VA 22314

  703-548-5387

  http://www.jets.org

  (sponsors activities to help students determine engineering readiness, has special outreach to minority students, and offers information about careers)

- **Society of Women Engineers**

  230 East Ohio Street, Suite 400

  Chicago, IL 60611-3265

  http://www.swe.org

  (offers scholarship and career guidance information as well as a guide to assist women who want to be engineers)

Industrial and Precision Production/Technology

Industrial and precision production/technology is the study of the design and production of tools and machines as well as consumer products. This area is usually referred to as the machine trades field. Students are exposed to intricate and precise techniques of machine and product development. Areas of focus include blueprint reading, machine function and operation, precision and accuracy, applied mathematics, production, materials applications, installation, repair, and service. Specialties include tool-and-die, machines, job setting, toolmaking, machine operating, moldmaking, diemaking, inspection, instrument making, computer-aided design (CAD), and computer-aided manufacturing (CAM).

High School Courses

Algebra	Graphic Arts
Applied Math	Industrial Arts
Blueprint Reading	Machine/Metal Shop
Drafting	Mechanical Drawing
Geometry	Trigonometry

Related Majors

Data Processing Technology	Environmental Control Technology
Design Technology	Machine Technology
Electrical/Electronics Technology	Mechanical Technology
Engineering Technology	Quality Control/Statistics Technology
Electromechanical Instrumentation and Maintenance Technology	

Related Occupations

See page 7 for detailed explanation of key.

Blacksmith—V	Machine Operator—V
Boilermaker—V	Machine Repairer—V
Butcher—V	Machine Tool Operator—V
Cabinetmaker—V	Machinist—V
CAD/CAM Operator—V	Millwright—V
Compositor—V	Photoengraver—V
Gunsmith—V	Printing Press Operator—V
Hand Molder—V	Set Up Worker—V

Instrument Maker—V
Jeweler—V
Layout Worker—V
Lithographer—V
Locksmith—V

Shoe Repairer—V
Tool and Die Maker—V
Tool Programmer—V
Upholsterer—V
Welder—V

Leisure Activities

- Working part-time or as a volunteer worker in a machine shop, school industrial arts or metal shop
- Fixing and repairing mechanical items such as household appliances
- Overhauling car engines or building race cars, go-carts, dune buggies, or other mechanical vehicles as a pastime
- Reading mechanically related manuals and books
- Belonging to an organization such as the Skills USA-VICA

Skills

- Aptitude for mathematics and mechanics
- Aptitude for spatial perception, precision, accuracy, and detail
- Good vision, motor coordination, and manual and finger dexterity
- Knowledge of machine operations and industrial practices and trends
- Ability to read and interpret blueprints, diagrams, and schematic drawings
- Ability to follow directions and work alone as well as with others
- Ability to meet deadlines
- Thorough knowledge and ability in an area of specialization
- Ability to make sound judgments and appropriate decisions and solve problems
- Proficiency with computerized equipment

Values and Attributes

- Achievement
- Security
- Desire to be exact and to the point
- Ability to adapt to awkward and uncomfortable positions
- Enjoyment of hands-on activities
- Thoroughness
- Patience
- Precision
- Carefulness

Resources

- **Association for Computing Machinery**

  1515 Broadway

  New York, NY 10036

  800-342-6626

  http://www.acm.org

  (offers student membership, curriculum recommendations, and accreditation information)

- **National Tooling and Machining Association**

  9300 Livingston Road

  Fort Washington, MD 20744

  301-248-6200

  http://www.ntma.org

  (promotes training programs)

- **Precision Machined Products Association**

  6700 West Snowville Road

  Brecksville, OH 44141

  http://www.pmpa.org

  (offers career information)

- **Skills USA-VICA**

  PO Box 3000

  Leesburg, VA 20177-0300

  703-777-8810

  http://www.skillsusa.org

- **Tooling and Manufacturing Association**

  1177 South Dee Road

  Park Ridge, IL 60068

  847-825-1120

  http://www.tmanet.com

  (provides information about careers, school activities, training programs, and an extensive list of related links)

Law

Law is the study of the rules and guidelines by which a society maintains order and cooperation. The effective development, implementation, interpretation, and modification of rules and guidelines is a requirement for transmitting societal values and expectations. Study in law exposes the student to civil and constitutional law, contracts, property, legal methods, research and writing, torts, criminal law and taxation, lawyer and client theory, law history, and many other areas. Specialties include civil, criminal, or labor law; real estate, corporate, or patent law; tort, taxation, or international law; entertainment, trust, or admiralty law; bankruptcy; and environmental law.

High School Courses

Civics	Psychology
Debate	Public Speaking
English	Sociology
Forensics	Speech
Government	

Related Majors

Bankruptcy Law	Foreign and International Law
Constitutional Law	Labor Law
Corporate Law	Law Education
Criminal Law	Paralegal/Legal Assisting
English	Political Science
Entertainment Law	Real Estate Law
Environmental Law	Tort and Insurance Law
Family Law	

Related Occupations

See page 7 for detailed explanation of key.

Adjudicator—P	Escrow Officer—B
Admiralty Lawyer—D/P	Insurance Attorney—P
Appeals Referee—P	Judge—P
Appellate Court Judge—P	Lawyer—P
Bankruptcy Attorney—P	Parole/Probation Officer—B
Bar Examiner—P	Patent Agent—B
Corporation Lawyer—P	Patent Lawyer—P
Criminal Lawyer—P	Real Estate Buyer—B
District Attorney—P	Tax Attorney—P
District Court Judge—P	Title Attorney—P

Employment Lawyer—P   Traffic Court Magistrate—P

Environmental Lawyer—P   Trial Court Judge—P

Leisure Activities

- Participating in activities that involve research
- Visiting libraries and attending court sessions
- Reading law publications
- Viewing dramas or documentaries about law on TV or at a theater
- Attending lectures or conferences related to law
- Working part-time or as a volunteer in a law office or department
- Joining a student government or newspaper staff
- Freelance or technical writing
- Participating in a community association
- Joining a debate or forensics team
- Competing in oratory contests
- Conversing with others

Skills

- Ability to speak articulately, read comprehensively, and write well
- Ability to persuade and influence others
- Broad background of general knowledge
- Ability to make keen observations and sound judgments
- Ability to research, collect, organize, and clearly present information to others
- Familiarity with legal practices, policies, and trends
- Intellectual capacity to perform well in most undergraduate and graduate college programs
- Ability to analyze and evaluate data, make appropriate decisions, and solve problems
- Ability to communicate abstract ideas to others
- Aptitude for accuracy and detail
- Aptitude for leadership

Values and Attributes

- Intellectual growth
- Power
- Prestige
- Desire for recognition and appreciation from others
- Ability to work under pressure, meet deadlines, and accept close public scrutiny and criticism
- High regard for and appreciation of the law and an orderly society
- Sensitivity to the needs of human beings
- Persistence
- Integrity
- Resourcefulness
- Persuasiveness

- Analytical mind
- Trustworthiness

Resources

- Abrams, Lisa L. *The Official Guide to Legal Specialties.* Orlando, FL: Harcourt Brace, 2000.
- National Association for Law Placement, ed. *National Directory of Legal Employers.* Orlando, FL: Harcourt Brace, 2001.
- **American Bar Association**
  Service Center
  514 North Fairbanks Court
  Chicago, IL 60611
  312-988-5522
  http://www.abanet.org
  (provides information about accredited law schools, exam preparation, an array of career publications, and student membership)
- **Law School Admission Council**
  661 Penn Street
  Newtown, PA 18940
  215-968-1001
  http://www.lsac.org
  (provides information on how to prepare for various law school exams, choosing a law school, and financial aid)

Legal and Protective Services

Legal and protective services is the study of several related fields which focus on the effective implementation of law and legal procedures, as well as the relationship of laws to the safety and protection of life and property. Legal services involves research and support related to the understanding and interpretation of law, legal procedures, and practices. Study in protective services concentrates on the implementation of laws aimed at ensuring the peaceful cooperation, security, and safety of human lives and property. Some specialties are legal assisting, criminal justice, public safety, corrections and rehabilitation, and law enforcement.

High School Courses

Civics	Psychology
Government	ROTC
Health	Social Studies
Physical Education	Sociology

Related Majors

Corrections	Military Science
Court Reporting	Military Technology
Criminal Justice	Paralegal/Legal Assisting
Fire Protection/Safety Technology	Physical Education
Fire Science	Safety and Security Technology
Law Enforcement/Police Science	

Related Occupations

See page 7 for detailed explanation of key.

Administrative Examiner—P	Lifeguard—V/AA
Bailiff—V	Military Officer—B
Border Patrol Officer—AA	Paralegal—AA/B
Case Worker—B	Parole/Probation Officer—B
Corrections Officer—AA	Penologist—B
Criminal Investigator—AA	Police Commissioner—B
Deputy Sheriff—AA	Police Officer—AA
Detective—AA	Polygraph Examiner—AA/B
District Attorney—P	Private Investigator—V
Drug Enforcement Officer—AA	Public Safety Captain—AA

Firefighter—AA   Security Officer—V
Fish and Game Warden—AA/B   Social Service Worker—V
Guard—V   Special Agent—B

Leisure Activities

- Working part-time or as a volunteer in a fire or police station, law office, or insurance firm
- Participating in individual or team sports
- Involvement in activities that require investigation and research
- Viewing law-related dramas and documentaries on TV
- Visiting libraries
- Reading publications related to legal or protective services
- Working as a security guard
- Writing reports
- Participating in student government
- Belonging to a debate or forensics team
- Serving in the armed forces

Skills

- Background of legal knowledge
- Ability to react spontaneously and maintain composure under pressure
- Proficiency in reading, writing, and speaking
- Ability to make appropriate decisions and sound judgments
- Ability to interact with people of different personalities and backgrounds
- Ability to solve problems and meet deadlines
- Proficiency in interpersonal communication
- Aptitude for accuracy and detail
- Ability to persuade and influence others
- Ability to conduct and clearly explain scientific research
- Good vision, health, physical stamina, and manual dexterity

Values and Attributes

- Security
- Wisdom
- Desire to help others
- Appreciation for order and thoroughness
- Analytical and logical thinking
- Interest in investigating and exploring for factual detail
- Integrity
- Persistence
- Alertness
- Trustworthiness
- Desire for challenges

Resources

- Ackerman, Thomas H. *Guide to Careers in Federal Law Enforcement: Profiles of 225 High-Powered Positions and Surefire Tactics for Getting Hired.* East Lansing, MI: Hamilton Burrows Press, 2001.

- Wagner, Andrea. *How to Land Your First Paralegal Job: An Insider's Guide to the Fastest Growing Profession of the New Millennium.* Upper Saddle River, NJ: Prentice Hall, 2000.

- **American Correctional Association**
  4380 Forbes Boulevard
  Lanham, MD 20706-4322
  800-222-5646
  http://www.corrections.com/aca
  (offers employment assistance, information about accreditation, and a helpful list of links to other resources)

- **American Jail Association**
  2053 Day Road, Suite 100
  Hagerstown, MD 21740
  617-471-4445
  http://www.corrections.com/aja
  (provides certification opportunities and informative online publications)

- **American Probation and Parole Association**
  2760 Research Park Drive
  Lexington, KY 40578
  859-244-8207
  http://www.appa-net.org
  (offers training opportunities, publications, and information resources)

- **Federal Bureau of Prisons**
  National Recruitment Office
  320 First Street, NW, Room 460
  Washington, DC 20534
  http://www.bop.gov
  (has information on entrance requirements, training, and career opportunities for corrections officers at the federal level)

- **International Association of Chiefs of Police**
  515 North Washington Street
  Alexandria, VA 22314-2357
  703-836-6767
  http://www.theiacp.org
  (has information about careers in law enforcement)

Library and Information Sciences

Library and information sciences are concerned with how information of all kinds is stored, organized, classified, and made available for use by others. Study in this area exposes you to the intricate logistics of acquiring, circulating, and maintaining massive amounts of information and materials. You also learn various ways to access information and techniques of promotion. Major concentrations in this field include materials for children and young adults, reference materials, audiovisual materials, school and college services, special library services, cataloging, special collections, material acquisitions, adult materials, community outreach, information systems, and administration.

High School Courses

Anthropology
English
History
Language Arts
Literature

Management
Social Studies
Sociology
Speed Reading
World History

Related Majors

History
Information Science
Information Management
Law Librarianship

Library Science Education
Linguistics
Museum Studies

Related Occupations

See page 7 for detailed explanation of key.

Academic Librarian—M
Acquisitions Librarian—M
Archivist—M
Bibliographer—M
Book Conservator—M
Cataloger—M
Children's Librarian—M
Classifier—M
Community Outreach Librarian—M
Information Scientist—M/D

Librarian—M
Library Assistant—V
Library Consultant—M/D
Library Director—M/D
Library Technician—C/AA
Media Center Manager—M
Medical Public Librarian—M
Reference Librarian—M
Special Collections Librarian—M
Systems Analyst—M

Leisure Activities

- Reading
- Freelance writing
- Attending book fairs, used book sales, and book stores
- Visiting libraries and museums
- Belonging to a book club, literary society, or professional organization, such as the American Library Association
- Attending lectures, workshops, and conferences related to library and information sciences
- Working part-time or as a volunteer in a library, bookstore, law office, or research firm
- Participating in activities that involve research
- Subscribing to a professional library publication
- Collecting items such as stamps or rare books

Skills

- Knowledge in an area of specialization as well as a background of general knowledge
- Proficiency in reading and grammar and having an extensive vocabulary
- Ability to organize, collect, classify, arrange, and coordinate materials of all kinds
- Ability to critically evaluate, make sound judgments and appropriate decisions, and solve problems
- Good vision and physical stamina
- Proficiency in interpersonal communication
- Ability to work with others as well as work quietly alone for long periods of time
- Ability to conduct and clearly explain scientific research
- Intellectual ability to perform well in most undergraduate and graduate college programs
- Aptitude for accuracy, detail, and memorization
- Proficiency with computers

Values and Attributes

- Intellectual growth
- Wisdom
- Desire to help others learn
- Love of reading and exploring for information
- Willingness to engage in lifelong learning
- Flexibility
- Resourcefulness
- Analytical mind
- Intellectual curiosity
- Perseverance
- Alertness

Resources

- **American Association of Law Libraries**
  53 West Jackson Boulevard, Suite 940
  Chicago, IL 60604
  312-939-4764
  http://www.aallnet.org
  (has information on law librarian careers, books, graduate student membership, and scholarships and grants)

- **American Library Association**
  50 East Huron Street
  Chicago, IL 60611
  800-545-2433
  http://www.ala.org
  (offers student membership, provides employment assistance and scholarship information, as well as a list of accredited programs)

- **American Society for Information Science and Technology**
  1320 Fenwick Lane, Suite 510
  Silver Spring, MD 20910
  301-495-0900
  http://www.asis.org
  (offers career information and a list of schools that have information science programs)

- **Association of Research Libraries**
  21 Dupont Circle, Suite 800
  Washington, DC 20036
  202-296-2296
  http://www.arl.org
  (has career information and other resources, including vacancy announcements)

- **Medical Library Association**
  65 East Wacker Place, Suite 1900
  Chicago, IL 60601-7298
  312-419-9094
  http://www.mlanet.org
  (has career information, a list of accredited schools, college student membership, and information on scholarships and grants)

- **Special Libraries Association**
  1700 18th Street, NW
  Washington, DC 20009-2514
  202-234-4700
  http://www.sla.org
  (offers student membership, scholarships, salary surveys, and sponsors student groups)

Marketing and Distribution

Marketing and distribution is a major field of business administration that involves the study of consumer needs and desires for products and services, consumers' willingness and ability to pay for those needs/desires, and consumer demographics. A strong focus is on the various strategies used to attract and motivate people to buy or subscribe to a product or service and the numerous methods of distribution. Specializations in this area include sales, advertising, sales promotion, retail management, brand management, and marketing research.

High School Courses

Advertising	Forensics
Business	Psychology
Debate	Sales
Economics	Speech
Fashion Merchandising	

Related Majors

Advertising	Fashion Merchandising
Business	Marketing Education
Business Marketing	Marketing Research
Economics	Retail Management

Related Occupations

See page 7 for detailed explanation of key.

Advertising Account Executive—B	Online Marketer—V/B
Advertising Manager—B	Package Designer—B
Advertising Salesperson—AA	Pharmaceutical Sales Representative—B
Assistant Buyer—B	Product Manager—B
Buyer—B	Purchasing Agent—B
Direct Salesperson—AA	Real Estate Agent—AA
Director of Marketing—V	Sales Manager—B
Economist—B	Sales Promotion Manager—B
Fashion Model—V	Sales Supervisor—B
Field Representative—AA	Securities Sales Agent—B
Human Resources Manager—B/M	Sports/Special Events Executive—B/M
Insurance Agent—V/B	Store Controller—B

Manufacturer Sales Workers—AA   Store Manager—B

Market Research Analyst—B   Wireless Sales Worker—V

Merchandise Manager—B

Leisure Activities

- Working part-time in a department store, advertising firm, warehouse, or wholesale/retail establishment
- Belonging to a Junior Achievement Club, the DECA (an association of marketing students), or professional organization, such as the American Marketing Association
- Participating in oratory contests
- Participating on a debate or forensics team
- Attending auctions, political rallies, or sales lectures
- Participating in a civic fund-raising event or in student government
- Writing promotional materials
- Reading publications related to marketing and distribution
- Attending sales and marketing workshops and conferences
- Serving as a student aide in a school or college distributive education or marketing department
- Selling products or services on a part-time basis

Skills

- Ability to work well with people of different personalities and backgrounds
- Ability to make appropriate decisions and sound judgments
- Ability to persuade and influence others
- A good vocabulary
- Articulacy
- Good knowledge of marketing techniques and consumer products and needs
- Ability to solve problems
- Physical stamina and emotional well-being
- Ability to conduct and apply the results of consumer research
- Aptitude for selling

Values and Attributes

- Achievement
- Prestige
- Wealth
- Desire for recognition and appreciation from others
- Creativity
- Outgoing, polite, and friendly attitude
- Desire to serve and please others
- Tendency to be alert and ambitious
- Competitiveness and flexibility
- Energy
- Patience

- Poise
- Neatness
- Self-confidence

Resources

- Basye, Anne. *Opportunities in Direct Marketing Careers.* New York, NY: NTC/Contemporary Publishing Company, 2000.
- Chen, Anne, editor. *The Harvard Business School Guide to Careers in Marketing.* Boston, MA: Harvard Business School Press, 2001.
- **American Marketing Association**
  311 South Wacker Drive, Suite 5800
  Chicago, IL 60606
  312-542-9000
  http://www.marketingpower.com
  (offers student membership and publishes a variety of marketing materials)
- **National DECA**
  1908 Association Drive
  Reston, VA 20191
  703-860-5000
  http://deca.org
  (an association of marketing students; sponsors high school and college chapters and offers scholarships)
- **Sales and Marketing Executives International**
  PO Box 1390
  Sumas, WA 98295-1390
  604-893-0751
  http://www.smei.org
  (provides information on sales/marketing careers in the form of career documents and career videos)

Mathematics

Mathematics is the study of quantitative relationships expressed in numbers and symbols. It focuses on mathematical concepts and theories and involves their formulation, testing, interpretation, and practical application. Mathematics is usually referred to as either pure (theoretical and abstract) or applied (practical and result-oriented). Mathematics is used by just about everyone in some manner. A minimal understanding and use of mathematics is considered basic to daily life. Major branches include arithmetic, algebra, geometry, trigonometry, calculus, probability, and statistics.

High School Courses

Accounting	Math
Algebra	Physics
Calculus	Statistics
Geometry	Trigonometry

Related Majors

Accounting	Economics
Actuarial Science	Engineering
Applied and Industrial Mathematics	Finance
Auditing	Mathematical Education
Banking	Mathematical Statistics
Computer Science	Physics

Related Occupations

See page 7 for detailed explanation of key.

Accountant—B	Financial Planner—B
Actuary—B/M	Market Research Analyst—B
Aerospace Engineer—B	Mathematician—B/D
Appraiser—B	Nuclear Scientist—B/D
Astronomer—D	Physicist—B/D
Bank Officer—AA/B	Radar Technician—AA
Bookkeeper—AA	Statistician—B
Cartographer—B	Surveyor—AA
Computer Programmer—B	Systems Analyst—B
Credit Manager—AA/B	Tool and Die Maker— V
Educator—B/M/D	

Leisure Activities

- Doing jigsaw puzzles and playing games of strategy
- Participating in tournaments, quiz bowls, and other competitive events
- Solving problems involving analytical and logical processes
- Joining a math club, science organization, or investment group
- Serving as a committee or church treasurer or as a financial officer for a civic or social agency
- Working as a part-time or volunteer sports statistician
- Reading math or science publications

Skills

- Ability to make sound judgments and decisions and to solve quantitative problems
- Ability to concentrate for long periods of time
- Proficiency in writing, speaking, and memorization
- Proficiency for accuracy and detail
- Ability to understand both concrete and abstract mathematical concepts
- Ability to organize, analyze, and interpret numerical data
- Ability to make keen observations
- Ability to conduct and clearly explain scientific research
- Proficiency in use of scientific calculator

Values and Attributes

- Independence
- Intellectual growth
- Achievement
- Security
- Ability to frame inquiry and respond objectively
- Tendency toward analytical and logical thinking
- Capacity for precision and detail
- Desire for challenges
- Thoroughness
- Imagination
- Patience
- Persistence
- Self-discipline

Resources

■ **American Mathematical Society**

201 Charles Street

Providence, RI 02940-6248

800-321-4267

http://www.ams.org

(helps those seeking employment, assistantships, and graduate fellowships; publishes salary surveys and provides helpful related links)

■ **American Statistical Association**

1429 Duke Street

Alexandria, VA 22314-3415

703-684-1221

http://www.amstat.org

(publishes *Careers in Statistics, Women in Statistics,* and *Minorities in Statistics*)

■ **Association for Women in Mathematics**

4114 Computer and Space Sciences Building

University of Maryland

College Park, MD 20742-2461

301-405-7892

http://www.awm-math.org

(promotes women and girls in mathematics; offers programs and workshops, a mentor network, and education and career information)

■ **Mathematical Association of America**

The MAA Service Center

1529 18th Street, NW

Washington, DC 20036-1385

800-741-9415

http://www.maa.org

(sponsors student chapters and offers a comprehensive array of career resources; see the Web site section Students)

■ **Society for Industrial and Applied Mathematics**

3600 University City Science Center

Philadelphia, PA 19104-2688

800-447-SIAM

http://www.siam.org

(has information on publications, conferences, activity groups, and programs)

Mechanical Engineering

Mechanical engineering focuses on the practical application of science, mathematics, and energy in the design and development of machines and related mechanical equipment that produce and use power as well as those used in manufacturing products. Internal combustion engines, motors of all types, nuclear reactors, refrigerators, elevators, robots, and a variety of medical equipment are some of the visible results of mechanical engineering. Specialties in this field include automotive, air-conditioning/refrigeration and heating, research, nuclear power, and aircraft.

High School Courses

Algebra
Blueprint Reading
Calculus
Geometry
Industrial Arts
Math

Mechanical Drawing
Mechanics
Physical Science
Physics
Small Engine Repair
Trigonometry

Related Majors

Aerospace Engineering
Automotive Engineering
Computer Engineering
Electrical/Electronics Engineering
Heating, Refrigeration, and Air-
    Conditioning Engineering

Industrial Engineering
Industrial Production Technology
Materials Engineering
Mechanical Design Technology
Mechanical Engineering Technology

Related Occupations

See page 7 for detailed explanation of key.

Aerospace Engineer—B/D
Astronaut—B/M
Automotive Engineer—B
Biomedical Engineer—B
Computer Science Engineer—B
Consulting Engineer—B/M
Electrical Engineer—B
Engineer—B
Engineering Mechanic—AA

Materials Handling Engineer—B
Mechanical Drafter—AA
Mechanical Engineer—B
Mechanical Engineering Technician—AA
Millwright—V
Packaging Engineer—B
Plastics Engineer—B
Research Engineer—B/D
Safety Engineer—B

Engineering Technician—AA

Heating and Air-Conditioning
Engineer—B

Industrial Engineer—B

Systems Analyst—B

Systems Engineer—B

Test Engineer—B

Leisure Activities

- Tinkering with electrical appliances or other mechanical devices
- Participating in a club or organization that requires you to make oral presentations and write reports
- Developing hobbies related to radios, stereos, building go-carts, fixing cars, and similar activities
- Reading publications related to mechanics or engineering
- Belonging to a student or professional engineering organization
- Working part-time or as a volunteer in an engineering firm, mechanics shop, or engineering department
- Attending lectures, workshops, and classes related to mechanical engineering

Skills

- Ability to make keen observations and sound judgments
- Proficiency in mathematics and science
- Ability to synthesize and integrate various factors of production
- Proficiency in written and oral communication
- Ability to conduct and clearly communicate scientific research
- Intellectual capacity to perform well in most undergraduate and graduate college programs
- Ability to work well with others
- Ability to solve problems and make appropriate decisions
- Aptitude for accuracy and detail, spatial perception, and abstract reasoning
- Manual dexterity and understanding of mechanics
- Proficiency with computers
- Proficiency in an area of specialization and knowledge of current practices and trends
- Sensitivity to economic considerations and human needs

Values and Attributes

- Creativity
- Achievement
- Knowledge
- Desire to help others live better
- Interest in seeing ideas developed into practical use
- Desire for challenges
- Imagination
- Flexibility
- Persuasiveness
- Curiosity

Resources

- **American Society for Engineering Education**
  1818 N Street, NW, Suite 600
  Washington, DC 20036
  202-331-3500
  http://www.asee.org
  (offers career information)

- **American Society of Heating, Refrigerating and Air-Conditioning Engineers**
  1791 Tullie Circle, NE
  Atlanta, GA 30329
  404-636-8400
  http://www.ashrae.org
  (offers student membership, scholarships, list of accredited programs, and information about careers in HVAC & R; see the Web site's Student Zone page)

- **American Society of Mechanical Engineers**
  3 Park Avenue
  New York, NY 10016-5990
  800-843-2763
  http://www.asme.org
  (offers student membership and internship, mentoring, and employment services)

- **Junior Engineering Technical Society**
  1420 King Street, Suite 405
  Alexandria, VA 22314
  703-548-5387
  http://www.jets.org
  (sponsors activities geared to assist students to determine engineering readiness, has special outreach to minority students, and offers information about careers)

- **National Society of Professional Engineers**
  1420 King Street
  Alexandria, VA 22314-2794
  703-684-2800
  http://www.nspe.org
  (offers career information)

Mechanics and Related Services

Mechanics involves the study of machine design, building, operation, repair, and service. Mechanics covers a broad range and includes appliances, communications and computer equipment, industrial machinery, and office machines as well as vehicle and mobile mechanics. Among the specialties within this area are automotive, aircraft, diesel, farm equipment, appliances, office machines, radio/TV, air-conditioning, refrigeration, and heating.

High School Courses

Algebra
Applied Math
Automotive Mechanics

Electronics
Mechanical Drawing
Small Engine Repair

Related Majors

Air Conditioning, Refrigeration, and Maintenance Technology
Data Processing Technology
Diesel Mechanics
Electrical/Electronics Technology

Electromechanical Instrumentation and Heating Mechanics
Mechanical Engineering Technology
Quality Control and Safety Technology

Related Occupations

See page 7 for detailed explanation of key.

Air-Conditioning, Refrigeration, and Heating Mechanic—AA
Aircraft Mechanic—AA
Automotive Body Repairer—V
Automotive Mechanic—V
Bicycle Repairer—V
Cable Splicer—V
Commercial/Industrial Electronic Equipment Repairer—V
Computer Service Technician—AA
Diesel Mechanic—V
Electronic Home Equipment Repairer—V
Engine Specialist—V
Farm Equipment Mechanic—V

General Maintenance Mechanic—V
Gunsmith—V
Industrial Machine Repairer—V
Instrument Mechanic—V
Instrument Repairer—V
Instrumentation Technician—AA/V
Line Installer—V
Locksmith—V
Millwright—V
Motorcycle Mechanic—V
Musical Instrument Repairer—V
Office Machine Servicer—V
Telephone Installer/Repairer—V
Vending Machine Servicer—V
Watchmaker—V

Leisure Activities

- Working part-time or as a volunteer mechanic in a service station or bicycle repair or small engine shop
- Repairing electric appliances or other mechanical gadgetry
- Reading manuals and books related to auto mechanics
- Developing hobbies and collections related to cars, model kits, or racing
- Doing your own car repair
- Building and/or repairing go-carts, mini-bikes, lawn mowers, or scooters
- Attending auto shows
- Racing

Skills

- Good health, vision, hearing, and coordination
- Aptitude for mechanics and computer instrumentation
- Ability to read and understand technical and service manuals and diagrams
- Good listening skills
- Ability to work alone as well as with others
- Ability to meet deadlines
- Ability to interact with people with different personalities and backgrounds
- Proficiency in spatial perception and mechanical dexterity
- Ability to make sound judgments and appropriate decisions and solve problems
- Proficiency in an area of mechanical specialization

Values and Attributes

- Skill
- Accomplishment
- Security
- Willingness to work with dirty, greasy materials and sometimes in awkward and hazardous positions
- Enjoyment of hands-on activities
- Willingness to continue training and education throughout life
- Dependability
- Precision
- Trustworthiness
- Carefulness
- Thoroughness

Resources

- Weber, Robert. *Opportunities in Automotive Service Careers*. New York, NY: VGM Career Horizons, 2001.

- **American Society of Certified Engineering Technicians**
  PO Box 1348
  Flowery Branch, GA 30542
  770-967-9173
  http://www.ascet.org
  (has information on training, certification, and employment)

- **Junior Engineering Technical Society**
  1420 King Street, Suite 405
  Alexandria, VA 22314
  703-548-5387
  http://www.jets.org
  (sponsors activities geared to assist students to determine engineering readiness, has special outreach to minority students, and offers information about careers)

- **National Automotive Technicians Education Foundation**
  101 Blue Seal Drive, Suite 101
  Leesburg, VA 20175
  703-669-6650
  http://www.natef.org
  (offers career information and certification programs)

- **National Institute for Automotive Service Excellence**
  101 Blue Seal Drive, SE, Suite 101
  Leesburg, VA 20175
  877-ASE-TECH
  http://www.asecert.org
  (publishes *ASE Blue Seal Tech News* as well as preparation guides and sample test questions; promotes high standards of automotive service)

- **Skills USA-VICA**
  PO Box 3000
  Leesburg, VA 20177-0300
  703-777-8810
  http://www.skillsusa.org
  (promotes high standards of workmanship and provides students with information on educational, job, and personal development skills)

Medicine

Medicine is a branch of the health sciences and focuses on the application of medicine and medical techniques in the treatment, care, and prevention of disease, illness, and injury in both humans and animals. The study of medicine focuses on procedures, drugs, and technology that help minimize pain and preserve health. Among the numerous specialties are anesthesiology, colon and rectal surgery, dermatology, family practice, internal medicine, neurology, obstetrics and gynecology, pediatrics, urology, gastroenterology, surgery, dentistry, psychiatry, and veterinary medicine.

High School Courses

Algebra	Health
Biology	Physical Education
Chemistry	Physiology
First Aid	Science
Geometry	Trigonometry

Related Majors

Athletic Training	Physician Assisting
Dermatology	Pre-Dentistry
Family Medicine	Pre-Optometry
Gynecology	Pre-Veterinary Medicine
Health Services	Psychiatry
Medical Technology	Psychology
Neurology	Sports Medicine
Pharmacy	Urology

Related Occupations

See page 7 for detailed explanation of key.

Allergist—P	Orthodontist—P
Anesthesiologist—P	Osteopath—P
Cardiologist—P	Pathologist—P
Chiropractor—P	Pediatrician—P
Dentist—P	Pharmacologist—P
Dermatologist—P	Physician—P
Endocrinologist—P	Physician Assistant—B
Gastroenterologist—P	Plastic Surgeon—P
Geriatrician—P	Podiatrist—P
Gynecologist—P	Psychiatrist—P
Immunologist—P	Radiologist—P

Internist—P
Neurologist—P
Obstetrician—P
Ophthalmologist—P
Optometrist—P

Reproductive Endocrinologist—P
Surgeon—P
Urologist—P
Veterinarian—P

Leisure Activities

- Attending medical science fairs and exhibits and visiting science museums
- Reading medically related publications
- Joining a health club
- Doing lab experiments and researching medically related topics
- Belonging to a medical science club or related professional organization
- Working part-time or as a volunteer in a local hospital, nursing home, or community health agency
- Actively participating in or financially supporting medical research efforts
- Attending lectures and conferences related to medicine

Skills

- High proficiency for accuracy and detail
- Ability to react quickly and maintain emotional and physical composure in stressful situations
- Proficiency in interpersonal communication
- Ability to work well and concentrate under pressure
- Proficiency in critical thinking, analyzing, and problem solving
- Physical stamina, good vision, and manual dexterity
- Intellectual capacity to perform well in most undergraduate and graduate college programs
- Thorough knowledge of medical theories and practices
- Ability to conduct and clearly explain scientific research
- Ability to make keen observations and appropriate decisions
- Aptitude for applied science
- Proficiency in reading and memorization

Values and Attributes

- Prestige
- Health
- Wisdom
- Achievement
- Desire to help others and make a contribution to humanity
- Interest in challenges
- Willingness to work long and irregular hours
- Desire to alleviate the pain and suffering of others
- Scientific inquiry
- Analytical mind
- Perseverance

- Dedication
- Imagination
- Alertness

Resources

- Sacks, Terrence. *Opportunities in Osteopathic Medicine.* New York, NY: NTC/Contemporary Publishing Company, 2001.
- **American Dental Association**
  211 East Chicago Avenue
  Chicago, IL 60611
  312-440-2500
  http://www.ada.org
  (offers information on dentistry careers, education requirements, and memberships for dentistry students)
- **American Hospital Association**
  1 North Franklin
  Chicago, IL 60606
  312-422-3000
  http://www.aha.org
  (has information on careers in medicine and health care)
- **American Medical Association**
  515 North State Street
  Chicago, IL 60610
  312-464-5000
  http://www.ama-assn.org
  (offers student membership and information on how to become a medical doctor)
- **American Osteopathic Association**
  142 East Ontario Street
  Chicago, IL 60611
  800-621-1773
  http://www.aoa-net.org
  (sponsors internships, provides information about accreditation, and publishes informative brochures)
- **American Veterinary Medical Association**
  1931 North Meacham Road, Suite 100
  Schaumburg, IL 60173-4360
  Attn: Education and Research Division
  800-248-2862 or 847-925-8070
  http://www.avma.org
  (has information on careers, schools, and other resources)
- **Association for Chiropractic Colleges**
  4424 Montgomery Avenue, Suite 102
  Bethesda, MD 20814
  http://www.chirocolleges.org
  (provides list of chiropractic colleges)

Metallurgical and Mining Engineering

Metallurgical and mining engineering is the practical application of science, mathematics, and energy in the extraction, treatment, and processing of metals, coal, and other nonmetallic resources from the earth. It involves the research and refinement of these natural materials as well as the discovery of new ways to use them in the development of new products. You may elect to concentrate in research, extractive engineering, processing, applications, management, or other areas.

High School Courses

Algebra
Blueprint Reading
Calculus
Chemistry
Earth Science
Geometry
Industrial Arts
Math
Mechanical Drawing
Physical Science
Science
Trigonometry

Related Majors

Chemical Engineering
Civil Engineering
Electrical/Electronics Engineering
Engineering Science
Engineering Technology
Environmental Engineering
Geological Engineering
Geophysical Engineering
Materials Engineering
Mathematics
Petroleum Engineering
Safety Engineering

Related Occupations

See page 7 for detailed explanation of key.

Ceramic Engineer—B
Chemical Engineer—B
Civil Engineer—B
Construction Engineer—B
Consulting Engineer—B/M
Electrical Engineer—B
Environmental Engineer—B
Geological Engineer—B
Geologist—B
Geophysical Engineer—B
Metallurgical Engineer—B
Metallurgical Engineering Technician—AA
Metallurgist—B
Mining Engineer—B
Nuclear Engineer—B
Petroleum Engineer—B
Pipeline Engineer—B
Plastics Engineer—B
Research Engineer—B
Safety Engineer—B

Geophysicist—B   Sanitary Engineer—B

Materials Handling Engineer—B   Systems Engineer—B

Leisure Activities

- Developing hobbies and interests related to building items out of metal or other materials, collecting rocks and minerals, and mechanics
- Reading publications about engineering or metallurgy
- Attending related lectures and workshops
- Doing experiments to see how materials react
- Working part-time with a mining company, in a foundry, or in a college engineering department
- Belonging to a student or professional engineering organization
- Solving analytic and logic problems
- Participating in clubs or organizations that require you to make oral presentations and write reports

Skills

- Ability to analyze, organize, and interpret scientific data
- Ability to work well with others
- Ability to make appropriate decisions and solve problems
- Ability to make keen observations and sound judgments
- Aptitude for accuracy and detail, spatial perception, and abstract reasoning
- Sensitivity to economic considerations and human needs
- Proficiency in an area of specialization and knowledgeable of current practices and trends
- Proficiency in written and oral communication
- Ability to conduct and clearly communicate scientific research
- Intellectual capacity to perform well in most undergraduate and graduate college programs
- Proficiency with computers

Values and Attributes

- Creativity
- Achievement
- Desire to help others live better
- Desire for challenges
- Interest in seeing ideas developed into practical use
- Curiosity
- Imagination
- Perseverance
- Flexibility
- Alertness

Resources

- **ASM International**
  9639 Kinsman Road
  Materials Park, OH 44073-0002
  440-338-5151
  http://www.asm-intl.org
  (offers student membership, college chapters, and networking opportunities)

- **Junior Engineering Technical Society**
  1420 King Street, Suite 405
  Alexandria, VA 22314
  703-548-5387
  http://www.jets.org
  (sponsors activities geared to assist students to determine engineering readiness, has special outreach to minority students, and offers information about careers)

- **The Minerals, Metals, & Materials Society**
  184 Thorn Hill Road
  Warrendale, PA 15086
  724-776-9000
  http://www.tms.org
  (has information on careers, schools, college student membership, scholarships and grants, and other resources)

- **National Mining Association**
  101 Constitution Avenue, NW, Suite 500 East
  Washington, DC 20001-2133
  202-463-2600
  http://www.nma.org
  (publishes educational brochures and sponsors mine tours)

- **Society for Mining, Metallurgy and Exploration**
  Career Information Department
  PO Box 277002
  Littleton, CO 80127
  303-973-9550
  http://www.smenet.org
  (offers career information)

Military Science

Military science is the study of the philosophies, theories, and practices of military leadership and warfare. Effective implementation of the principles of military science is considered vital to the protection of a country's citizens. Military science exposes you to military history, the nature of war, leadership and management skills, organization, customs and traditions, first aid, life-saving and survival techniques, weaponry, marksmanship, equipment use and design, methods of combat, offensive and defensive strategies, and communications. The five major concentrations within military science are communications, engineering, logistics, strategy, and tactics. Keep in mind that some of the occupations listed below are limited to simulated or actual war environments. However, many of the skills developed in preparation for them (particularly leadership, administration, and management skills) are transferable to civilian occupations such as engineering, clerical, maintenance, and mechanics.

High School Courses

Civics	Psychology
Government	Social Studies
History	Sociology
Law	ROTC
Physical Education	World History

Related Majors

Business Administration	Mechanical Engineering
Communications	Military Technologies
Corrections	Physical Education
Criminal Justice	Political Science
Geography	Psychology
Law Enforcement/Police Science	ROTC

Related Occupations

See page 7 for detailed explanation of key.

Administrative Officer—B	Intelligence Specialist—B/D
Airplane Engineer—V/B	Interpreter/Translator—B
Airplane Pilot—V/B	Journalist—AA/B
Air Traffic Controller—V	Medical Lab Technician—AA
Career Counselor—B/M	Musician—V/B
Cartographer—AA/V	Public Information Specialist—AA/B

Computer Programmer—AA   Radio Equipment Technician—AA/V
Diver—V   Recruiter—AA/B
Educator—B/M   ROTC Instructor—B
Electronics Technician—AA/V   Ship's Pilot—B
Engineering Officer—B   Systems Analyst—B
Graphic Designer—AA   Topographic Engineer—B
Human Rights Counselor—B/M   Trainer—AA/B

Leisure Activities

- Participating in an ROTC program
- Belonging to a national guard unit
- Playing games of logic, strategy, and warfare
- Serving in a branch of the armed forces
- Reading publications related to the military
- Attending military-related lectures and conferences
- Viewing war-related TV programs and movies
- Working part-time or as a volunteer in a police station or as a security guard
- Visiting military exhibits
- Participating in competitive team and individual sports

Skills

- Intellectual capacity to do well in most undergraduate and graduate college programs
- Aptitude for leadership
- Proficiency for analytical and logical reasoning
- Ability to react instantly and maintain composure in stressful situations
- Proficiency in reading and understanding directions
- Ability to make sound judgments and appropriate decisions
- Ability to interact with people of different personalities and backgrounds
- Good vision and health
- Physical stamina, good motor coordination, and manual dexterity
- Ability to clearly communicate ideas and concepts to others
- Ability to motivate and extract loyalty from others
- Background in military history, principles, and procedures

Values and Attributes

- Loyalty
- Independence
- Security
- Achievement
- Willingness to follow orders and take risks
- Courage
- Ability to respond well in emergencies
- Order and discipline
- Perseverance

- Analytical mind
- Competitive drive
- Spontaneity
- Responsibility
- Determination

Resources

- United States Department of Defense (Compiler). *America's Top Military Careers: The Official Guide to Occupations in the Armed Forces.* 3rd Edition. Indianapolis, IN: JIST Works, 2000.
- **Air Force Web Site**
  http://airforce.military.com
- **Army Web Site**
  http://army.military.com
- **Coast Guard Web Site**
  http://coastguard.military.com
- **Marine Corps Web Site**
  http://marinecorps.military.com
- **Navy Web Site**
  http://navy.military.com
- **Association of Military Colleges and Schools of the United States**
  9429 Garden Court
  Potomac, MD 20854-3964
  301-765-0695
  http://www.amcsus.org

In addition, contact the area recruiting office of the military branch you are interested in. (See Recruiting in the Yellow Pages.)

Nursing and Related Services

Nursing and related services is the study of the direct personal care, support, and condition monitoring (usually accompanied by frequent hands-on activities) of those who are sick, injured, disabled, or elderly. You learn the day-to-day skills and practices involved in quality patient care. Study includes human anatomical and physiological processes; human growth, development, and behavior; teamwork, observation, and referral; responding to emergencies; health care facility operations, philosophy, and management; and diet and nutrition. Some of the specialties of nursing and related services are midwifery, occupational nursing, public health nursing, physical therapy, occupational therapy, school nursing, private duty nursing, and family practice nursing.

High School Courses

Algebra	Geometry
Applied Math	Health
Biology	Physiology
Chemistry	Science
First Aid	

Related Majors

Family Practice Nursing	Physical Therapy
Nursing Administration	Practical Nursing
Nursing Anesthetist	Psychiatric/Mental Health Nursing
Nursing Education	Public Health Nursing
Nursing Midwifery	Registered Nursing
Occupational Therapy	

Related Occupations

See page 7 for detailed explanation of key.

Art Therapist—B	Nurse Practitioner—M
Athletic Trainer—B	Nurse Supervisor—B
General Duty Nurse—AA/B	Occupational Therapist—B
Head Nurse—B/M	Physical Therapist—B
Licensed Practical Nurse—C	Private Duty Nurse—AA/B
Music Therapist—B	Recreational Therapist—B
Nurse Anesthetist—M	Registered Nurse—AA/B

Nurse Clinician—M   Respiratory Therapist—AA

Nurse Instructor—B   School Nurse—B

Nurse-Midwife—M

Leisure Activities

- Attending lectures, workshops, and conferences related to nursing
- Belonging to a health guild, club, or advisory board
- Watching TV programs or movies related to hospitals, nursing, or medicine
- Reading nursing publications
- Belonging to a professional organization such as the National League for Nursing or American Nurses Association
- Working part-time or as a volunteer in a hospital, nursing home, health agency, or college nursing department
- Actively supporting health care and charitable efforts

Skills

- Aptitude for applied science
- Ability to make keen observations, sound judgments, and appropriate decisions
- Thorough knowledge of nursing and/or related practices and techniques
- Proficiency for accuracy and detail
- Physical stamina, good vision, and manual dexterity
- Ability to solve problems
- Proficiency in reading, writing, and following directions
- Understanding of normal human behavior, growth, and development
- Ability to react spontaneously and maintain emotional and physical composure in stressful situations
- Ability to work cooperatively with people of different backgrounds and personalities

Values and Attributes

- Health
- Wisdom
- Desire to work directly with people and to help others
- Warm, understanding, and friendly attitude
- Sensitivity to the needs and pain of others
- Willingness to work irregular hours and on weekends
- Patience
- Self-confidence
- Poise
- Responsibility
- Capability

Resources

- **American Academy of Nurse Practitioners**
  PO Box 12846
  Capitol Station, LBJ Building
  Austin, TX 78711
  512-442-4262
  http://www.aanp.org
  (has information on accredited training programs, scholarships, certification, and employment)

- **American Association of Colleges of Nursing**
  1 Dupont Circle, Suite 530
  Washington, DC 20036
  202-463-6930
  http://www.aacn.nche.edu
  (has a list of member schools and an online pamphlet entitled "Your Nursing Career: A Look at the Facts")

- **American Nurses Association**
  600 Maryland Avenue, SW, Suite 100 West
  Washington, DC 20024
  800-274-4ANA
  http://www.ana.org
  (an excellent resource for aspiring nurses)

- **Discover Nursing**
  http://www.discovernursing.com
  (provides information on nursing careers, nursing schools, and scholarships)

- **National League for Nursing**
  61 Broadway
  New York, NY 10006
  800-669-1656
  http://www.nln.org
  (has information on nursing education programs)

- **National Student Nurses Association**
  45 Main Street, Suite 606
  Brooklyn, NY 11021
  718-210-0705
  http://www.nsna.org
  (offers scholarships, career advice, and much more)

Performing Arts

Study in the performing arts offers exposure to creative, dramatic expression, primarily in front of live audiences. It involves all types of artistic performance in theaters, in educational institutions, on TV, in movies, and outdoors. All major aspects of performance preparation are studied, including music dance, acting, set design, stage setup, scenery, decorations, light and sound production, costumes, and makeup. Speaking techniques and developing stage presence are also taught. Major specializations include acting, singing, playing musical instruments, comedy, and dance.

High School Courses

Arts	Forensics
Band	Orchestra
Choir	Physical Education
Dance	Public Speaking
Debate	Speech
Drama	Theater

Related Majors

Cinematography and Production	Film/Video Making
Dance	Music
Dance Therapy	Music Therapy
Design and Applied Art	Physical Education
Drama and Dance Education	Speech
Dramatic/Theater Arts and Stagecraft	

Related Occupations

See page 7 for detailed explanation of key.

Actor/Actress—AA/B	Magician—V
Announcer (Radio, TV)—AA/B	Merchandise Displayer—AA
Choreographer—B	Motion Picture Photographer—B
Circus Performer—V	Music Director—B
Comedian—V	Music Teacher—B/M
Composer—B	Musician—B
Costumer—V	Orchestra Conductor—B/V
Dance Instructor—B/V	Producer—B
Dancer—V	Public Relations Specialist—B
Drama Coach—B/M	Puppeteer—V
Educator—B/M/D	Set Designer—B

Fashion Model—V   Singer—B

Film Director—B   Stage Manager—B

Leisure Activities

- Participating in local theater productions
- Attending plays, concerts, lectures, and movies
- Working part-time or as a volunteer for a radio or TV station
- Joining a choir, glee club, marching band, orchestra, cheerleading team, or popular music group
- Practicing aerobics, modeling, or sports
- Participating in a talent or variety show, skit, or play
- Joining the student council or a debate team
- Serving as an assistant in a theater arts or communications department
- Running for political office or competing in an oratory contest
- Reading publications related to the performing arts

Skills

- Ability to concentrate and practice intensely for long periods of time
- Ability to speak articulately, listen introspectively, and make keen observations
- Good health, physical stamina, and body coordination
- Ability to work well under pressure and meet deadlines
- Ability to maintain composure when faced with the unexpected
- Ability to communicate emotions and ideas creatively
- Ability to relate to people of varying backgrounds
- Proficiency in memorization
- Ability to attract the attention of others
- Ability to analyze and interpret the emotions and motives of others

Values and Attributes

- Aesthetic awareness
- Independence
- Self-expression and fulfillment
- Desire for recognition and influence
- Creativity
- Ability to withstand close scrutiny and criticism
- Ability to adjust to ups and downs
- Sense of drama and showmanship
- Physical stamina
- Patience
- Determination
- Imagination
- Self-discipline
- Analytical mind
- Dedication
- Poise

Resources

- **American Federation of Musicians of the United States and Canada**
  Paramount Building
  1501 Broadway, Suite 600
  New York, NY 10036
  212-869-1330
  http://www.afm.org
  (offers information on job opportunities, news about developments in the music field, and the journal *International Musician*)

- **Dance USA**
  1156 15th Street, NW, Suite 820
  Washington, DC 20005-1726
  202-833-1717
  http://www.danceusa.org
  (has a directory of dance companies and related organizations and other information on professional dance)

- **National Association of Schools of Theater**
  11250 Roger Bacon Drive, Suite 21
  Reston, VA 20190
  703-437-0700
  http://www.arts-accredit.org/nast
  (accrediting agency for postsecondary programs in theater)

- **Screen Actors Guild**
  5757 Wilshire Boulevard
  Los Angeles, CA 90036-3600
  323-954-1600
  http://www.sag.com
  (provides a list of FAQs; see the Web site's Getting Started section)

- **Theater Communications Group**
  355 Lexington Avenue
  New York, NY 10017
  212-697-5230
  http://www.tcg.org
  (promotes nonprofit theaters and theater artists and awards grants)

Philosophy

Philosophy is a branch of the language arts and involves the study of the truths or principles underlying all knowledge. Philosophical study involves the analysis, interpretation, and logical explanation of what people believe, value, and do. While the Related Occupations below are generally only indirectly linked to the study of philosophy, a number of other disciplines, avocations, and leisure activities offer additional pursuits for interested students. Among the major sub-branches are metaphysics (the study of reality and being), epistemology (the study of knowledge), logic (the study of the formal principles of reasoning), and ethics (the study of values and morals).

High School Courses

Anthropology	Language Arts
Debate	Literature
English	Psychology
Forensics	Religion
Government	Social Studies
History	Sociology

Related Majors

Anthropology	Literature
English	Psychology
History	Religion
Humanities	Sociology
Liberal Arts	Theology

Related Occupations

See page 7 for detailed explanation of key.

Anthropologist—D	Lawyer—P
College Administrator—B/D	Lecturer—B/M
College Instructor—M/D	Librarian—M
Diplomat—B	Market Research Analyst—B
Film Editor—AA	Political Scientist—B/D
Foreign Correspondent—B	Psychologist—D
Freelance Writer—B	Public Administrator—B
Historian—B/D	Publisher—B
Journalist—B	Research Assistant—B
Judge—P	Social Worker—B/M

Leisure Activities

- Participating on a debate or forensics team
- Writing
- Playing word games and games of strategy
- Participating in oratory contests
- Joining an organization such as the American Philosophical Association
- Subscribing to professional publications related to philosophy
- Visiting libraries
- Working part-time or as a volunteer research assistant or in a philosophy department
- Attending lectures
- Listening to radio talk shows
- Participating in political campaigns
- Joining a student government or student association group

Skills

- Ability to formulate and defend positions
- Ability to make keen observations, evaluations, and appropriate decisions
- Ability to summarize complicated materials and solve problems
- Ability to concentrate for long periods of time
- Ability to speak articulately
- Objectivity
- Ability to organize, conduct, and clearly explain research
- Proficiency in analytical reasoning
- Ability to synthesize information
- Broad background of general knowledge
- Comprehensive command of grammar and vocabulary

Values and Attributes

- Intellectual growth
- Logical thought and self-expression
- Desire for recognition and to influence others
- Independence
- Tendency to question and seek answers
- Tendency to support beliefs with facts and logic
- Thoughtfulness
- Persuasiveness
- Objectivity
- Imagination

Resources

- **American Philosophical Association**

  31 Amstel Avenue

  University of Delaware

  Newark, DE 19716-4797

  302-831-1112

  http://www.udel.edu/apa

  (publishes "A Nonacademic Career?," "The Philosophy Major," and "So, You Want to Teach Precollege Philosophy?")

- **EpistemeLinks.com**

  http://www.epistemelinks.com/Main/MainOrgs.asp

  (links to more than 300 philosophy-related organizations)

- **Society of Christian Philosophers**

  Calvin College

  Department of Philosophy

  Grand Rapids, MI 49546-4388

  http://www.siu.edu/departments/cola/philos/SCP

  (provides forum for discussion of Christian and philosophical issues)

Physics

Physics is a major branch of the physical sciences and involves the study of matter and energy. It attempts to find out how and why physical matter and energy interact, as well as how to describe force, motion, and gravity. Physics is considered to be the foundation of science and technology. It is closely related to astronomy, engineering, chemistry, mathematics, geology, and biology.

High School Courses

Algebra	Math
Biology	Physical Science
Calculus	Physics
Chemistry	Science
Earth Science	Statistics
Geometry	Trigonometry

Related Majors

Astronomy	Geophysics
Astrophysics	Geophysical Engineering
Biophysics	Mathematics
Chemistry	Nuclear Engineering
Geology	Physics Education

Related Occupations

See page 7 for detailed explanation of key.

Aerodynamist—B/D	Geophysicist—B/D
Aeronautical Engineer—B	Laboratory Technician—AA
Aerospace Engineer—B/D	Mathematician—B/D
Airplane Pilot—AA/B	Metallurgical Engineer—B
Astronomer—B/D	Metallurgist—B
Astrophysicist—B/D	Meteorologist—B
Biophysicist—B	Nuclear Engineer—B/D
Civil Engineer—B	Nuclear Medicine Technologist—AA
Computer Programmer—B	Nuclear Technician—AA
Educator—B/M/D	Optical Technician—AA
Electrical Engineer—B	Physicist—B/D
Environmental Engineer—B	Seismologist—B

Leisure Activities

- Joining a science club, the American Physical Society, the Society of Physics Students, or another physics club
- Reading physics or science publications
- Computer programming
- Operating a ham radio
- Repairing radios, TVs, or stereos
- Playing board games and doing puzzles
- Performing lab experiments
- Solving analytic and logic problems

Skills

- Ability to organize, analyze, and interpret scientific data
- Intellectual capacity to perform well in most undergraduate and graduate college programs
- Ability to make keen observations and appropriate decisions
- Ability to conduct and clearly explain scientific research
- Proficiency with computers
- Aptitude for accuracy and detail
- Proficiency in questioning and problem solving
- Proficiency in reading, writing, memorization, and speaking
- Strong background in mathematics
- Good vision and manual dexterity

Values and Attributes

- Achievement
- Independence
- Intellectual growth
- Recognition
- Strong desire to know why and how things work
- Fondness for mathematics and science
- Analytical mind
- Curiosity
- Dedication
- Imagination
- Perseverance

Resources

- **American Association of Amateur Astronomers**
  PO Box 7981
  Dallas, TX 75209-0981
  http://corvus.com
  (offers career books and information as well as recommendations for beginning astronomers)

- **American Institute of Physics**
  One Physics Ellipse
  College Park, MD 20740-3843
  301-209-3100
  http://www.aip.org
  (offers an outstanding career information link; see Education & Student Service section)

- **American Physical Society**
  One Physics Ellipse
  College Park, MD 20740-3844
  301-209-3280
  http://www.aps.org
  (offers student membership and provides career information which includes a special focus on minorities and women)

- **Society of Physics Students**
  One Physics Ellipse
  College Park, MD 20740
  301-209-3007
  http://www.aip.org/education/sps/index.html
  (offers scholarships, internships, networking opportunities, publications, and a career development center)

Physiology

Physiology is a branch of the biological sciences that involves the study of life processes and functions. This study requires the close observation, recording, and analysis of cellular and sub-cellular constructions, tissues, and organs to understand how they function and why. Research into the way these systems respond within and between organisms and to environmental influences is important to physiological study. Major branches of this discipline include plant physiology and animal physiology. Physiology also overlaps with chemistry, physics, and mathematics.

High School Courses

Algebra	Health
Biology	Physics
Chemistry	Physiology
First Aid	Science
Geometry	Trigonometry

Related Majors

Animal Physiology	Medicine
Biochemistry	Microbiology
Biology	Nutritional Science
Botany	Pharmacology
Chemistry	Physics
Genetics	Physiology Education
Health	Veterinary Science
Mathematics	Zoology

Related Occupations

See page 7 for detailed explanation of key.

Anatomist—B	Nutritionist—V
Anesthesiologist—P	Osteopath—P
Biochemist—B	Pathologist—P
Biophysicist—B/D	Pediatrician—P
Botanist—B	Pharmacist—P
Cardiologist—P	Pharmacologist—D/P
Chemist—B/D	Physician Assistant—AA/B
Dietitian—B	Physiologist—B/D
Emergency Medical Technician—AA	Psychiatrist—P
Funeral Director—AA/B	Respiratory Therapist—AA
Geneticist—D	Surgeon—P

Gynecologist—P   Toxicologist—B/D

Internist—P   Urologist—P

Medical Assistant—AA   Veterinarian—P

Microbiologist—B/D

Leisure Activities

- Attending science fairs or exhibits
- Visiting museums or zoos
- Reading science journals, magazines, and books
- Joining a health club
- Doing lab experiments and researching science topics
- Volunteering for the American Red Cross, American Cancer Society, or a local mental health association, hospital, or nursing home
- Owning or caring for pets
- Watching medical shows on TV or at a theater
- Actively or financially supporting blood donor drives or medical research efforts

Skills

- Ability to concentrate for long periods of time
- Ability to conduct and clearly explain scientific research
- Ability to make keen observations and appropriate decisions
- Ability to work under pressure
- Good understanding of mathematical principles and basic knowledge of chemistry and physics
- Proficiency in reading, writing, speaking, and memorizing
- Intellectual capacity to perform well in most undergraduate and graduate college programs
- Thorough knowledge of basic biological theories and practices
- Proficiency in critical thinking, analysis, and problem solving
- Physical stamina, good vision, and manual dexterity

Values and Attributes

- Achievement
- Creativity
- Helpful attitude
- Independence
- Intellectual growth
- Prestige
- Desire to help improve our world
- Interest in public health and safety
- Strong interest in how and why living organisms function
- Curiosity
- Empathy
- Endurance

- Patience
- Persistence
- Self-discipline
- Thoroughness

Resources

- **American Physiological Society**

  9650 Rockville Pike

  Bethesda, MD 20814-3991

  301-634-7164

  http://www.the-aps.org

  (offers student membership and provides career information)

- **American Society for Microbiology**

  1752 N Street, NW

  Washington, DC 20036

  202-737-3600

  http://www.asmusa.org

  (provides career information, minority programs, student section, student membership, and links to other helpful resources)

Political Science

Political science is the study of government and focuses on its structure and function and the need for social order. Political science study provides you with a better understanding of political parties, interest groups, international relationships, public law, public administration, liberty, freedom, justice, and power. Major sub-branches include political theory and philosophy, comparative government, American government and politics, public administration, international relations, and political behavior.

High School Courses

Civics

Debate

English

Forensics

Government Economics

History

Psychology

Public Speaking

Social Studies

Sociology

Speech

Related Majors

Criminal Justice

Economics

History

International Relations

Law

Military Science

Philosophy

Political Science Education

Psychology

Public Administration

Public Health

Public Relations

Sociology

Urban Studies

Related Occupations

See page 7 for detailed explanation of key.

Announcer—B

Campaign Worker—V

Chamber of Commerce Manager—B

City Manager—B

Diplomat—B/M

Educator—B/M/D

FBI/CIA Agent—B/M

Foreign Service Officer—B/M

Geographer—B/D

Judge—P

Labor Relations Specialist—B

Military Officer—B

News Reporter—B

Parole/Probation Officer—B

Penologist—B

Political Consultant—B

Political Scientist—B/D

Politician—B

Public Health Official—B

Public Recreation Director—B

Research Assistant—B

School Administrator—B

Lawyer—P   Surveying Technician—V
Lobbyist—B   Technical Writer—B
Mayor—V   Urban Planner—B

Leisure Activities

- Attending political rallies or lectures
- Serving as a part-time worker or volunteer precinct clerk, party worker, or poll watcher
- Running for or serving in a public school or municipal office
- Joining a debate or forensics team
- Participating in fund-raising or writing promotional materials for a political campaign
- Participating in student government
- Chairing a public panel discussion
- Working part-time or as a volunteer news broadcaster for a school radio or TV station
- Joining a school newspaper staff
- Participating in a neighborhood association
- Freelance writing
- Reading political publications
- Joining a professional group such as the American Political Science Association

Skills

- Ability to conduct and clearly explain research clearly
- Ability to effectively communicate ideas to others
- Intellectual capacity to perform well in most undergraduate and graduate college programs
- Ability to relate to people from varying backgrounds
- Ability to speak articulately, read comprehensively, and write well
- Charisma and public appeal
- Aptitude for leadership
- Ability to organize and interpret social, economic, and political data
- Understanding of and sensitivity to community needs
- Broad background of general knowledge
- Ability to effectively evaluate problems and make appropriate decisions

Values and Attributes

- Achievement
- Desire for recognition and to influence others
- Prestige
- Tendency to be ambitious and outgoing
- Desire to render public service
- Willingness to take risks
- Poise

- Tactfulness
- Patience
- Perseverance
- Flexibility
- Competitive drive

Resources

- **American Political Science Association**
  1527 New Hampshire Avenue, NW
  Washington, DC 20036-1206
  202-483-2512
  http://www.apsanet.org
  (publishes monthly guide to jobs in political science and *Earning a Ph.D. in Political Science* and offers other valuable information)
- **National Association of Schools of Public Affairs and Administration**
  1120 G Street NW, Suite 730
  Washington, DC 20005
  202-628-8965
  http://www.naspaa.org
  (provides information about degree programs in public administration and other tips related to public service)

Psychology

Psychology is the study of human and animal behavior. It seeks to understand and explain both normal and abnormal behavior, mental ability, perception, development, and differences in individuals. Psychological study also explores human emotions, thoughts, and motives. Among the major sub-branches within this field are educational psychology, social psychology, psychometrics, developmental psychology, comparative psychology, psychology of the personality, abnormal psychology, applied psychology, differential psychology, statistics, and child psychology.

High School Courses

Economics

Government

Health

History

Psychology

Religion

Social Studies

Sociology

Related Majors

Anthropology

Criminal Justice

Economics

Guidance Counseling

History

Philosophy

Political Science

Psychiatry

Psychology Education

Religion

Social Work

Sociology

Related Occupations

See page 7 for detailed explanation of key.

Advertising Manager—B

Educator—B/M/D

Employee Assistance
  Administrator—B

Employment Counselor—B

Guidance Counselor—M

Human Resource Manager—B

Industrial Psychologist—M/D

Job Analyst—B

Market Research Analyst—B

Mental Health Worker—B

Minister—P/V

Occupational Therapist—B

Outplacement Specialist—B/D

Penologist—B

Police Officer—AA

Probation Officer—B

Psychiatric Nurse—B

Psychiatric Social Worker—M

Psychiatrist—P

Psychologist—D

Psychometrist—B/M

Public Relations Specialist—B

Speech Pathologist—M

Vocational Rehabilitation Counselor—B/M

Leisure Activities

- Serving as a peer advisor
- Working part-time or as a volunteer in a mental health agency, psychology department, or senior citizens' home
- Assisting with college recruitment efforts
- Serving on a student council or as a tutor
- Participating in Junior Achievement
- Serving as a leader or chairperson in a community or school organization
- Working part-time or as a volunteer in an advertising firm, sales department, special education class, or day care center
- Serving as a camp counselor or hotline assistant
- Freelance writing
- Reading psychology-related publications.

Skills

- Ability to interpret and clearly explain psychological research and tests of all types
- Proficiency in reading comprehension, writing, and speaking
- Understanding of human development and behavior
- Ability to observe and analyze introspectively
- Sensitivity to and understanding of the needs and emotions of others
- Ability to evaluate personal problems and make appropriate decisions
- Intellectual capacity to do well in most undergraduate or graduate college programs
- Proficiency in interpersonal communication

Values and Attributes

- Intellectual understanding
- Helpfulness
- Mental and emotional well-being
- Sensitivity to the inconsistencies of human behavior
- Desire to continue learning throughout life
- Warm and personable character
- Tactfulness
- Inquisitiveness
- Integrity
- Patience

Resources

- Super, Charles M., Donald E. Super, and Blythe Camenson. *Opportunities in Psychology Careers*. New York, NY: NTC/Contemporary Publishing Company, 2001.

- **American Psychological Association**

  750 First Street, NE

  Washington, DC 20002-4242

  202-336-5510

  http://www.apa.org

  (provides information about psychology careers, including nonacademic careers, minority interests, useful skills, and salaries; see the Students section of the Web site)

- **National Association of School Psychologists**

  4340 East West Highway, Suite 402

  Bethesda, MD 20814

  301-657-0270

  http://www.nasponline.org/index2.html

  (offers scholarships and includes a special outreach to minorities; publishes *What Is a School Psychologist?*)

Recreation and Leisure

Recreation and leisure focuses on the design, management, implementation, supervision, expansion of, and need for recreational and leisure activities among individuals and groups of all ages and backgrounds. The recreation and leisure field encompasses a broad range of events and activities related to camping, natural resources, outdoor activities, tourism, amusement parks, sporting events, and community recreation programs. A few of the many specialties within this growing field are gerontology, youth organizations, parks and forestry, public recreation, tourism, commercial enterprise, therapeutic recreation, professional sports, resource management, and recreation and parks administration.

High School Courses

Arts	Psychology
First Aid	Social Studies
Health	Sociology
Physical Education	Theater

Related Majors

Dance	Psychology
Gerontology	Recreation/Leisure Facilities
Forest Management	Management
Health	Recreation Therapy
Music	Sociology
Natural Resources	Theater Arts/Drama
Physical Education	Travel/Tourism Management

Related Occupations

See page 7 for detailed explanation of key.

Armed Forces Recreation Leader—AA	Lifeguard—V/AA
	Municipal Recreation Director—B
Athletic Trainer—B	Music Therapist—B
Camp Director—B	Park Ranger—B
Church Recreation Director—V	Physical Education Instructor—B
Circus Performer—V	Playground Leader—AA
Coach—V	Prison Recreation Specialist—B
College Recreation Instructor—B/M	Professional Athlete—V
Community Center Director—AA/B	Recreation Facility Manager—B
Concert Promoter—B/V	Recreational Therapist—B
Dance Instructor—B/V	Resort Manager—B

Dance Therapist—B   Ski Instructor—V

Exercise Physiologist—B   Sports Marketer—B

Fitness Instructor/Specialist—B   Sports Reporter—B

Game Official—B

Leisure Activities

- Playing or participating in sports
- Working as a camp counselor or at a fitness club, playground, or other recreational facility
- Engaging in physical and outdoor activities
- Serving as a part-time coach, official, or scorer
- Reading publications related to recreation, sports, health, and fitness
- Organizing and participating in community recreational activities
- Attending lectures and workshops related to recreation and leisure
- Serving as an aide in a school physical education or recreation department

Skills

- Ability to relate to and interact with people of varying ages and backgrounds
- Ability to lead, supervise, and direct others
- Ability to react spontaneously and maintain emotional composure in stressful situations
- Understanding of human nature
- Good health, vision, and physical stamina
- Ability to solve problems and make appropriate decisions
- Proficiency in written and oral communication
- Ability to organize and coordinate activities
- General knowledge of recreational and leisure theories and practices
- A high level of athletic ability (for a career as a fitness instructor or athlete)

Values and Attributes

- Health
- Achievement
- Emotional well-being
- Sensitivity to the human need for recreation and balance
- A good sense of humor and fondness for being around people
- Friendliness
- Tactfulness
- Dedication
- Patience
- Outgoing personality

Resources

- **American Alliance for Health, Physical Education, Recreation, and Dance**
  1900 Association Drive
  Reston, VA 20191-1598
  800-213-7193
  http://www.aahperd.org
  (offers scholarships, student membership, and career information and publishes a student newsletter)
- **American Association for Leisure and Recreation**
  1900 Association Drive
  Reston, VA 20191
  703-476-3472
  http://www.aahperd.org/aalr/template.cfm
  (has information regarding industry trends, education, and scholarships)
- **American Therapeutic Recreation Association**
  1414 Prince Street, Suite 204
  Alexandria, VA 22314
  703-683-9420
  http://www.atra-tr.org
  (offers career information and resources)
- **National Recreation and Park Association**
  22377 Belmont Ridge Road
  Ashburn, VA 20148-4501
  703-858-0784
  http://www.nrpa.org
  (provides information about university programs, community recreation, natural resources, park management, recreation administration, therapeutic recreation, and accreditation)
- **National Therapeutic Recreation Society**
  22377 Belmont Ridge Road
  Ashburn, VA 20148
  703-858-0784
  http://www.nrpa.org/branches/ntrs.htm
  (has information on careers in therapeutic recreation)

Rehabilitation Therapy and Related Services

Rehabilitation therapy is the study of the history, theories, practices, and medical issues related to rehabilitation and disability. It includes a careful look at how rehabilitation efforts impact individual evaluation, case management activities, and society at large. A primary focus is on the rehabilitative needs of individuals and how to deliver these services. Students learn about a variety of supportive programs as well as the special needs of clients seen regularly by rehabilitation specialists. Clients served usually have one or more physical, mental, or emotional disabilities.

High School Courses

Algebra	Health
Biology	Math
Chemistry	Physical Education
Economics	Psychology
First Aid	Social Studies
Geometry	Sociology

Related Majors

Art Therapy	Pharmacy
Athletic Training	Physical Therapy
Horticultural Therapy	Recreational Therapy
Medicine	Rehabilitative Counseling
Music Therapy	Special Education
Nursing	Speech Therapy
Occupational Therapy	

Related Occupations

See page 7 for detailed explanation of key.

Art Therapist—B	Nurse—AA/B
Athletic Trainer—B	Occupational Therapist—B
Audiologist/Speech Pathologist—M	Orthotics/Prosthetics Technician—AA
Consultant—M/D	Pharmacist—B/M
Dance Therapist—B	Physical Therapist—B
Educator—M/D	Recreational Therapist—B
Exercise Physiologist—B	Respiratory Therapist—B

Horticultural Therapist—B   Special Education Teacher—B

Music Therapist—B   Vocational Rehabilitation Counselor—M

Leisure Activities

- Attending lectures, workshops, conferences, and other events related to rehabilitation and/or individuals with special needs
- Working part-time or volunteering at an assisted living center, nursing home, veteran's or children's hospital
- Reading biographies, periodicals, and other publications about people with special needs
- Belonging to an organization such as the National Rehabilitation Association
- Regular observation/attendance at Special Olympic events, wheelchair basketball, or arts programs for people with disabilities

Skills

- High proficiency in a therapeutic area of expertise (art, music, occupational, physical, etc.)
- Aptitude for applied science
- Thorough knowledge of the theories, practices, and techniques of a specialty
- Ability to make keen observations, sound judgments, and appropriate decisions
- Ability to think outside of the box, go beyond, and be innovative
- Ability to work with people of differing backgrounds and personalities
- Understanding of normal human behavior, growth, and development

Values and Attributes

- Sensitivity and compassion, particularly for those with special needs
- Empathy
- Patience
- Self-confidence
- Being responsible
- Creativity
- Health

Resources

- Garner, Geraldine O. *Careers in Social and Rehabilitation Services.* 2nd Edition. New York, NY: NTC/Contemporary Publishing Company, 2001.
- **American Art Therapy Association**
  1202 Allanson Road
  Mundelein, IL 60060-3808
  888-290-0878
  http://www.arttherapy.org

- **American Music Therapy Association**

  8455 Colesville Road, Suite 1000

  Silver Spring, MD 20910

  301-589-3300

  http://www.musictherapy.org

- **The American Occupational Therapy Association**

  4720 Montgomery Lane

  PO Box 31220

  Bethesda, MD 20824-1220

  301-652-2682

  http://www.aota.org

- **American Physical Therapy Association**

  1111 North Fairfax Street

  Alexandria, VA 22314-1488

  703-684-2782

  http://www.apta.org

- **American Rehabilitation Counseling Association**

  5999 Stevenson Avenue

  Alexandria, VA 22304-3300

  800-545-2223

  http://www.nchrtm.okstate.edu/arca

  (has general information on careers in rehabilitation counseling)

- **American Speech-Language Hearing Association**

  10801 Rockville Pike

  Rockville, MD 20852

  800-638-8255

  http://www.asha.org

- **American Therapeutic Recreation Association**

  1414 Prince Street, Suite 204

  Alexandria, VA 22314

  703-683-9420

  http://www.atra-tr.org/atra.htm

- **National Rehabilitation Association**

  633 South Washington Street

  Alexandria, VA 22314

  703-836-0850

  http://www.nationalrehab.org

  (offers student membership and publishes a journal)

Religion and Theology

Religion and theology is the study of human beliefs, practices, and worship activities related to a supreme power or deity. Study includes religious history, doctrine, theological concepts, and worship practices as well as issues related to faith, virtue, and morality. Focus may be on a particular denomination or faith or in a specialization such as youth work, religious education, mission work, clerical studies, administration and leadership, evangelism, or outreach.

High School Courses

Anthropology	Religion
Government	Religious History
History	Social Studies
Philosophy	Sociology

Related Majors

Biblical Languages/Literature	Philosophy
Biblical Studies	Religious Education
History	Social Work
Missionary Studies	Sociology
Pastoral Counseling	

Related Occupations

See page 7 for detailed explanation of key.

Campus Minister—B	Rabbi—P
Campus Religious Coordinator—D	Religious Brother—V/B
Chaplain—P	Religious EducationTeacher—B
Church Camp Director—B	Religious Educational Administrator—V/B
Director of Religious Education—B	Religious Researcher—B
Evangelist—V/P	Religious Sister—V/B
Minister of Music—B	Religious Writer—V/B
Missionary—V/B	Salvation Army Officer—V/B
Pastor—V/P	Social Worker—B/M
Priest—P	Youth Minister—V

Leisure Activities

- Regularly participating in church or synagogue activities
- Working part-time or as a volunteer in a religious institution or bookstore
- Attending religious retreats, conferences, revivals, or workshops
- Listening to religious lectures, tapes, and music

- Participating in and financially contributing to religious and charitable endeavors
- Visiting shut-ins or those who are sick or in jail
- Belonging to a religious club or fellowship group
- Attending Bible study
- Reading publications related to religion or theology
- Viewing religious programs on TV
- Engaging in activities that help others

Skills

- Knowledge and proficiency in some area of personal ministry
- Ability to interact with people of varying ages and backgrounds
- General knowledge of the practices, procedures, guidelines, and doctrine of your faith
- Ability to persuade and influence others
- Ability to carry out and integrate occupational responsibilities with religious faith
- Proficiency in reading, writing, and oral communication
- Proficiency in interpersonal communication
- Understanding of human spiritual and social needs
- Sensitivity to and compassion for others
- Ability to make appropriate decisions and solve problems

Values and Attributes

- Religious faith
- Desire to do God's will and love others
- Wisdom
- Morality
- Willingness to continue learning throughout life
- An inner spiritual conviction or calling to serve in a religious capacity
- Sensitivity and concern for the spiritual welfare of others
- Dedication
- Perseverance
- Integrity
- Faith
- Determination

Resources

- Nelson, John, Ph.D. *Opportunities in Religious Service Careers*. New York, NY: VGM Career Horizons, 1998.
- **Intercristo**
  19303 Fremont Avenue, North
  Seattle, WA 98133
  800-251-7740
  http://www.jobleads.org
  (offers Christian employment assistance and career development services and publishes salary comparisons; see the Web site's FAQs)
- **National Council of Churches**
  475 Riverside Drive, Suite 880
  New York, NY 10115
  212-870-2227
  http://ncccusa.org
  (represents 52 million members of Protestant, Anglican, and Orthodox denominations; publishes a variety of religious and educational materials)
- **National Religious Vocation Conference**
  5420 South Cornell Avenue, Suite 105
  Chicago, IL 60615
  773-363-5454
  http://www.visionguide.org
  (offers various materials on religious vocations within the Roman Catholic Church, including the annual *Vision Guide* in print and online)
- **Judaism and Jewish Resources**
  http://www.shamash.org/trb/judaism.html
  (has substantial list of links to Judaism-related Web sites)

Secretarial (Management and Information) Services

Secretarial services include administrative, clerical, information management, and human relations activities associated with and necessary for the efficient operation of an office or workplace. You learn keyboarding, filing, stenography, and word processing and other computer programs. You are also introduced to methods of information management, organization, schedule coordination, problem solving, decision-making, accounting, and communication as well as general office procedures. Specialties in this area are legal, medical, executive, technical, and school.

High School Courses

Accounting	Math
Bookkeeping	Office Operations/Practices
Business	Psychology
Business Machines	Speech
Computers	Word Processing

Related Majors

Accounting	Legal Administrative Assistant
Business Data Processing	Medical Assisting
Business Education	Office Management
Court Reporting	Paralegal Assistant
Dental Assisting	

Related Occupations

See page 7 for detailed explanation of key.

Accounting Clerk—V	Legal Secretary—AA
Administrative Assistant—AA	Medical Assistant—C/AA
Bank Teller—V	Medical Assistant Secretary—C/AA
Cashier—V	Office Clerk—AA/B
Court Reporter—AA/B	Office Manager—AA/B
Data Input Operator—V	Paralegal—AA
Dental Assistant—AA	Receptionist—V
Educational Secretary—C/AA	Records Manager—AA
Educator—V/B	Secretary—V

Executive Secretary—AA/B	Stenographer—AA
File Clerk—V	Typist—AA
Foreign Service Secretary—AA	Word Processor—V

Leisure Activities

- Working as a part-time or volunteer student aide, secretarial assistant, or office clerk
- Reading materials on administrative and secretarial careers
- Volunteering as an office helper for a local church, neighborhood association, club, or community agency
- Belonging to a student or professional office personnel organization
- Writing reports and making oral presentations
- Working on a school newspaper
- Providing a word processing, resume-writing, or editing service
- Organizing social events

Skills

- Good vision and health
- Proficiency for memorization, accuracy, and detail
- Ability to work independently as well as interact effectively with people of different backgrounds
- Ability to work quickly, with distractions, and under tight deadlines
- Ability to take the initiative, make sound judgments and appropriate decisions, and solve problems
- Proficiency with computers
- Strong office skills, including proficiency in operating electronic office equipment, such as scanners, fax machines, and copiers
- Knowledge of practices and trends in office procedures
- Ability to understand and interpret written and oral communication
- Proficiency in spelling, grammar, punctuation, and editing
- Ability to maintain emotional composure under stressful circumstances

Values and Attributes

- Security
- Recognition
- Achievement
- Neatness and flexibility
- Pleasant, positive, and friendly attitude
- Fairness
- Sense of professionalism
- Willingness to perform tasks that may be repetitive or tedious
- Organization
- Self-confidence
- Dependability

Resources

- Ettinger, Blanche. *Opportunities in Secretarial Careers.* New York, NY: VGM Career Horizons, 1999.

- **American Association for Medical Transcription**
  100 Sycamore Avenue
  Modesto, CA 95354-0550
  800-982-2182
  http://www.aamt.org
  (provides online resources, including suggestions on how to prepare for a career in medical transcription, a career overview, and tips for students)

- **International Assistants and Administrative Professionals**
  10502 NW Ambassador Drive
  PO Box 20404
  Kansas City, MO 64195-0404
  816-891-6600
  http://www.iaap-hq.org/about.htm
  (runs job placement service for administrative support personnel and publishes free career booklets on salaries in the field, temporary service, professional trends, and tips for success)

- **National Association of Legal Secretaries**
  314 East 3rd Street, Suite 210
  Tulsa, OK 74120
  918-582-5188
  http://www.nals.org
  (has information on certification and job openings)

Social Work

Social work is the study of the processes that assist people who are unable to cope with serious personal and social problems. Study is aimed at helping the needy and disadvantaged in such areas as child abuse, substance abuse, juvenile delinquency and crime, hunger, financial budgeting, unemployment, health care, mental illness, disability education, parenting, family problems, and homelessness. Some of the areas of specialization are health care and mental health, education, family services, child welfare, drug abuse, gerontology, clinical practice, and occupational counseling.

High School Courses

Civics	History
Economics	Psychology
Government	Social Studies
Health	Sociology

Related Majors

Community Services	Political Science
Criminal Justice	Protective Services
Demography	Psychology
Economics	Public Affairs
Education	Sociology
Gerontology	Urban Studies
History	

Related Occupations

See page 7 for detailed explanation of key.

Child Welfare Worker—B	Minister—P
Community Service	Peace Corps/VISTA Volunteer—B
Agency Director—B	Probation Officer—B
Cooperative Extension Worker—B	Psychiatric Social Worker—M
Drug Rehabilitation Counselor—B	Psychologist—D
Educator—M/D	Residential Counselor—AA
Employee-Assistance	School Counselor—M
Administrator—M	School Psychologist—D
Family Services Social Worker—B	Social Service Aide—AA
Geriatric Case Worker—M	Social Service Director—M
Gerontologist—B/D	Social Worker—B/M
Group Home Director—AA/B	Sociologist—D
Home Economist—B	Technical Writer—B

Human Services Worker—B   Vocational Rehabilitation Counselor—M
Marriage Counselor—B

Leisure Activities

- Working part-time or as a volunteer in a community social agency
- Participating in charitable outreach endeavors and church activities
- Serving as a peer counselor, tutor, or hotline assistant
- Donating money to social concerns
- Reading publications that focus on social problems and issues
- Belonging to a professional organization such as the National Association of Social Workers, Inc.
- Attending lectures and conferences related to social work
- Participating in a Big Brother/Big Sister program

Skills

- Understanding of human behavior and familiarity with community services
- Familiarity with social work theories, practices, and trends
- Ability to interact with people of different backgrounds in a variety of situations
- Proficiency in interpersonal communication
- Intellectual capacity to do well in most undergraduate and graduate college programs
- Proficiency in reading comprehension, writing, and speaking
- Ability to respond spontaneously and maintain composure in stressful situations
- Ability to keenly observe, evaluate, and solve problems
- Ability to conduct and clearly explain social research
- Ability to make appropriate decisions and sound judgments

Values and Attributes

- Achievement
- Desire for recognition and appreciation from others
- Desire to work directly with those challenged by social problems
- Sensitivity to the needs and pains of others
- Ability to work under unpleasant and stressful conditions
- Patience
- Resourcefulness
- Empathy
- Tactfulness
- Integrity
- Discretion

Resources

- Krannich, Ron, and Caryl. *Jobs & Careers with Nonprofit Organizations: Profitable Opportunities with Nonprofits.* 2nd Edition. Manassas Park, VA: Impact Publications, 1999.
- Brophy, Paul C., and Alice Shabecoff. *Guide to Careers in Community Development.* Washington, DC: Island Press, 2001.
- **American Association of State Social Work Boards**
  400 South Ridge Parkway, Suite B
  Culpepper, VA 22701
  540-829-6880
  http://www.aswb.org
  (provides information about licensure and certification standards as well as examination study guides and registration materials)
- **Council on Social Work Education**
  1725 Duke Street, Suite 500
  Alexandria, VA 22314
  703-683-8080
  http://www.cswe.org
  (has information on social work careers and educational programs)
- **National Association of Social Workers, Inc.**
  750 First Street, NE, Suite 700
  Washington, DC 20002-4241
  202-408-8600
  http://www.naswdc.org
  (reported to be the largest social work organization in the United States with more than 150,000 members; provides information about accredited schools, licensure, and social work careers)

Sociology

Sociology is the study of social life and focuses on the interaction between population groups and institutions and their influences on each other. Sociology ranges from the study of relationships in family units in the most primitive cultures to the research of large bureaucratic institutions in major industrialized nations. Among the specialties within sociology are criminology, demography, cultural traditions, family relations, social psychology, gerontology, social welfare, race relations, education, social status, and social change.

High School Courses

Anthropology	History
Civics	Psychology
Economics	Religion
Government	Social Studies
Health	Sociology

Related Majors

Anthropology	History
Criminology	Political Science
Demography	Psychology
Economics	Religion
Education	Urban Affairs
Gerontology	

Related Occupations

See page 7 for detailed explanation of key.

Anthropologist—M/D	Minister—V/P
Case Worker—AA	Peace Corps/VISTA Volunteer—B
City Manager—B	Political Scientist—B/D
Consultant—D	Probation Officer—B
Counselor—M	Psychologist—D
Criminologist—B	Public Administrator—B
Demographer—B	Public Relations Manager—B
Educator—B/M/D	Research Assistant—B
Foreign Service Worker—V	Social Worker—B/M
Gerontologist—B	Sociologist—D
Historian—M/D	Surveying Technician—AA/B
Human Services Worker—V/B	Urban Planner—B
Labor Relations Specialist—B	

Leisure Activities

- Participating in charitable outreach endeavors
- Joining church activities
- Donating money toward social concerns
- Working as a part-time or volunteer in a day care center or community service agency
- Organizing games, parties, or get-togethers
- Joining a professional organization such as the American Sociological Association
- Serving as a camp counselor, on a school board, or as a social research aide
- Freelance writing
- Reading social-issue publications
- Joining a school or community club

Skills

- Proficiency in interpersonal communication
- Intellectual capacity to do well in most undergraduate and graduate college programs
- Ability to conduct and clearly explain sociological research
- Ability to interact with people of different backgrounds in various situations
- Knowledge of community resources
- Ability to maintain composure in stressful situations
- Proficiency in reading comprehension, writing, and speaking
- Ability to evaluate problems and make appropriate decisions
- Proficiency with computers

Values and Attributes

- Desire for recognition and appreciation from others
- Desire to help humanity
- Intellectual growth
- Strong interest in human problems and events
- Sensitivity to and understanding of social problems
- Desire to solve social problems
- Curiosity
- Resourcefulness
- Empathy
- Tactfulness
- Integrity
- Independence

Resources

- **American Sociological Association**

  1307 New York Avenue, NW, Suite 700

  Washington, DC 20005

  202-383-9005

  http://www.asanet.org

  (offers student membership, publishes a student newsletter and career brochures, and provides a directory of sociology departments)

- **Society for Applied Sociology**

  Florida Parishes Social Science Research Center

  Southeastern Louisiana University CB 10686

  Department of Sociology & Criminal Justice

  Hammond, LA 70402

  985-549-5984

  http://www.appliedsoc.org

  (has information on employment of sociologists outside academia)

- **Sociological Practice Association**

  http://www.socpractice.org

  (publishes *The Practicing Sociologist* newsletter and provides information about certification and jobs)

Transportation

Transportation is the field that focuses on the movement of people, materials, and equipment from one place to another. The logistics required for the numerous methods of transportation in an industrialized society are complex. Study in transportation concentrates on how automobiles, buses, trucks, trains, waterways, airplanes, pipelines, and industrial equipment are scientifically, technologically, and creatively manipulated to effectively meet the location needs and deadlines of materials and people. Transportation students specialize in such areas as trucking, automobiles, busing, railroads, waterways, construction machine operation, industrial machine operation, and aircraft.

High School Courses

Business

Driver's Education

Economics

Health

Mathematics

Physical Education

Statistics

Related Majors

Air Transportation

Business

Computer Engineering

Construction Trades

Diesel Mechanics

Electrical/Electronics Technology

Engineering Mechanics

Marketing and Distribution

Quality Control and Safety Technologies

Water Transportation

Related Occupations

See page 7 for detailed explanation of key.

Air Traffic Controller—AA

Airplane Pilot—AA/B

Ambulance Driver—V

Bus Driver—V

Chauffeur—V

Coal Pipeline Operator—V

Deep Submergence Vehicle
  Operator—AA

Dispatcher—AA

Driving Instructor—V

Educator—B/M/D

Ferryboat Operator—V

Industrial Truck Operator—V

Locomotive Engineer—V

Merchant Mariner—AA/B

Motorboat Operator—V

Oil Pumper—V

Operating Engineer—V

Physical Distribution Manager—B

Service Station Worker—V

Taxi Driver—V

Traffic Manager—B

Train Conductor—V

Transportation Engineer—B

Truck Driver—V

Leisure Activities

- Working part-time in a service station, parking garage, or at a truck, bus, or airport terminal
- Engaging in activities that involve moving, hauling, or driving
- Reading publications related to transportation
- Developing hobbies, collections, and interests related to model cars, trains, aircraft, or other vehicles
- Participating in or visiting racing events or car, truck, or boat shows or exhibits
- Operating farm equipment

Skills

- Ability to clearly understand and apply instructions for operating vehicular or mobile equipment
- Manual dexterity and mechanical aptitude
- Aptitude for accuracy and detail
- Knowledge of transportation and safety codes and regulations in an area of specialization
- Good health and physical stamina
- Good vision, color perception, and eye-hand-foot coordination
- Ability to give and understand directions
- Ability to make keen observations, sound judgments, and appropriate decisions
- Ability to react quickly, work under pressure, and meet deadlines
- Good understanding of computerized instrumentation

Values and Attributes

- Power
- Sense of adventure
- Achievement
- Ability to work in stressful situations and awkward positions
- Enjoyment and appreciation of the importance of moving and maintaining vehicles and equipment
- Enjoyment of challenges
- Patience
- Responsibility
- Dependability
- Competence
- Endurance
- Alertness

Resources

- Heitzmann, William. *Opportunities in Marine and Maritime Careers.* New York, NY: VGM Career Horizons, 1999.

- **Air Transport Association of America**

  1301 Pennsylvania Avenue, NW, Suite 1100

  Washington, DC 20004-1707

  202-626-4000

  http://www.air-transport.org

  (organization of airlines that transport people and goods; provides job listings and helpful hints)

- **American Public Transportation Association**

  1666 K Street, NW, Suite 1100

  Washington, DC 20006

  202-496-4800

  http://www.apta.com

  (publishes *Transit Industry Career* newsletter that lists job opportunities)

- **American Trucking Association**

  2200 Mill Road

  Alexandria, VA 22314-4677

  703-838-1700

  http://www.trucking.org

  (provides information on trends in transportation, publishes job listings, and offers resume posting service; see the Web site's Career Center section)

- **Brotherhood of Locomotive Engineers**

  1370 Ontario Street, Mezzanine

  Cleveland, OH 44113

  216-241-2630

  http://www.ble.org

  (sponsors a job bank; see the Web site's Becoming An Engineer section)

- **U.S. Department of Transportation**

  400 7th Street, SW

  Washington, DC 20590

  202-366-4000

  http://www.dot.gov

Zoology

Zoology is a major branch of the biological sciences and involves the study of animals. Zoology ranges from the subatomic and cellular level of the smallest organism to the largest mammal. Zoological study focuses on embryonic development, body structure and function of parts, habitat, and ecological interactions with other living organisms. Specializations within this subject include embryology, cytology, ecology, entomology, ornithology, anatomy, physiology, paleontology, genetics, herpetology, parasitology, mammalogy, marine biology, and wildlife fisheries biology.

High School Courses

Algebra

Biology

Chemistry

Geometry

Math

Physiology

Science

Related Majors

Agriculture

Animal Science

Biology

Entomology

Environmental Science

Marine Biology

Museology

Pathology

Pharmacology

Physiology

Veterinary Science

Wildlife Management

Zoology Education

Related Occupations

See page 7 for detailed explanation of key.

Animal Breeder—V

Animal Control Officer—AA

Animal Laboratory Technician—AA

Biochemist—B

Conservationist—B

Curator—B

Ecologist—B

Educator—B/M/D

Farm/Ranch Manager—V/B

Fishery Biologist—B

Forester—B

Humane Society Worker—AA

Kennel Operator—V

Museum/Zoo Worker—AA

Nature Photographer—AA/B

Park Ranger—B

Pathologist—D

Pest Control Worker—AA

Pet Shop Manager—V

Public Health Specialist—B

Range Manager—AA/B

Taxonomist—B

Technical Writer—B

Veterinarian—P

Veterinary Assistant—V/AA

Wildlife Biologist—B

Marine Biologist—B   Zookeeper—AA/B
Microbiologist—B   Zoologist—B/D

Leisure Activities

- Browsing through 4-H exhibits, pet shops, and science displays
- Attending animal shows or the circus
- Belonging to a zoological society, National FFA Organization, wildlife preservation group, or the Humane Society
- Visiting aquariums, museums, zoos, and nature centers
- Hiking, camping, nature photography, bird watching, fishing, or horseback riding
- Owning and caring for pets
- Working part-time or as a volunteer for the American Society for the Prevention of Cruelty to Animals, a national park or forest, zoo, or veterinary office
- Watching animal shows on TV
- Reading animal-related publications
- Collecting shells, butterflies, insects, or other natural specimens

Skills

- Proficiency in observing, collecting, and analyzing data
- Ability to concentrate for long periods of time
- Proficiency in reading, writing, speaking, and memorization
- Ability to conduct and clearly explain scientific research
- Proficiency in problem solving and decision making
- Proficiency for accuracy and detail
- Ability to work with and relate to animals
- Intellectual capacity to perform well in most undergraduate and graduate college programs
- Thorough knowledge of general biology
- Good health, physical stamina, agility, and manual dexterity

Values and Attributes

- Achievement
- Desire to help others
- Creativity
- Courage, respect, and determination
- Deep appreciation for and kindness toward animals
- Interest in animal protection and preservation
- Curiosity
- Endurance
- Patience
- Perseverance
- Self-control
- Compassion

Resources

- Lee, Mary Price, and Richard Lee. *Opportunities in Animal and Pet Care Careers.* New York, NY: NTC/Contemporary Publishing Company, 2001.
- Maynard, Thane, and Jane Goodall. *Working with Wildlife: A Guide to Careers in the Animal World (Science, College and Career Guidance).* London, UK: Franklin Watts, Inc., 2000.

American Association of Zoo Veterinarians

6 North Pennell Road

Media, PA 19063

610-892-4812

http://www.aazv.org/aazv_001.htm

(offers student membership, a journal, job listings, and links to related sites)

American Institute of Biological Sciences

1444 Eye Street, NW, Suite 200

Washington, DC 20005

202-628-1500

http://www.aibs.org

(has information on careers in biology)

American Zoo and Aquariums Association

8403 Coleville Road, Suite 710

Silver Springs, MD 20910-3314

301-562-0777

http://www.aza.org

(lists employment opportunities and publishes information about careers in zoos and aquariums, as well as in mammal, aquatic, and marine science)

National Wildlife Federation

11100 Wildlife Center Drive

Reston, VA 20190-5362

800-822-9919

http://www.nwf.org

(has information on employment, internships, and volunteer opportunities)

Society for Integrative and Comparative Biology

1313 Dolly Madison Boulevard, Suite 402

McLean, VA 22101

703-790-1745

http://www.sicb.org

(offers student membership and educational programs; provides career information, job listings, and fellowships)

U.S. Fish and Wildlife Service

1849 C Street, NW

Washington, DC 20240

202-208-5611

http://www.fws.gov

(has information on careers and educational requirements for working in this agency)

SECTION V

Career-Related Questions and Answers

1 What does the word "career" mean?

For many people, career means the part of life that is concerned with employment. From an occupational standpoint, it means the sum total of the various jobs you may hold during your lifetime. However, these definitions do not fully capture the meaning of career. We would like you to think of career in a broader, more life-encompassing way. Think of the decisions you make about a job or a college major as valuable components of a lifelong process. When viewed in this manner, career can be defined as the sum total of decisions that direct your educational, social, economic, political, and spiritual endeavors and reflect your unique personality characteristics and basic life values.

2 What is career decision making?

You can best understand good decision making by first defining the term decision. A decision can be defined as the act of choosing. A decision, whether you are aware of it or not, is a response to a question, concern, or problem. Appropriate career decisions can be further defined as the ongoing lifelong process of making choices that complement your personal attributes and help you to realize your basic life values. Indeed, career decisions (particularly those pertaining to an occupation) should be made with great care, for they will significantly influence your direction, personal satisfaction, and fulfillment in life.

3 Is career development different for an older adult than for a younger person?

While the basics of career development (self-assessment, decision-making, occupational awareness, exploration, and implementation) are the same regardless of age, variations in maturity and life experiences necessitate different approaches. Some career specialists believe that most adults, like children and young people, go through a number of developmental stages. Consequently, they consider the life stage of a person before selecting a counseling strategy.

4   What is career success?

Career success really depends on the individual. For some, career success is measured by financial and material accumulation. Others base career success on recognition and popularity. Still others believe that real career success comes only through helping others or making a contribution to society.

It is my belief that career success comes when you achieve inner satisfaction (reflected in a generally positive attitude) through the continuing realization

- of your deepest and most cherished life values in every major endeavor (home, work, school, and leisure).
- that you have the opportunity and inspiration to use and develop current and desired skills.
- that you are excited about what you have achieved, are achieving, and can achieve in the future.

5   What is a career resource or information center?

A career resource or information center is an office or agency that provides you with career and life development information, materials, and services. Career resource or information centers can be either public or private, and they can be independent or part of a larger institution. Many such centers are located on college campuses and within placement services. Others are found in libraries and high schools. The goal of most centers is to maintain accurate, up-to-date career information and provide support services like seminars and workshops, which enable you to make more effective life and career decisions.

6   Are career development and placement services the same?

Not really. However, career development and placement services are often cited by many in the same breath. This is understandable in light of their close relationship. Services and programs often overlap and many colleges and universities offer career development and placement functions jointly through the same office. Nevertheless, while there are a number of program similarities, there are several distinguishing characteristics. Career development is primarily concerned with helping someone make the most appropriate decisions to ensure a fulfilling life. Job placement, on the other hand, focuses on helping a person to actually locate a position and participate and succeed in both career- and noncareer-related work. One might refer to career development as the beginning or foundation stage of the career development and placement process, while job placement is the final or practical application stage. However, particularly in America, both functions are usually intertwined in realizing a more meaningful life.

7   What are career development services?

Career development services usually offer the following:
- Life and career advising, consultation, and counseling
- Computerized career guidance activities
- Administration and interpretation of career interest and personality surveys and ability-and-achievement tests.
- Access to up-to-date occupational files and a career resource library
- Seminars and workshops related to self-awareness, decision making, goal setting, and other career development areas
- Development and distribution of career-related handouts and similar materials
- Access to test information files
- Career lectures presented to classrooms and community groups
- Career information for school administration, faculty, students, and the community at large
- Help in appropriately integrating home life, work, and leisure activities

8   What are job placement services?

Job placement services usually offer the following:
- Employment advice and counseling
- Information about local, state, and national job openings
- Placement of individuals into part-time and full-time jobs
- Creation and maintenance of individual qualification files
- Job hunting, resume, and interviewing services (an increasing number offer online resume and job placement assistance)
- On-campus interviews with potential employers
- Creation and maintenance of employer information files
- Information about career fairs and career days
- Help in establishing professional relationships with local employers
- Information about internships, co-ops, work-study experiences, and on-site visitations
- Follow-up studies related to job placement results and trends
- Lectures to groups on and off campus on job hunting, labor market trends, and other pertinent topics

9   What does a good career counselor do?

Most of the information cited below was developed by the National Career Development Association (NCDA), which can be contacted at http://ncda.org. A good career counselor:
- Conducts individual and group counseling sessions to help clarify life and career goals

- Administers and interprets tests and inventories to assess abilities and interests and to identify career options
- Encourages exploratory activities through assignments and planning exercises
- Evaluates, organizes, and provides educational, occupational, and personal resources and information to clients engaged in life development
- Utilizes career development and occupational information systems to help individuals better understand the world of work
- Helps to improve decision-making skills
- Assists in developing individualized career plans
- Assists with job-search planning and resume development
- Fosters an understanding of the integration of work and other life roles
- Provides support for persons experiencing job stress, job loss, or career transition

10 What is a self-assessment?

A self-assessment entails a serious and honest look at yourself. Self-assessment is a process that requires prioritizing, deep thinking, discovery, and acceptance of personal realities. It may or may not include the help of a career counselor. However, if you want to conduct your assessment in a comprehensive manner, it is strongly recommended that you secure the assistance of a qualified professional. It is not always easy to identify personal aspects of oneself or to use the information discovered to make effective life-changing decisions. However, once you successfully start this process (and it is an ongoing process), it can result in a more focused and fulfilling life. At minimum, self-assessment should include the accurate identification of physical and personal attributes, temperament, abilities and aptitudes, strengths and weaknesses, attitudes, life values, work values, interests, and goals.

Once you have identified, defined, and summarized the above in writing, you will have a beginning blueprint of who you are and what you want in life. You can then compare your decisions with this self-assessment to determine how close they are. Keep in mind that you will need to continually monitor, revise, and update your blueprint. This will ensure that it stays current with your changing reality.

11 What is a college major?

A college major is a specialized field of study that usually reflects your strongest interests and involves the largest number of courses you elect to take. While the term "major" applies to college or university study, its equivalent would be the largest concentration of related courses elected by a student engaged in any postsecondary educational experience (e.g., trade or vocational school, military, etc.).

12 What should I know before selecting a major?

Choosing the appropriate major requires more preparation than many people realize. Contrary to what many think, most of the work needed to effectively select a major should be done prior to entry into a college or university. Ideally, the selection of a major should take place only after you have a fairly good grasp of the techniques for determining, monitoring, and adjusting to who you are and what is most important in your life. Your major area of study should represent only one of a number of important areas in your life, completing the broader life direction previously established. Unfortunately, this advance work is not done by most people, resulting in avoidable frustration due to frequent changes in majors as well as wasted time, energy, and money. You can significantly improve your chances of selecting the most appropriate major if you carefully do the following, in order, beforehand:

I. Identify who you are and what is most important to you in life. In other words, conduct a thorough self-assessment, and if necessary, seek the help of a qualified career counselor.

II. Learn the steps of good career decision making. A good decision-making model might be:
    Step 1. Become aware of the need to make a decision.
    Step 2. Identify what you value and determine whether or not you need more information.
    Step 3. Gather any additional information you believe you need to make a more informed and wise decision.
    Step 4. After you have gathered this information, consider the possible results of each alternative.
    Step 5. Select the one alternative that you believe will most appropriately complement the results of your self-assessment.
    Step 6. Develop and implement a plan of action.
    Step 7. If circumstances make it necessary, review and repeat steps 1 through 6.

III. Identify significant factors (including disability, need for more training, family problems, or recent job loss) that you must consider before deciding what to do.

IV. Applying the steps of good decision making, choose from the following alternatives:
- enter college or trade school
- enter an apprenticeship program

- join the military
- travel
- work for VISTA or the Peace Corps
- get a job
- keep doing what you are doing

It is only at this point (assuming the results of your self-assessment clearly indicate the need for some type of additional training or education) that you are ready to address the next question.

13 How do I select a major?

Choosing a major area of study is often one of the most important and difficult decisions you have to make during your lifetime. A genuine effort to determine a suitable major can serve as the catalyst for comprehensive career planning activities. The results can have lifelong implications in terms of learning how to establish and monitor life direction. There are four main steps in the decision-making process. (If you plan to enter a one- or two-year program of study, apprenticeship, or similar endeavor that requires that the major area of study be decided immediately, then you should complete steps 1, 2, and 3 before entry.)

Step 1. Apply the steps of good decision making to determine what type of curriculum most adequately complements your self-assessment. More than likely, particularly if you have elected to enter a four-year college program-after selecting a suitable curriculum, you will find that a number of related majors can possibly fit. A specific major preference may not crystallize until later.

Usually, this comes about after you have taken a variety of courses, have had fulfilling experiences in certain courses, and have explored several options in depth through discussions with advisors and reading relevant materials.

Step 2. As you continue to apply the steps of good decision making, select the training institution, college, or university you believe offers the curriculum and environment that best support your self-assessment and accommodate any significant influencing factors.

Step 3. Next, continuing to apply the steps of good decision making, select the major that best supports your self-assessment and accommodates any significant influencing factors.

Step 4. Finally, continue to monitor the results of your self-assessment. This is important due to the possibility that one or more significant influencing factors could alter your profile. You should always be ready and willing to refigure previous decisions.

14 What should I do if I want a college degree but don't know what to pick for my major?

Regardless of whether you are in high school or college, there are basic courses that are required in order to earn a diploma or degree. Take these first, as they are likely to apply to the curriculum or major you eventually select. (Be sure to check the basic requirements in the school's handbook or catalog.) In addition to the basics, you may want to take one or more liberal arts or practical electives (computer science, interpersonal communications, writing, speech) that are increasingly important in our changing society. Although these courses may not directly apply to your eventual major or profession, the information acquired can be applied to other areas of your life. Since you will take these courses, at least initially, as electives, it is recommended that you don't enroll in too many before you've reached a decision on your curriculum focus. The extra time you gain as a result will provide you with the opportunity to engage in unrushed self-assessment and other career planning activities. Then, the next time you select courses, you can make informed and wise decisions.

15 What should I do if I only want to pursue a short-term program of a year or less?

Most short-term programs are highly specialized, and courses taken rarely transfer to other programs. Entering into a short-term program without a clear indication that it will most realistically support your self-assessment could prove to be a significant waste of time, energy, and money. Therefore, comprehensive career planning activities are recommended before enrolling in any one- or two-year programs. (You can elect to do this yourself or seek help from a qualified career counselor.)

16 I must register for a full load of classes tomorrow but don't know what to take. What should I do?

There are many variables to consider. Do you plan to graduate from this institution? If so, have you completed all of the basic required courses? Do you have self-assessment results from recent career development activities? If so, what courses seem to complement what you know about yourself? Do you have room for electives? Do you want to attend days? Nights? Part-time? Full-time? Try to answer these questions first. Then, although it may be difficult to talk with someone at short notice, present this concern to a qualified career counselor or academic advisor. Some career counselors have short exercises, checklists, or tests that you can complete in an hour or less, which may point out some general directions. A discussion with a qualified counselor and/or the completion of such exercises may result in a tentative emergency decision. However, this should be viewed as a temporary measure only!

While it may be true that more comprehensive career development activities later will verify the general direction that you arrived at as a result of the above emergency efforts, it does not negate the need to engage in more comprehensive career development. While such "Band-Aid" measures are often required to meet the sometimes overwhelming demands of a fast-moving society, the most successful professionals will strongly recommend follow-up activities.

17 What is an MBA?

MBA stands for Master's of Business Administration. Traditionally, the acquisition of an MBA, particularly if it has been earned at one of the nation's top business schools (e.g., Harvard, University of Michigan, Yale), signifies that you have been well-educated and are highly qualified to step into the world of business. For years, MBA candidates, as well as many professionals, have regarded this degree as the one to acquire if you expect to succeed in corporate America. The MBA has been touted as the key to higher salaries and upper-level executive positions. Indeed, some would probably say that the MBA is to business what the PhD is to college teaching. While some have expressed concerns about how adequately many business schools are keeping pace with the times, the MBA remains a cherished goal for most aspiring business students and still appears to carry considerable weight in the business community (particularly if it comes from an Ivy League school).

18 Should I earn an MBA?

This is probably a question that is asked by most, if not all, undergraduate business majors. Before you make a decision, carefully consider the following:

Age. Do you believe that the years you will have to benefit from having the MBA will outweigh the projected time and effort required to earn it?

Cost. Will you be able to recoup the expenses incurred from attending an MBA program for several years?

Values and Family Lifestyle. Will the pursuit of an MBA, as well as projected benefits later on, support your desired values and lifestyle?

The following is a brief summary of the pros and cons of pursuing an MBA:

Pros
- MBAs usually enjoy a higher salary than non-MBAs.
- In larger corporations, an MBA may improve your chances for advancement and promotion.
- MBA programs usually involve a broad-based (often including an international aspect) and future-directed perspective, which is greatly needed in an increasingly competitive and global market.

- The MBA saves job candidates the frustration of being passed over because of a lack of credentials.
- The MBA is still viewed by many as desirable and may provide opportunities in unrelated areas.

Cons

- Some employers may shy away from MBA grads, believing that they are overrated, lack technical skills, expect higher salaries, and that they may quickly move on to another company.
- An MBA program can be very expensive, possibly costing as much as two years of lost salary that may never be recouped.
- The pursuit of an MBA may place a significant strain on family time and finances.
- You may find out after completion of an MBA program that the sacrifice was not required, particularly if you start your own business or remain in a smaller one.
- If your MBA is not earned from one of the nation's top business schools, you may experience difficulty in landing the type of position you desire.
- You may have unrealistic expectations regarding what the MBA will do for you.

19 Should I earn a PhD?

Whether you should go for the PhD (Doctor of Philosophy)—or for that matter, any graduate degree—depends on how you answer the following questions:

- Do the values, lifestyle, and occupation your are seeking require that you go on to graduate school?
- Do you have the money and/or can you afford the expense of going on to graduate school?
- Will the outlay of money, time, and energy be worth the expected benefits later on?
- Are you willing to do the rigorous and time-consuming research usually required for the final dissertation?
- Do you have to work while you pursue this degree or can you quit work and attend school full-time?
- What is the likelihood you will get a job related to your studies?
- Will the pursuit of a PhD come into severe conflict with your other life values, particularly concerning your family?

These questions should be answered by the potential PhD candidate prior to starting a program of study. A thorough self-analysis should be the first priority. If the results clearly point to areas such as university teaching, higher education administration, research, computer science, or engineering supervision, then a PhD should be a definite consideration. In order to obtain the highest level professional jobs in mathematics, physics, psychology, sociology, engineering, and many other academic disciplines, a PhD is required. The PhD might also be your goal if you have a continuing desire to learn and be intellectually stimulated through research, discovery, and publishing. You may choose this route in order to obtain the status and job advantages often associated with the PhD. However, you may want to avoid such a rigorous academic endeavor if you dislike or are weak in the areas of language, writing, and research. Listed below are some of the pros and cons of pursuing a PhD.

Pros

- A doctorate may open up many more professional and/or supervisory employment possibilities.
- A PhD may increase your prestige and status; you may be considered an expert in your area.
- You may have an opportunity to earn more income.
- A PhD usually increases your credibility in terms of published materials and research.
- A doctorate will probably put you in a good position to take advantage of an increasingly complex and knowledge-oriented society in terms of being able to apply skills learned.
- You have the satisfaction of learning at a highly specialized level.

Cons

- A great deal of time is normally required. It is estimated that the average candidate takes about six or seven years beyond the bachelor's degree to complete the PhD.
- After receiving a PhD, and if employed in a university setting, you may be pressured to "publish or perish."
- The cost of obtaining a PhD can be very high.
- You may experience discrimination from some employers who consider you overqualified.
- The written dissertation is a major obstacle for many.
- You may not be able to find the most desired employment and thus may experience underemployment.

Finally, if you are seriously considering the pursuit of a PhD, be sure to get input from postdoctoral and current graduate students in your area of interest before making a decision.

20 What is an apprenticeship?

An apprenticeship is an arrangement between an employer and an individual (referred to as an apprentice) whereby the apprentice agrees to be trained and supervised by a skilled craftsperson for a specified period of time. Apprenticeship experiences combine classroom instruction and on-the-job training, which must add up to a minimum number of required hours (usually around 8,000 hours or four years of on-the-job experience and a minimum of 576 hours of related instruction). During this time, the apprentice is paid at a progressively higher rate of pay. If the apprenticeship is successfully completed, the apprentice usually applies for and receives his or her Journey Worker's Card, which represents full status as a skilled craftsperson in a particular area of training. (However, be aware that one may acquire a Journey Worker's Card, usually through a union, and not have completed an official apprenticeship program.)

Some occupations that offer apprenticeship training include: Automobile-Body Repairer, Electronics Mechanic, Automobile Mechanic, Emergency Medical Technician, Baker, Firefighter, Biomedical Equipment Technician, Furniture Finisher, Boilermaker, Glazier, Butcher, Hazardous Waste Material Technician, Bricklayer, Instrument Mechanic, Cabinetmaker, Legal Secretary, Carpenter, Machinist, Cement Mason, Millwright, Cosmetologist, Painter, Drafter, Plumber, Electrician, and Sheet-Metal Worker.

21 What is co-op education?

Co-op (short for cooperative) education is a joint venture between an educational institution and an employer to provide a learning experience for one or more students, combining classroom studies with related on-the-job work activities. Normally, the student is paid and the work experience is supervised by representatives from both of the parties involved. Co-op programs are widespread and are administered through many high school, college, and university job placement offices or business departments. The co-op student may spend part of his or her day or semester on the job while the other part is spent in the classroom. In some cases, students rotate between terms of full-time study and terms of full-time work. Many co-op programs grant academic credits.

Pros
- It may lead to a job with the employer.
- It prepares you for the real world due to the large block of time required for work.
- You can earn money for school fees and other expenses.
- A co-op program can help you determine your career direction.
- Work experience can enhance your resume and interviews.

- Co-ops can help you develop work experiences and contacts.
- Co-ops can enrich your personal development.

Cons

- You may not be able to take other academic courses.
- You may find out that the area is not suited for you and thus waste valuable time and energy.
- You may not be able to participate in as many school-related or campus activities due to a full schedule.

22 What are home study (distance learning) courses?

Traditionally, home study courses (sometimes referred to as correspondence courses or distance learning) have been off-campus courses taken by individuals via mail. However, the mode of delivery has changed dramatically due to computerization. A growing number of classes can now be taken via the correspondence route, from elementary through the graduate level. Correspondence courses can be particularly attractive to those who are shut-in. John Bear's book entitled *College Degree by Mail or Modem* (Ten Speed Press, 1999) comprehensively covers this topic.

Pros

- Most home-study courses provide a one-on-one teaching experience.
- They are flexible and convenient for faculty and students.
- You can work at your own pace.
- You can usually enroll at any time.
- You can experience personal growth and satisfaction from achievements.
- You can save time and money (transportation, housing, etc.).
- There are no scheduling hassles.

Cons

- In-person interactions are reduced.
- You need strong self-discipline.
- There may be distractions at home.
- You may not be able to transfer course credits to a traditional program later.
- Your isolation is increased.

23 What is virtual education?

Virtual education can be considered an outgrowth of distance learning, resulting from widespread technological advances. In essence, it is taking academic classes and/or training electronically (primarily via the computer) instead of in an educational institution.

This form of educational training has experienced phenomenal growth and there is no end in sight for the foreseeable future. Various technologies are utilized, although the computer is the primary tool. Depending upon the school, program, and class, other methods or technologies used may include interactive TV, computer conferencing, audiographics, audiocassettes, tele-courses, videotape courses, email, teleconferencing, and fax machines. Colleges that offer entire programs of study online are now commonplace. Students at many of these virtual colleges can now access libraries around the world virtually.

For more information, contact the U.S. Distance Learning Association (USDLA) at http://www.usdla.org.

24 What is an internship?

An internship is an experience offering an individual an opportunity to work in a real job situation for a prescribed period of time to gain knowledge, skills, and work experience. Internships are usually related to your area of study and can be served with or without financial compensation or other work benefits. While many internships take place during the summer months, they may take place anytime during the year and last for a much longer period of time. Some professional internships last a year or more. A growing number of college programs now require the successful completion of an internship before a certificate or degree is granted. Some internships offer academic credits.

Pros
- You can learn job-holding behaviors.
- You can establish contacts for future employment.
- An internship can help you make career decisions.
- You can gain experience valuable on resumes and in interviews.

Cons
- An internship may offer reduced or no pay.
- It may take time away from paid work experience.
- You may find during the internship that the area is not for you and thus waste valuable time and energy.

25 What is mentoring?

Mentoring occurs when an experienced and/or skilled adult (often in an influential leadership position) takes another individual (or mentoree) who is less experienced, knowledgeable, and skilled under his or her wing for the purpose of:

1. Instructing, coaching, and advising in order to help the mentoree overcome potential obstacles and increase the chances for career success;

2. Sharing important inside information about a company, organization, agency, or institution; or

3. Being a contact and support person as well as an advocate for the mentoree in terms of future employment possibilities or promotions.

Having a mentor appears to be extremely advantageous for a growing number who seek to get a foot in the door and learn what it takes to experience upward career mobility within a particular organization. But mentoring relationships have both pros and cons:

Pros

- There is an increased chance to be noticed and thus permanently employed or promoted.
- You have an opportunity to learn from the inside of a company.
- You can pick up skills of use in other situations.
- You can learn valuable tips that will prevent mistakes later.
- You can cut down on the amount of time you need to move up.
- You can build a support base.

Cons

- There is danger of becoming too intimate with or dependent on your mentor.
- The relationship may create friction among your mentor's co-workers.
- Advice from your mentor may conflict with advice from others.
- You may be perceived as a threat by some.
- You may be unfairly used by your mentor.
- If the experience doesn't turn out well, it may hamper your prospects at the company.

26 What is networking and can it help me?

Networking is simply establishing as many relevant personal contacts as possible in order to enhance future career possibilities and personal growth. This could include a wide range of individuals, from family members, friends, and job or school associates to professional acquaintances developed at conventions and meetings and through referrals. Most people engage in networking, whether they realize it or not, through discussions about mutual interests, fellowship, and other interchanges. Networking is viewed negatively by some people because they feel the individual who seeks to network may selfishly take advantage of others. Unfortunately, this may be true of some. However, networking can and should be a give-and-take arrangement wherein both persons involved derive benefit from the interaction and each assists the other.

27 What are "high-tech" jobs?

According to the U.S. Department of Labor, high-tech jobs represent one of the fastest growing occupational areas in the country. These jobs, while they make up only a small percentage of the labor force, continue to increase. Most of us probably associate high-tech with computers, robotics, and automated processes, but there is some difference of opinion as to really what constitutes a high-tech job. The definition used by the Department of Labor says that high-tech jobs are characterized by:

- A significant (higher than the average) number of scientific or technical employees
- A higher-than-average allocation of monies for research and development
- Workers with a good command of the theories and principles of mathematics, science, and engineering

While there are numerous jobs that fit the above criteria, some of the more common ones are computer analysts, engineers, and technicians; science technicians; physical scientists; engineers and engineering technicians; and mathematicians.

28 How do I know if a program or institution is good?

While in some instances this may require considerable investigation, a general evaluation of an academic/training program or institution can be obtained by checking its accreditation status. Most college directories, such as Peterson's guides, include accreditation status. Accreditation procedures are usually thorough and comprehensive and normally include on-site observations and periodical evaluations. To obtain accreditation, an institution or program has to meet previously determined acceptable standards of quality in:

- Academic performance of students
- Competence level of the faculty and administration (amount of training, degrees earned, recognitions, etc.)
- Appropriateness of curriculum
- Quality of library and technology resources
- Quality of student support services (such as assistance for students with disabilities, tutoring, career development and job placement services, foreign student support, and student activities)
- Adequacy of physical facilities

In addition, you can evaluate a program or institution by:

- Seeing how closely it complements your personality attributes and helps you to realize your fundamental life values (determined with a self-assessment or by consulting a career counselor.)

- Obtaining a sampling of opinions from current and past students and instructors
- Checking the institution's job placement records for information on how many of the recent graduates in your interest area are employed in related fields
- Ascertaining the institution's public image and credibility; in other words, what do professionals in your community, past and present students, friends, and community residents say about it?
- Taking note of the ratio of applicants accepted to students enrolled

29 What is a liberal arts major?

A liberal arts major refers to a concentration of courses in nontechnical, non-specialized areas such as anthropology, art, foreign language, political science, communications, literature, religion, English, history, music, economics, journalism, philosophy, psychology, and sociology.

Students who have successfully completed liberal arts curricula normally demonstrate proficiencies in many, if not most, of the following knowledge and skill areas, which are important for occupational flexibility, advancement, and overall life fulfillment:
- Ability to analyze and synthesize information
- Critical thinking and reasoning ability
- Ability to read analytically and speak articulately
- Active listening
- Ability to make good judgments and keen observations
- Ability to solve problems and apply the steps of good decision making
- Interpersonal communication
- Tolerance for change and ambiguity
- Understanding underlying causes and ability to see the "big picture"
- Self-discipline and good organizational skills
- Flexibility
- Appreciation for diversity
- Identifying trends and implications
- Ability to get along with people of different racial and ethnic backgrounds and personalities

30 What are career tests?

It may help to first define "test." Any procedure that attempts to measure or evaluate in order to determine quality, achievement, or ability level can be said to be a test. Career tests are actually surveys, in that they attempt to help you identify interests, skills, and various personality characteristics that will help you make appropriate career-related decisions.

31 Should the results of my career tests determine what I do in the future?

Absolutely not! This is an incorrect assumption that is believed by people far too often. Career tests results should only verify other information you have obtained about yourself so that you can make a better and more informed decision. The intricately complex nature of the human being as well as the highly technical and changing society we live in can never be fully measured by human-devised evaluations. However, when the appropriate career or aptitude test is used, it can be highly beneficial.

Even if it were possible to determine precisely what you should do in the future, it is probably more important to answer the following questions:
- Are my career interests or aptitude test results generally supportive of my most cherished life values?
- Do the results complement my personality attributes?
- Do the results provide me with enough additional information and insight to help me make a better decision about my career direction?

Once again, the most important thing to remember is to combine the results of any career assessment you take with as much additional information as you need to be able to make an informed and wise decision.

32 Should I accept career test results that point to a single field?

Possibly, although you should not act too hastily, even if the results seem to verify your career focus. Also, if you have not had a qualified career counselor assist you in your interpretation, I would strongly encourage you to do so. It is usually wise to have several indicators clearly point in the same direction. I would recommend three to five verifications of direction (e.g., career survey results, favorite school courses and/or those in which you have the highest grades, career worksheet results, feedback from credible others, your own personal beliefs, etc.). Multiple verifications usually minimize the tendency for you to doubt or have continuing second thoughts. They should increase your confidence as well as the chances for you to realize personal satisfaction in life. Finally, using several clear indicators may help you avoid spending time, effort, and money moving in an inappropriate direction.

33 What does it mean when the results of my career testing show that I am interested in just about everything?

While there are a number of possible reasons for such a profile, it is more than likely that one or more of the following is true:

- You may have purposely put down answers that would show a high interest in everything so as not to miss out on anything exciting or interesting.
- You have broad and strong interests in many different areas but may not know enough about yourself to identify those areas that represent the highest priority.
- You lack decision-making skills.
- You simply marked all of the items "favorable" in order to just get through.
- You genuinely have strong interests in many areas, but, unrealistically, want to do everything.
- You may have misunderstood or responded incorrectly.
- There may have been a mechanical (or computer) malfunction or a human recording error.

In such cases, if you cannot identify the reason (and eventually resolve your confusion) from among the above possibilities, it is suggested that you seek the help of a qualified career counselor or do what you most want to do (given that other verifications support the decision).

34 Am I required to take a battery of tests to effectively plan my career?

No. There are a number of resources that can help you determine career direction. Some people, because of family influences, their past experiences with counselors, and other career-directing activities, have developed a clear understanding of themselves and their values. Certain individuals have been fortunate to have had interested and knowledgeable teachers who continually encouraged them in self-analysis, exploration, and good decision making, or maybe a family member just happened to be a career counselor. Still others have benefited from a variety of career-oriented family friends or comprehensive home libraries or enriching trips and vacations. Consequently, they not only monitor change within and around themselves continually, but also they have learned effective decision-making skills.

Some find the results of career-related worksheets, exercises, and written questionnaires sufficient to make appropriate career decisions. Others simply develop over time the necessary motivation and direction by reading books and other publications and doing Internet research. Finally, certain individuals develop an effective system of career decision making through career-oriented audiovisuals; seminars, workshops, and conferences; clubs; classroom and community lectures and discussions; computer software programs; work, volunteer, co-op, or internship experiences; and talking to others.

As you can see, career tests represent only one of a variety of career development activities for you to consider. Testing may not be required or even appropriate for you due to time constraints, cost, language difficulty, reading level, or availability, just to name a few reasons. However, you will want to be absolutely sure you have enough information about yourself and the world around you to better ensure that you are making wise career decisions.

35 What is the difference between an aptitude test and an interest inventory?

While these two types of tests attempt to measure something quite different, I have found that many individuals do not know the difference and are confused. A frequently heard statement is, "I'd like to take one of those aptitude tests." This statement could be referring to an occupational interest inventory, abilities test, or a personality survey. Quite often, after some clarifying questions, it is discovered that the individual actually desired a more comprehensive test to help him or her make a better decision.

Aptitude Tests—According to Harcourt Brace Jovanovich, Inc., publishers of the popular *Differential Aptitude Tests* (DAT), aptitude is "the capacity to learn given appropriate training and environmental input." Aptitudes are considered by this leading test publisher as learned and not inherited. Its tests attempt to measure your degree of "readiness or potential to perform or do" in some identified area(s). An aptitude test seeks to establish if you have a strong, average, or weak tendency to perform well, based on natural and/or learned abilities in selected areas (e.g., spatial, verbal, numerical, mechanical, abstract reasoning, clerical, etc.). Normally, the results of an aptitude test do not provide enough diagnostic information for those seeking to establish career direction, unless they are added to other relevant data.

Interest Inventories (Surveys)—These tests are widely used and may be mistakenly perceived by some as having more comprehensive career development application than they have been designed for. Interest inventories attempt to identify significant trends toward or away from selected occupational areas, the objective being to compare the inventory-taker's interests with the general interests of individuals in designated occupations. Interest inventories are based on the premise that the more your interests are like/unlike individuals in selected occupations, the more compatible/incompatible the occupational area is likely to be. Nevertheless, just as it is true for aptitude tests, interest inventory results are limited, no matter how accurate, and represent only one of a number of important aspects that should be considered in career decision making.

36 Should I "test out" of a required course?

It depends on your particular circumstance, but it may be to your advantage to test out if one or more of the following is true:

- You are thoroughly proficient in the basic knowledge and/or skills that will be covered in the course; to take the course would be a rehash of what you already know and thus may be a waste of valuable time. For example, if you've been a freelance writer for five years, testing out of a basic composition course in your degree program makes good sense.
- Extenuating circumstances, such as disabilities that keep you from taking on-campus courses or serious time conflicts due to family or job obligations, demand that an alternative to regular classroom attendance be explored.
- You have taken an advanced placement (AP) class during high school in the area you want to test out of, and you are quite knowledgeable and/or highly capable in that area. In this instance, testing out may allow you to move into advanced courses and thus shorten the time required to earn your degree. Remember, the rationale here for testing out is that you are already highly capable. If this is not true, then maybe taking the course would be the wiser choice. If in doubt, see a qualified counselor.

On the other hand, testing out may not be the best option if one or more of the following reflects your present situation.

- Due to a lack of effort, knowledge, or ability, you have failed a required course and thus would like to test out of it to avoid taking it over again.
- You believe you can pass the test and are looking for a quick and easy way to obtain a degree. Not only is there a good chance you will not pass, but you may very well find out later that you have unnecessarily shortchanged yourself in terms of the enriching educational experiences that often result from classroom exposure.
- The course is in an important foundation area that will give you knowledge and skills you will later need to apply regularly and with significant proficiency. In such instances, it is recommended that you take the actual class. It is unlikely that a test will be able to duplicate the formal and informal discussions between instructor and student that a classroom experience affords. A great deal of learning, as well as valuable networking opportunities, can be lost if you are not exposed to such experiences. To test out of courses that

demand depth and breadth in all aspects could eventually put you at a disadvantage in the future.

If you are interested in testing out, contact your high school or college counselor and ask about Advanced Placement, CLEP Tests, GED Tests, and/or any Challenge Tests (faculty made) that may be available.

37 Can occupational projections be trusted?

Some would answer, "Well, yes!" and others would say, "Probably not." Whatever position you take, it must be clearly understood that occupational projections are merely educated guesses, although they may be based on extensive research. No human being can foretell the future perfectly; many variables can and do, often unexpectedly, affect outcomes (e.g., supply and demand, technological advances, weather, war). Predictions have often been known not to hold up. Nevertheless, job projections can be quite helpful when coupled with other related data, particularly if information is obtained from a reliable source. A key resource, considered to be credible by most, is the U.S. Bureau of Labor Statistics (BLS), a government agency that specializes in occupational predictions. Many college and university career development and placement centers, as well as state employment service offices, maintain a file of updated labor market projections from the BLS and other sources. Also, many career specialists believe that jobs are available in most occupational areas, regardless of job predictions. However, to acquire these jobs, you must learn and effectively implement the skills of job hunting (including via the Internet) and self-marketing. I am inclined to agree.

38 What are some common problems that often hamper career development?

There is a limitless number of obstacles that can seriously jeopardize career progress. The following represent some of those frequently voiced by our clients over the years. For most we have included some general suggestions on how you can begin to overcome such obstacles. In addition, several positive qualities that might develop, should the obstacle be overcome, have been cited in some instances. Finally, a suggested resource may be included for a few of the obstacles listed. However, it is strongly recommended that if any of the problems below persist, please seek the help of a qualified professional. Suggestions are provided as starting points only.

Procrastination—An ex-procrastinator could become thorough, analytical, and cautious before acting. A helpful little booklet published by Pathway Books is James R. Sherman's *Do It*.

Work-Family Conflict—Effectively coping with conflicts arising between work and family can help you develop time-management, self-discipline, and conflict management skills. Several books on the topic are available and individual counseling can be helpful.

Lack of Information, Education, or Training—Conduct a thorough self-assessment and engage in related career development activities; read career materials and talk to people in your area of interest; if necessary, enroll in a related course of study. Those who lack information, education, or training can develop self-confidence and the ability to sift through unnecessary information and thus avoid a significant waste of time, money, and energy. See a qualified professional counselor.

Financial Need—Explore scholarship and grant options and consider going to school part-time, attending a community college, or taking courses through correspondence programs. It is my belief that you should avoid taking out a loan to attend college. However, should you determine that a loan is absolutely necessary, be sure the program or major selected is appropriate and obtainable. When acquiring loans under such circumstances, it can usually be considered an investment which will provide a positive return.

Perfectionism—With professional counseling, a former perfectionist can develop into someone who is neat, exact, precise, and thorough.

Lack of Self-Confidence—Very often, if you obtain knowledge about yourself and what you want in life, along with information about acquiring a more fulfilling life, it will serve to build confidence (particularly if you also develop new skills). Minimize or eliminate negative images of yourself; realistically list accomplishments, no matter how small they may appear; associate with those who encourage rather than discourage you. A person who formerly lacked self-confidence may become conscientious, reliable, and encouraging to others.

Indecisive—Conduct a thorough self-assessment and engage in related career development activities; learn and apply the steps of good decision making. A person who formerly made haphazard and generally poor decisions may develop the qualities of patience, courage, and wisdom (particularly with the assistance of a qualified career counselor).

Stress—Often characterized by frustration, fear, and general discomfort due to conflicts in relationships, time, responsibilities, and values, some possible solutions include physical exercise, recreation, rest, self-assessment identification and implementation, and time management. Very often, college counseling and career centers as well as women's resource centers distribute materials on this topic.

Appendix A
Self-Assessment Survey

Feel free to duplicate any of the following self-assessment sheets for your own personal use. Responses can also be simply written on a sheet of paper.

TEMPERAMENTS

Temperaments are personality attributes that relate to your way of thinking, feeling, and behaving and determine whether you are comfortable or uncomfortable in a given situation. Please read the directions and complete the temperaments profile below.

Directions: Weigh each of the temperaments below on a comfort scale of 1 to 12 (1 being the situation in which you feel the MOST COMFORTABLE). Place your rating on the black line beside the appropriate letter. If you feel equally comfortable about more than one, do not hesitate to use the number twice.

___A. Situations involving a VARIETY of duties often requiring frequent CHANGE (doing different activities).

___B. Situations involving REPETITION or REPEATING SOMETHING FREQUENTLY according to set procedures or sequences (doing the same task over and over).

___C. Situations involving DOING THINGS only UNDER SPECIFIC INSTRUCTION, allowing little or no room for independent action or judgment in working out job problems (little or no personal input required).

___D. Situations that involve DEALING WITH PEOPLE in actual job duties beyond giving and receiving instructions (high degree of interaction and cooperation with people).

___E. Situations that involve DIRECTING, CONTROLLING, and PLANNING of entire activities or the activities of others.

___F. Situations involving WORKING ALONE and apart from others although the activity may be integrated with that of others (doing most or all of your work by yourself although it may be done around others).

___G. Situations that involve INFLUENCING PEOPLE in their opinions, attitudes, or judgments about ideas or things (being able to persuade others in the way they think, act, and behave).

___H. Situations involving PERFORMING ADEQUATELY WHILE WORKING UNDER PRESSURE or when confronted with the critical or unexpected or when taking risks (being challenged, taking challenges and coming through on challenges).

___I. Situations that require you make an evaluation based on PERSONAL JUDGMENT (making decisions based on personal experiences and through the use of your senses, e.g., sight, smell, hearing, taste, or touch).

___J. Situations requiring you to make a decision using MEASURABLE OR VERIFIABLE CRITERIA (making decisions based on something that has been or can be measured based on facts, rules, or standards).

___K. Situations in which you INTERPRET AND EXPRESS FEELINGS, IDEAS, OR FACTS IN A PERSONALLY CREATIVE WAY (such as through song, acting, writing, painting, etc.).

___L. Situations involving PRECISION in terms of set limits, tolerances, or standards (being detailed and exact).

PRIMARY SOURCE: *Dictionary of Occupational Titles*

STRENGTHS (Circle those you believe are most like you and rank order your strongest five.)

Active	Enduring	Industrious	Punctual
Affectionate	Energetic	Intelligent	Respectful
Ambitious	Enthusiastic	Joiner	Self-confident
Analytical	Expressive	Kind	Sense of humor
Assertive	Fair	Like challenges	Sensitive
Caring	Faithful	Logical	Sharing
Charming	Flexible	Loyal	Speak well
Cheerful	Forgiving	Mannerly	Spontaneous
Comforting	Friendly	Neat	Steadfast
Compassionate	Generous	Objective	Tactful
Competent	Gentle	Observant	Talented
Cooperative	Good listener	Open-minded	Team player
Courageous	Good with hands	Optimistic	Thoughtful
Creative	Good-natured	Organized	Thrifty
Dedicated	Graceful	Patient	Tolerant
Dependable	Grateful	Peacemaker	Trustworthy
Determined	Helpful	Perform well under pressure	Understanding
Disciplined	Honest		Unselfish
Discreet	Hospitable	Persistent	Witty
Efficient	Humble	Poised	
Encouraging	Independent	Productive	

WEAKNESSES (Circle those that are most like you and rank your weakest five.)

Apathetic	Disrespectful	Liar	Rarely finish
Argumentative	Do dumb things	Moody	anything
Aggressive	often	Not dependable	Rude
Bossy	Domineering	Obnoxious	Sarcastic
Braggart	Drug abuser	Often negative	Secretive
Can't concentrate	Easily offended	Overly critical	Selfish
Can't make	Fearful	Overly talkative	Shy
decisions	Flippant	Panicky	Stingy
Can't say no	Gullible	Perfectionist	Stubborn
Can't take	Hateful	Perform poorly	Sulky
criticism	Hostile	under pressure	Tactless
Clumsy	Impatient	Pessimistic	Uncouth
Cruel	Impulsive	Picky	Unrefined
Complainer	Inflexible	Poor listener	Swear a lot
Cocky	Insensitive	Poor loser	Wasteful
Condescending	Intolerant	Prejudiced	Whiny
Confronter	Irresponsible	Prideful	Wimpy
Deceptive	Jealous	Put things off	Worry a lot
Dependent	Judgmental	Quick-tempered	
Dishonest	Lack of courage	Racist	
Disorganized	Lazy		

Top Five Strengths

1. _____
2. _____
3. _____
4. _____
5. _____

Top Five Weaknesses

1. _____
2. _____
3. _____
4. _____
5. _____

SKILLS (ABILITIES and APTITUDES)

Skills can be divided into two major categories:

ABILITIES—An ability can be defined as something you can do as a result of rehearsal and/or practice. Abilities and skills are often thought of as being the same; being skilled, though, usually implies that you can do something well. A specific knowledge of your strongest abilities can greatly increase your sense of confidence.

APTITUDES—Aptitudes are those activities you have the potential to perform well and seem to come easily and naturally. Some people have aptitudes they are either unaware of or have been unable to develop to their fullest. Becoming aware of your aptitudes can help you to better understand who you are on the inside.

Directions: Place an "A" in front of the area(s) in which you believe you have ABILITY or APTITUDE. Feel free to write in any ability/aptitude you may have in addition to or instead of the sampling listed. Leave blank any area you are not sure of. As you go through, keep in mind that you will be asked when finished to list your five strongest abilities/aptitudes.

___Understanding instructions, facts, and underlying reasoning; being able to reason and make judgments

___Understanding the meaning of words and ideas; being able to present information or ideas clearly

___Doing arithmetic operations quickly and correctly

___Looking at flat drawings or pictures of objects and forming mental images of them in three dimensions or in terms of height, width, and depth (such as in reading blueprints, patterns, etc.)

___Observing details in pictorial or graphic material and effectively making visual comparisons; good at noticing differences in shapes, shading, etc.

___Observing details and recognizing errors in numbers, spelling, and punctuation in written materials, charts and tables; good at avoiding errors when copying

___Moving the eyes and hands or fingers together to perform a task rapidly and correctly

___Moving the fingers to work with small objects rapidly and correctly

___Moving the hands with ease and skill, as in placing and turning

___Moving hands and feet together in response to visual signals, etc.

___Seeing likenesses and differences in colors or shades; matching colors

___Finding errors in writing

___Following instructions

___Asking the right questions

___Improving what others have done

___Explaining things clearly

___Planning and organizing

___Operating mechanical equipment

___Expanding on what others have started

___Exploring and doing research

___Budgeting

___Being exact and to the point

___Spelling

___Accepting constructive advice

___Being creative

___Getting along with others

___Counseling others

___Doing artistic things

___Keeping records

___Leading and supervising others

___Teaching others

___Gardening

___Typing

___Giving others helpful advice

___Being flexible

___Drawing or designing things

___Mechanical things

___Training others to do things

___Driving vehicles

___Performing in front of others

___Taking risks

___Solving conflicts

___Noticing shapes, sizes, etc.

___Staying with a task until done

___Repairing and servicing computers

___Getting others to believe in something

___Making good decisions during emergencies

___Simplifying what appears to be complex

___Learning from mistakes and past experiences

___Working alone for long periods of time

___Understanding and reading blueprints, maps, drawings, etc.

___Listening or picking up on what others say

___Seeing the underlying reasons for behavior or events

___Estimating costs

___Interpreting the feelings and emotions of others

___Reading and comprehending

___Doing activities that require heavy physical work

___Writing

___Copying things or activities done by others

___Collecting things

___Constructing things out of wood or metal or other materials

___Speaking in public

___Working with numbers/solving accounting-type problems

___Operating computers

___Motivating others to perform or do something

___Being thorough

___Expressing feelings

___Managing time

___Distinguishing sounds

___Doing things for others

___Communicating to others

___Controlling own emotions

___Thinking before acting

___Team sports (basketball, football, etc.)

___Individual sports (tennis, golf, etc.)

___Leading and supervising people and activities

___Using your fingers to work with small objects or instruments

___Studying English or related subjects (name related subject(s))

_____

___Studying social studies or related subjects (name related subject(s))

_____

___Studying science or related subjects (name related subject(s))

_____

___Other (Include any additional or alternative skills.)

_____   _____

_____   _____

_____   _____

List your five STRONGEST abilities/aptitudes.

1. _____

2. _____

3. _____

4. _____

5. _____

The skills list represents just a sampling of possibilities. For a more comprehensive and personalized list, you may want to read the latest edition of Richard Bolles's *What Color is your Parachute?* (Ten Speed Press, 2001).

LIFE VALUES

Life values are those deeply cherished things, activities, or relationships you place the most importance on and aspire to obtain or engage in. Life values provide us with the necessary motivation to endure many of life's hardships. Please read the directions and complete the life values survey below.

Directions: Read through the entire list. After reading, go back and place in the blank to the left of each value the code that best describes its level of importance to you:

NVI = Not Very Important   I = Important   VI = Very Important

Next, circle the items marked VI that you consider MOST IMPORTANT (identify at least five but no more than seven).

___ACHIEVEMENT (accomplishment; being able to see or experience results that have been brought about by persistence or hard work)

___AESTHETICS (the appreciation and enjoyment of beauty for beauty's sake, as in the arts and/or in nature)

___ALTRUISM (having a special regard for or dedication to the welfare of others; service to others)

___AUTONOMY (independence; the ability to make your own decisions; self-directed; not being dependent on others)

___CREATIVITY (being able to try out new ideas; being different from the traditional; being innovative)

___EMOTIONAL WELL-BEING (having peace of mind and inner sense of security; the ability to identify and resolve inner conflict; being relatively free from anxiety)

___HEALTH (maintaining an acceptable condition in terms of your physical body; being relatively free from pain, discomfort, sickness, etc.)

___HELPING MANKIND (engaging in activities or inventing, developing, or producing something that will positively influence the lives of many; making a significant contribution of lasting or continuing value)

___HONESTY (being frank, genuine, and truthful with yourself and others)

___JUSTICE (treating others fairly or impartially; holding to truth or reason)

___KNOWLEDGE (desire to learn or know; to seek truth; to acquire information about)

___LOVE (warmth, caring, and unselfish devotion that freely accepts others without conditions)

___LOYALTY (maintaining allegiance to a person, group, or institution; not abandoning; sticking with during difficult times)

___MORALITY (believing and keeping ethical standards; personal honor; integrity; doing what you truly believe is right)

___PHYSICAL APPEARANCE (concern for your attractiveness; being neat, clean, and well-groomed)

___PLEASURE (having satisfaction, fun, joy, gratification)

___POWER (having possession or control; authority or influence over others)

___RECOGNITION (to be regularly recognized and positively noticed; receive attention)

___RELIGIOUS FAITH (having religious beliefs; having a personal relationship with God)

___SECURITY (being sure of most endeavors or involvements in life; having visible or concrete support or back-up before taking risks)

___SKILL (being very good at something; being better than average; performing at a high proficiency level)

___WEALTH (having many possessions and plenty of money)

___WISDOM (having mature understanding; deep insight; good sense and judgment; being able to make appropriate and effective decisions)

WORK VALUES

Work values are those things, activities, and relationships you place the most importance on and aspire to obtain or engage in, relative to an occupation. While work values are often similar to life values, many are specifically related to an occupational setting. Work values tend to reflect much of who you are on the inside. Please read the directions and complete the work values survey below.

Directions: Read through the entire list. After reading, go back and place in the blank to the left of each value the code that best describes its level of importance to you:

NVI = Not Very Important   I = Important   VI = Very Important

Next, circle the items marked VI that you consider MOST IMPORTANT (identify at least five but no more than seven).

___ADVANCEMENT (the ability to advance and move up; opportunity for higher position or training or education, etc.)

___ACHIEVEMENT (accomplishing something everyone can't do or will not do; doing something that requires considerable effort and/or difficulty)

___ASSISTING OTHERS (being directed and supervised by others; preferring not to have the responsibility of leading or directing people or activities)

___BENEFITS (having good hospital and life insurance, etc.; unemployment and vacation benefits)

___COMPETITION (being in an environment where you have to compete or be matched against in rivalry; being challenged to produce or perform)

___CREATIVITY (being able to try out new ideas; to be innovative)

___ENVIRONMENT (being in physical or social surroundings that are suitable to your temperaments and values, e.g., beautiful, neat, friendly, warm, etc.)

___HANDS-ON CONTACT (working with things, objects, and/or equipment; using hands and other body parts to perform tasks and activities that are primarily of a physical nature)

___HELPING OTHERS (engaging in activities that directly aid and assist others)

___INDEPENDENCE (having little or no supervision; freedom to guide your own activities and make your own decisions)

___INDUSTRY (work that keeps you busy and active continuously; could include physical and/or mental tasks; having little or no down time)

___INTERESTING (being positively excited and motivated most of the time in what you are doing; not likely to be bored for any significant span of time; doing something you can continuously enjoy with few exceptions)

___LEADERSHIP MANAGEMENT (being in a leadership, supervisory, or managerial position; being in charge of others)

___LEARNING (using mental abilities; gaining knowledge and understanding; being intellectually stimulated)

___MONEY (earning a high salary)

___NUMBER CONTACT (working with numbers; charting; doing statistical reports and summaries)

___POSITIVE RELATIONSHIPS (being able to get along very well with co-workers and supervisors; working with people whom you generally like; being in an environment that is characterized by warm and cooperative relationships)

___PRESTIGE (having a position that is recognized as being very important and influential by most; being in a position that commands great respect)

___PEOPLE CONTACT (high interaction and cooperation with people; being around people most of the time)

___RELIGIOUS FAITH (work that is in line with your religious beliefs; work that does not interfere with your ability to practice your religious principles)

___SECURITY (being relatively free from the fear of frequent layoffs, job loss, reduced hours, etc.)

___SELF-DIRECTION (being able to determine what you are going to do and how you are going to do it in terms of work tasks, procedures, pace, etc.)

___SKILL (having the ability to perform one or more tasks at an extremely high proficiency level; being able to do something that requires special effort or training or education)

___SUPPORT (being in a work environment where you receive emotional support, praise, and backing)

___TRAVEL (being able to travel within a local community as well as from city to city as a part of your job responsibilities; having a travel budget)

___VARIETY (doing different things or activities; not doing repetitive tasks)

___WHOLE LIFE SENSITIVITY (working in a situation that allows or provides reasonable flexibility and choice in terms of overtime, time off, vacation selection, length of workday, family priorities, and outside concerns; being able to engage in non-job-related activities without hindrances)

___WORDS/IDEAS INFORMATION (working with oral, visual, and written information, knowledge, facts, ideas, and/or symbols (may include numbers))

___OTHER (Include any value that has not already been mentioned. If you desire to add more, please feel free to do so.)

_____

_____

INTERESTS

Interests are those things, activities, and experiences you enjoy and are excited about. Much of what we do during our leisure time tends to reflect our interests. Interests often reveal some of our most important values. Also, you can be interested in an activity, experience, etc., without actually being involved in it. A selected list of interests and/or leisure-time activities has been included below and on the next several pages. Please read through the directions and complete the interests survey below.

Directions: Go through the entire list and circle those things, activities, or experiences that represent a STRONG INTEREST for you. Keep in mind that you will be asked when you finish to list your strongest interests.

being the leader

cooking

acting

gardening

solving math problems

visiting museums

organizing community events

working with people

water sports and games

canoeing, sailing, etc.

doing hard physical work

working with words or ideas

participating in church activities

drawing cartoons or real-life pictures

helping those who are poor

hunting, fighting, trapping, etc.

biology, life science, etc.

working on cars or other mechanical things

team sports (basketball, baseball, football, hockey, etc.)

individual sports (swimming, golf, jogging, tennis, racquetball, etc.)

reading

writing

beading

selling things

going to plays

driving vehicles

music

teaching

canning

parenting

earning money

competing with others

video games

electronic gadgets

board games

listening to the radio

watching TV

eating out

bowling

arts and crafts

traveling

antiques

talking

foreign languages

movies

politics

guns

knitting

collecting (butterflies, leaves, stamps, coins, etc.)

designing clothes

ham radio operation

interior decorating

backpacking

bird watching

camping

exploring

flying

hiking

horseback riding

nature walks

sailing

sightseeing

walking

yard work

Big Brother/Big Sister or similar program

charitable drives

counseling others

neighborhood associations

house plants and flowers

Peace Corps

military involvement

war games

Red Cross

spending time with the elderly or visiting the sick and shut in

VISTA

YMCA/YWCA

browsing through bookstores

conferences/conventions/workshops

debating

editing

jigsaw puzzles

lab experiments

lectures

organizing activities

preparing taxes

researching

science exhibits

studying and going to school

talk shows

working in a nursery or day care center

writing in a diary

antique shows

art galleries

auctioning

auto shows

religious study

boat shows

singing in a choir

playing or singing with a group

circuses

composing

concerts

macramé

needlepoint

photography

pottery

sculpting

typing

dancing

entertaining others

fairs

fashion shows

festivals

marching band

nightclubs

parties

pen-pal exchange

plays

poetry

talent shows

variety shows

visiting libraries

zoos

planetariums

4-H

archery

club leader

conservation

health

nutrition

investments

Junior Achievement

Masons

astrology

motorcycles

scouting

sororities/fraternities

broadcasting

doing housework

exercising

learning new things

comic books

magazines

newspapers

professional journals

sleeping

window shopping

shopping

teaching a craft or sport

visiting flea markets

viewing travelogues

auto racing

fitness activities

gymnastics

ice skating

skiing

weightlifting

fencing

cross country

In the blanks below, write any interests or leisure-time pursuits that you strongly enjoy but were not included above.

_____   _____

_____   _____

_____   _____

What do you like the most? Write your STRONGEST (at least five but no more than seven) interests below.

1. _____

2. _____

3. _____

4. _____
5. _____
6. _____
7. _____

Are there any things, activities, or experiences (listed in the sampling or not) that you strongly dislike? If so, write these in the blanks below.

1. _____
2. _____
3. _____
4. _____
5. _____
6. _____
7. _____

SELF-ASSESSMENT PROFILE SHEET (SAPS)

A Self-Assessment Profile Sheet appears on the next page. On this sheet record the summary information you were asked to identify in each section. If you feel there are items that should be added to the number requested because you believe they are of equal weight (or tied in terms of rank order) please feel free to do so. A sample of a completed SAPS has been included.

Remember, your profile is subject to change in time due to Significant Influencing Factors (SIF). SIF are situations or events that significantly alter your thinking patterns, activities, and relationships and consequently motivate you to make adjustments in important occupational decisions. Examples of SIF include sickness, disease, accident, flood, famine, war, change in religious beliefs, divorce, drug abuse problem, loss of a job, new legislation, among others. Therefore, it is suggested that you periodically review this profile and, whenever necessary, update it.

After completing your SAPS you will probably want to identify the occupation and/or college major you believe the results most realistically reflect (minus the weaknesses and dislikes, of course). You can generate your own list of occupations and majors to pick from or take a Career Interest Survey, such as the Kuder or Strong-Campbell surveys, from a career counselor. It is our hope that after you complete the reading and exercises in this book, as well as follow the suggestions given, you will be well on your way toward a more directed and fulfilling life.

SELF-ASSESSMENT PROFILE SHEET

LIFE VALUES (p. 228) List the five to seven items you circled.

1.
2.
3.
4.
5.
6.
7.

WORK VALUES (p. 229) List the five to seven items you circled.

1.
2.
3.
4.
5.
6.
7.

INTERESTS (p. 231) List your five to seven STRONGEST interests.

1.
2.
3.
4.
5.
6.
7.

TEMPERAMENTS (p. 223) List in order from 1 to 12 your MOST COMFORTABLE temperaments.

1.
2.
3.
4.
5.
6.
7.
8.
9.
10.
11.
12.

SKILLS (p. 225) List your five STRONGEST abilities/aptitudes.

1.
2.
3.
4.
5.

STRENGTHS (p. 224) List your top five strengths.

1.
2.
3.
4.
5.

WEAKNESSES (p. 225) List your top five weaknesses.

1.
2.
3.
4.
5.

SELF-ASSESSMENT PROFILE SHEET

(Sample of Completed Form)

LIFE VALUES

1. Achievement
2. Emotional well-being
3. Love
4. Morality
5. Religious faith
6. Wisdom

WORK VALUES

1. Support
2. Variety
3. Words/ideas/info
4. Advancement
5. Money
6. Benefits
7. Achievement

INTERESTS

1. Being the leader
2. Sports
3. Making money
4. Biology
5. Talking
6. Religious study and prayer/meditation
7. Being with friends

TEMPERAMENTS

1. Measurable/verifiable
2. Directing/controlling
3. Variety/change
4. Influencing people
5. Precise

SKILLS

1. Solve conflicts
2. Doing for others
3. Knowing what to say/do
4. Leading/supervising
5. Being exact and budgeting

STRENGTHS

1. Independent
2. Dependable
3. Competent
4. Ambitious
5. Organized

WEAKNESSES

1. Moody
2. Perfectionist
3. Argumentative
4. Judgmental
5. Often negative

APPENDIX B

Descriptions of Selected Occupations

The following descriptions should encompass the least familiar occupations mentioned in this book. Most of the occupational definitions cited are based to some extent on information provided in the *Dictionary of Occupational Titles* (DOT) and the *Occupational Outlook Handbook*. For a comprehensive and detailed list of occupational definitions, consult the latest edition of the DOT or the Occupational Information Network (O*NET), which is being developed by the U.S. Employment and Training Administration as the new, automated replacement for the DOT. When it is completed, it will provide a comprehensive database that identifies and describes important information about occupations, worker skills, and training requirements. (See http://www.doleta.gov/programs/onet/)

ABSTRACTOR—A worker who analyzes pertinent legal or insurance details or sections of statute or case law to summarize for purposes of examination, proof, or ready reference—may specialize as a title examiner.

ACCOUNTING CLERK—A clerical worker who performs any combination of routine calculating, posting, and verifying of financial information for use in maintaining accounting records.

ACQUISITIONS LIBRARIAN—A librarian who selects and orders books, periodicals, films, and other materials for a library.

ACTIVITIES SUPERVISOR—A recreation therapist who specializes in the organization, direction, and supervision of recreational activities for those individuals who are elderly, ill, or disabled to assist in their overall rehabilitation.

ACTUARY—A professional who applies knowledge of mathematics, probability, statistics, and principles of finance and business to various forms of insurance, annuities, and pensions.

ADJUDICATOR—A government worker who adjudicates (gives an opinion on) claims filed by the government against individuals or organizations.

ADMINISTRATIVE EXAMINER—A worker who supervises and oversees polygraph examiners who question and screen individuals to detect deception or to verify truthfulness using polygraph equipment and techniques.

ADMIRALTY LAWYER—A lawyer who specializes in legal matters pertaining to inland navigable waters or on the high seas.

ADULT AND VOCATIONAL EDUCATION TEACHER—A teacher who specializes in preparing students for a particular vocation such as welding, food service, or horticulture.

ADVERTISING ACCOUNT EXECUTIVE—A professional who plans, coordinates, and directs advertising campaigns for the clients of an advertising agency.

AERODYNAMIST—An engineering specialist who plans and conducts the analyses of aerodynamic, thermodynamic, aerothermodynamic, and aerophysics concepts, systems, and designs to resolve problems and determine suitability and application to aircraft and spacecraft.

AERONAUTICAL ENGINEER—An engineer who applies engineering principles and techniques to design, develop, and test aircraft, space vehicles, surface effect vehicles, and missiles.

AEROSPACE ENGINEER—An engineer who designs, develops, tests, and helps produce commercial and military aircraft, missiles, and spacecraft.

ARCHIVIST—A professional who appraises and organizes permanent records and historically valuable documents, participates in research activities involving archival materials, and directs the safekeeping of archival documents and materials.

ART THERAPIST—A health care specialist who plans, coordinates, and supervises art techniques, projects, and programs to assist in the rehabilitation of mentally or physically challenged patients.

ASTROPHYSICIST—A physicist who specializes in the study of the physical aspects of the heavenly bodies or space such as the sun, stars, and planets.

AUDIOLOGIST—A professional therapist who specializes in diagnostic evaluation of hearing, prevention research, and rehabilitative services for people with hearing problems and related disorders.

AUDITOR—An accounting professional who examines or audits financial records and controls operating procedures to determine effectiveness and efficiency; may specialize in internal, external, county, tax, or other kinds of auditing.

BACTERIOLOGIST—See Microbiologist.

BAILIFF—A court officer who maintains order in a courtroom during trials and guards the jury from outside contact, can arrest persons violating the law, and is responsible for overall security.

BAR EXAMINER—A professional who determines the qualifications of candidates seeking to practice law; prepares written exams, corrects and marks papers, announces those who pass, and makes recommendations.

BIBLIOGRAPHER—A professional who compiles lists of books, periodicals, articles, and audiovisual materials on specialized subjects.

BIOCHEMIST—A professional scientist who studies chemical processes of living organisms and conducts research to determine the influence of foods, drugs, serums, and other substances on tissues and vital processes.

BIOMEDICAL ENGINEER—An engineer who specializes in using medical and biological ideas and principles in the design, development, production, and supervision of medical equipment and devices.

BIOMEDICAL EQUIPMENT TECHNICIAN—A worker who specializes in the inspection, maintenance, calibration, and modification of the electronic, electrical, mechanical, hydraulic, and pneumatic equipment and instruments used in medical therapy.

BIOPHYSICIST—A biological scientist who studies the physical principles of living cells and organisms, their electrical and mechanical energy, and related phenomena.

BIOSTATISTICIAN—See Statistician.

BLACKSMITH—A worker who creates and repairs various metal articles such as tongs, edged tools, hooks, chains, machine and structural components, and agricultural articles.

BLOOD BANK SPECIALIST—A health care worker who specializes in both simple and advanced blood techniques such as drawing blood, classification, collection and transfusion, testing, evaluation, preservation and storage, and other related activities.

BOILERMAKER—A worker who assembles, analyzes defects in, and repairs boilers, pressure vessels, tanks, and vats by using power and hand tools.

BOOKBINDER—A worker who cuts, sews, and glues the pages of a book to its cover, using a sewing machine, hand press, and hand cutter.

BOTANIST—A biological scientist who studies the development and life processes, physiology, heredity, environment, distribution, anatomy, morphology, and economic value of plants for application in such fields as agronomy, forestry, horticulture, and pharmacology.

BUYER—A professional who purchases merchandise or commodities for resale, inspecting, selecting, ordering, and authorizing payment for them.

CABLE SPLICER—A worker who splices overhead, underground, or sub-marine multiple-conductor cables used in telephone and telegraph communications and electric power transmission systems.

CARDIOLOGIST—A medical doctor who specializes in the diagnosis, treatment, and prevention of diseases of the heart.

CARTOGRAPHER—A professional drafter who specializes in drawing maps of geographical areas to show natural and constructed features, political boundaries, and other features.

CATALOGER—A librarian who compiles information and materials, such as books and periodicals, and prepares catalog cards and computer records to identify materials and integrate information into a library's collection.

CATERER—One who coordinates the food service activities of a hotel, restaurant, or other similar establishment or at a social function; includes food preparation, budgeting, menu planning, managing staff, and maintaining food quality.

CERAMIC ENGINEER—An engineer who specializes in developing new non-metallic, inorganic materials and new methods for making ceramic materials into useable products.

CHAMBER OF COMMERCE OFFICER—One who represents a local asso-ciation of businesspeople who aim to promote commercial and industrial interests in the community; involves analyzing of market trends, economic conditions, and tax issues; advising businesses; supporting economic and civic growth; and other activities.

CHAPLAIN—A clergy worker who conducts and coordinates worship ser-vices, evangelism activities, and religious education endeavors in the armed forces, correctional institutions, hospitals, and on college campuses.

CHEMICAL LABORATORY TECHNICIAN—A worker who conducts chem-ical and physical laboratory tests and makes qualitative and quantitative analyses of materials, liquids, and gases for the purpose of research, new prod-ucts, health and safety standards, criminology, environmental concerns, and more.

CHIEF EXECUTIVE OFFICER (CEO)—The top executive or administrator of a large corporation or government.

CHILD WELFARE WORKER—A social worker (caseworker) who aids par-ents with child-rearing problems and children who have difficulties in social adjustments; investigates home conditions; refers clients to community resources; coordinates foster care or adoption activities; provides counsel to families; and supervises and monitors placements.

CHIROPRACTOR—A physician, but not a medical doctor, who specializes in the adjustment of the spinal column and other body parts to improve health and correct abnormalities of the human body believed to be caused by interferences with the nervous system.

CHOREOGRAPHER—A dance director who creates and teaches original dances for ballet, musical, or revue to be performed for stage, TV, motion picture, or nightclub production.

CINEMATOGRAPHER—A photography director who plans, directs, and coordinates the filming of a motion picture.

CIRCULATION MANAGER—A manager who directs the sales and distribution of newspapers, books, and periodicals.

CITY MANAGER—A government administrator who directs and coordinates the administration of a city or county government in accordance with policies determined by a city council or other authorized officials.

CIVIL ENGINEER—An engineer who plans, designs, and directs the construction and maintenance of structures and facilities such as roads, railroads, airports, bridges, harbors, channels, dams, irrigation projects, pipelines, power plants, water and sewage systems, and waste disposal units.

CLIMATOLOGIST—A meteorologist who specializes in the study of climate and climate conditions.

CLINICAL CHEMIST—A biochemist who studies the chemical processes of living organisms and uses complex chemical tests and procedures to analyze body tissues and fluids.

COAL PIPELINE OPERATOR—A worker who controls, from a master panel, a semiautomatic processing plant that pulverizes and mixes coal with water and sends the resulting slurry into a pipeline for transportation.

COLLEGE DEAN—A college administrator who directs and coordinates a specific area of responsibility such as student affairs, academics, occupational programs, continuing education, men, or women.

COLUMNIST—An individual who analyzes news and writes a column or commentary based on personal knowledge and experience with the subject matter for publication or broadcast.

COMMERCIAL ARTIST—A professional artist who draws or paints illustrations for use by various media to explain or enhance the printed or spoken word.

COMMUNITY SERVICE AGENCY DIRECTOR—An individual who directs the activities of a community health or social service agency concerned with community problems such as teen pregnancy, child abuse, substance abuse, or disease.

COMPOSITOR—A worker who assembles and sets type by hand or machine and creates galleys for printed materials.

COMPUTER SECURITY SPECIALIST—An individual who evaluates the security of computer systems; also trained to prevent, safeguard against, and investigate computer-related crimes.

CONSERVATIONIST—A worker who is concerned with the protection and care of natural resources such as streams, rivers, lakes, and forests.

CONSULTANT—A professional who has developed a proficiency or expertise in a particular area and is consulted by clients to define a need or problem, conduct studies or surveys to obtain information, and analyze data to give advice on or recommend a solution.

CONTRACTOR—A manager who contracts to perform specified construction work in accordance with architectural plans, blueprints, and codes; may be classified as a building contractor, landscape contractor, engineering contractor, or other specialized contractor.

CONTROLLER/COMPTROLLER—An individual who directs the financial affairs of an organization such as a bank, hospital, governmental office, or hotel.

COOPERATIVE EXTENSION WORKER—An agricultural agent who organizes meetings to advise farmers and individuals engaged in agribusiness in application of agricultural research findings; may direct 4-H club activities, give lectures, and prepare articles; sometimes called an agricultural extension agent.

COPYWRITER—A professional who writes or revises material (copy) for use by print or broadcast media to promote the sale of goods and services.

CORONER—A medical examiner who directs investigations of death occurring within a particular jurisdiction as required by law. Coroners conduct inquests, perform autopsies and laboratory analyses, and may testify at hearings or trials.

CORRECTIONS OFFICER—An individual who is responsible for guarding inmates in jails and prisons in accordance with established policies, regulations, and procedures.

COUNTY PROSECUTOR—See District Attorney.

COURT REPORTER—A clerk who performs clerical duties in a court of law, including preparing a calendar of cases, examining legal documents, explaining procedures, securing information, recording minutes of court proceedings, and other tasks.

CREDIT MANAGER—A worker who directs and coordinates the activities of a federal or state chartered credit union that provides savings and loans services to members.

CRIMINOLOGIST—A professional sociologist who specializes in the study of crime and criminal behavior.

CURATOR—A professional who oversees the collection, research, authentication, preservation, maintenance, and information dissemination activities of operating and exhibiting institutions such as museums, botanical gardens, arboretums, art galleries, herbariums, and zoos.

CURRICULUM SUPERVISOR—A professional educator who supervises and oversees the implementation of an instructional materials program in an elementary, junior high, or high school in accordance with guidelines.

CUSTOMS INSPECTOR—A government worker who inspects cargo, baggage, and articles worn or carried by persons on vessels, vehicles, or aircraft entering or leaving the country to enforce customs and related laws.

CYTOLOGIST—A biological scientist who studies plant or animal cells.

CYTOTECHNOLOGIST—A health care specialist who assists pathologists through the process of staining, mounting, and studying cells of the human body to determine pathological conditions.

DANCE THERAPIST—A specialist who plans, organizes, and directs dance activities and learning experiences as part of the care and treatment of patients to produce positive behavioral changes.

DATA-ENTRY EQUIPMENT OPERATOR—A worker who enters information into a computer system.

DATABASE MANAGER—A worker who supervises and manages the designing, creating, and operating activities in the formulation of a computerized information storage bank.

DENTAL HYGIENIST—A health care worker who specializes in removing plaque and tartar from teeth and beneath the gumline; also does preliminary examinations for the dentist.

DENTAL LAB TECHNICIAN—A health care worker who builds and repairs full and partial dentures (sets of teeth), bridges, crowns, and other dental apparatus using hand tools, molding equipment, and bench fabricating machines.

DERMATOLOGIST—A medical doctor who specializes in the diagnosis and treatment of diseases and conditions of the skin.

DESIGN/BUILDING SPECIALIST—An architect who specializes in both the design and physical building aspect of a project; may work with a contractor or make modifications on his or her own.

DESKTOP PUBLISHER—A professional who produces printed materials via computer using the techniques of layout and graphic design.

DIAGNOSTIC MEDICAL SONOGRAPHER—A health care specialist who uses ultrasound diagnostic procedures, which make use of sonic energy to identify or determine the extent of disease or injury in body tissue.

DIETETIC TECHNICIAN—A worker under the direction of a dietitian who assists in food service management, nutrition education, and dietary counseling.

DIETITIAN—A health care specialist who directs, plans, and supervises programs for menu planning, food preparation, nutritional care, serving of meals, and specialized diets.

DIPLOMAT—See Foreign Service Officer.

DIRECTOR OF ADMISSIONS—A professional who directs and coordinates a student admissions program at private schools or public and private colleges or universities according to policies developed by a governing board, determines who will be accepted, prepares and distributes materials about the institution and its programs, and conducts recruitment programs.

DIRECTOR OF CAREER PLACEMENT—A professional who directs and supervises job placement services for students and employees; usually arranges for interviews, posts or publicizes listings of job openings, supervises and coordinates campus work-study programs, offers seminars and workshops related to job seeking/holding skills, develops and distributes occupational information, etc.

DIRECTOR OF GUIDANCE—A professional counseling administrator who directs and coordinates educational and vocational guidance and counseling programs for students and graduates.

DISPATCHER—A worker who dispatches buses, cabs, trains, airplanes, trucks, and other transporting vehicles; supervises, coordinates, and relays schedules and instructions regarding movement and location; also maintains an operational log.

DISTRICT ATTORNEY—A lawyer who conducts prosecutions in court proceedings on behalf of the city, county, state, or federal government; presents evidence against the accused to a grand jury and before a judge or other judiciary or jury.

DRAFTER—A worker who prepares clear, complete, and accurate working plans and detail drawings from rough or detailed sketches or notes for engineering or manufacturing purposes according to specified dimensions; may specialize in architectural, aeronautics, electrical, or other area.

ECOLOGIST—A biological scientist who studies the relationship between organisms and their environments and the effects of pollutants, rainfall, temperature, altitude, and other variables on organisms.

ECONOMIST—A professional who plans, designs, and conducts research to aid in interpretation of economic relationships and develops solutions for problems arising from the production and distribution of goods and services; may specialize in health, agriculture, labor, or other areas.

EDITOR—A person who prepares materials for publication or release, making revisions or other modifications.

EEG (Electroencephalographic) TECHNOLOGIST—A health care worker who measures impulse frequencies and differences in electrical potential from the brain for use in diagnosis of brain disorders using the electroencephalograph.

EKG (Electrocardiograph) TECHNICIAN—A health care worker who records electromotive variations in the action of heart muscle, using the electrocardiograph machine, to help determine the causes of heart complications.

EMERGENCY MEDICAL TECHNICIAN—A health care worker who administers first aid, including life support, while transporting sick or injured persons to a medical facility.

ENDOCRINOLOGIST—A doctor who specializes in diseases that affect glands (thyroid, parathyroid, pancreas, ovaries, testes, adrenal, pituitary and hypothalamus).

ENGINEER—A professional who applies mathematical and scientific principles in an economical and efficient manner to the design, planning, development, production, supervision, repair, and maintenance of the products, equipment, structures, processes, systems, and programs of industrial societies. The main branches of engineering are civil, electrical/electronics, mechanical, industrial, metallurgical, chemical, aerospace, agricultural, and nuclear.

ENTOMOLOGIST—A professional scientist who studies insects and their relation to plant and animal life, identifies and classifies insects, and helps to develop pesticides and other methods to control pests.

ENTREPRENEUR—An individual who starts and owns his or her own business.

ENVIRONMENTAL ENGINEER—Usually a civil, chemical, or mechanical engineer who specializes in some aspect of the environment (e.g., soil testing, air pollution, water pollution, toxic substances, etc.).

ENVIRONMENTAL HEALTH TECHNICIAN—A worker who conducts tests and field investigations to obtain information for use by environmental engineering and scientific personnel in determining sources and methods of controlling pollutants in air, water, and soil.

ENVIRONMENTALIST—A professional who studies, analyzes, and evaluates environmental problems and applies scientific knowledge to prevent pollution, solve problems, and make predictions about the air, water, land, noise, and radioactivity.

ERGONOMIST—A professional who specializes in designing products and arranging work environments to adapt to the behaviors of human beings and to ensure their health and safety on the job.

ESCROW OFFICER—A professional worker who holds in escrow (safekeeping) funds, legal papers, or other collateral posted by contracting parties to ensure fulfillment of contracts or trust agreements.

ESTIMATOR—An accounting specialist who prepares cost estimates for products or services requested to aid management in bidding on jobs or determining the price of those products or services.

EXECUTIVE HOUSEKEEPER—An administrator who directs an institutional housekeeping program to ensure clean, orderly, and attractive conditions; may be employed by hospitals, hotels, or motels.

FBI AGENT—See Special Agent.

FINANCIAL AID DIRECTOR—A professional who directs the scholarship, grant, and loan programs at a college or university to provide financial assistance to students.

FINANCIAL ANALYST—A worker who conducts statistical analyses of information affecting an investment program of a public, industrial, or financial institution such as a bank, insurance company, brokerage, or investment house.

FINANCIAL PLANNER—A professional who specializes in helping individuals and companies invest their income in the most efficient and economical manner to better prepare for future needs, goals, and emergencies.

FLORICULTURIST—A professional horticulturist who specializes in the research, breeding, production, storage, processing, and transit of flowers.

FOOD AND DRUG INSPECTOR—A government worker who inspects establishments where food, drugs, cosmetics, and similar consumer items are manufactured, handled, stored, or sold to enforce legal standards of sanitary conditions and health and hygiene habits of persons handling such products.

FOOD SCIENTIST—A professional scientist who applies scientific and engineering principles in the research, development, production technology, quality control, packaging, processing, and utilization of foods; may specialize in dairy products, poultry, cereal, grains, etc.

FOOD SERVICE MANAGER—An individual who manages, supervises, and coordinates a program of serving food in a hospital, nursing home, college, or other institution.

FOREIGN SERVICE OFFICER—A government worker who represents the interest of the United States government and citizens by conducting relations with foreign governments and international organizations, protecting and advancing political, economic, and commercial interests, and rendering personal services to Americans abroad and to foreign nationals traveling to the United States; may be termed diplomat, consultant, ambassador, etc.

FORESTER—A professional who manages and protects forest lands and their resources for economic, educational, and recreational purposes.

FORESTRY TECHNICIAN—A worker who gathers information pertaining to size, content, condition, and other characteristics of forest tracts and under the direction of a forester, leads workers in forest propagation, fire prevention and fighting, and maintenance of facilities.

4-H CLUB AGENT—A worker who organizes and directs the educational projects and activities of a 4-H club; recruits farm volunteer leaders; directs selection of projects such as sewing, woodworking, photography, and livestock raising; and develops and arranges exhibits in county or state fairs.

FREELANCE WRITER—A self-employed writer who submits his or her work to various sources for publication and/or writes on a contract basis.

FUNERAL DIRECTOR—An individual who arranges, coordinates, and directs burial preparations and funeral services.

GENEALOGIST—A historian who conducts research into the background of an individual or family in order to establish descent or to discover and identify forebears of the individual or family.

GENERAL CONTRACTOR—See Contractor.

GENERAL PRACTITIONER—A medical doctor who treats a variety of medical problems without specializing in any one area.

GENERAL SUPERINTENDENT—A manager who directs the activities of workers in the construction of buildings, dams, highways, pipelines, or other structures; usually directs and oversees other supervisory personnel.

GENETICIST—A professional scientist who studies the hereditary variation of characteristics in forms of life; may specialize in molecular, population, human, medical, animal, or plant genetics.

GEODESIST—A professional who studies the size, shape, and gravitational field of the earth.

GEOGRAPHER—A professional who studies nature and the features of the earth, relating and interpreting interactions of physical and cultural phenomena.

GEOMORPHOLOGIST—A geologist who specializes in the history, structure, and changes of the earth's surface.

GEOPHYSICIST—A physical scientist who studies the physical aspects of earth, including its atmosphere and hydrosphere. Specialties include oceanography, glaciology, and volcanology.

GEOTECHNICAL ENGINEER—A civil engineer who specializes in the evaluation of soil and rocks that support structures and assists in the design and construction of foundations, dams, tunnels, and other structures.

GERIATRIC CASE MANAGER—A professional social worker who specializes in diagnosing the physical and mental health needs and arranging for the proper care of the elderly.

GERONTOLOGIST—A sociologist who specializes in the study of aging and older adults.

GLAZIER—A construction worker who installs glass in windows, skylights, store fronts, display cases, building fronts, interior walls, ceilings, and table tops; may specialize in auto glass, aircraft, plate glass, etc.

GRAPHIC DESIGNER—An artist who designs books, magazines, newspapers, packaging, and other printed materials as well as artwork for TV and other media.

GREENSKEEPER—A worker who oversees a staff in preserving the grounds and turf of golf courses.

GROUNDSKEEPER—A caretaker who maintains the grounds of industrial, commercial, or public property and performs a combination of tasks such as cutting lawns, trimming hedges, pruning trees, fertilizing and spraying, raking and planting, watering, and shoveling snow.

GYNECOLOGIST—A medical doctor who specializes in the diagnosis, treatment, and prevention of diseases and disorders of the female genital, urinary, and rectal organs.

HAND MOLDER—A worker who tends a stuffing machine that fills molds with meat emulsion to form meat loaves; may stuff bologna and sausages into casings by hand.

HEALTH ADVOCATE—A health care professional who serves as a liaison between patients and health care institutions; provides a link to appropriate services.

HEALTH MICROBIOLOGIST—See Microbiologist.

HOME ECONOMIST—A professional who organizes and conducts consumer education services or research programs for equipment, food, textile, or utility companies utilizing principles of home economics (preparing food, recipe testing, using household equipment and products, home management, etc.); may specialize as a nutritionist, equipment specialist, or in another area.

HOME HEALTH AIDE—A worker who cares for elderly, convalescent (recovering from illness), or people with disabilities in their homes, performing any combination of tasks such as changing beds, ironing, washing, purchasing food items, giving massages, assisting patients in walking, and monitoring their patients' conditions.

HORTICULTURIST—A professional who conducts experiments and investigations in the breeding, production, storage, processing, and transport of fruits, nuts, berries, vegetables, flowers, bushes, and trees.

HOTEL/MOTEL MANAGER—A person who manages a hotel or motel to ensure it is an efficient and profitable operation and is meeting the guests' service needs.

HYDRAULICS ENGINEER—A civil engineer who specializes in the area of hydraulics (operation or motion by means of water or liquid).

HYDROGRAPHER—An individual who analyzes hydrographic data to determine trends in movement and utilization of water.

HYDROLOGIST—A geologist who studies the distribution, circulation, and physical properties of underground and surface waters.

ILLUSTRATOR—A worker who creates drawings or other images for display, book or magazine illustration, or advertising purposes using pencil, pen, charcoal, watercolors, air brush, or computer.

INDUSTRIAL DESIGNER—A professional who conceives and designs the forms of manufactured products.

INDUSTRIAL HYGIENIST—A health care professional who develops, conducts, and evaluates the health program in an industrial setting or governmental organization in an effort to identify, eliminate, and control health hazards such as dust, gases, vapors, lighting, noise, ventilation, and diseases.

INDUSTRIAL TRUCK OPERATOR—A worker who drives a gasoline, natural gas, or electric-powered industrial truck equipped with lifting devices (forklifts, boom, scoop, lift beam, swivel hook, fork-grapple, clamps, elevating platform, or trailer hitch) to push, pull, stack, tier, or move products, equipment, or materials in a warehouse, storage yard, or factory.

INFORMATION SCIENTIST—A professional who designs computerized information systems to provide management or clients with specific electronic data utilizing data processing principles, mathematics, and computer capabilities.

INSTRUMENT REPAIRER—A worker who repairs and calibrates speedometers and other automotive gauges and meters using hand tools and test equipment.

INSTRUMENTATION TECHNICIAN—A skilled worker who develops and operates electronic equipment and related apparatus to test mechanical and/or electrical equipment.

INSURANCE ADJUSTER—A worker who investigates claims against insurance or other companies for personal, casualty, or property loss or damages, and attempts to effect an out-of-court settlement with the claimant; may be called a claims adjuster.

INTERIOR DESIGNER—A professional who plans, designs, and finishes interior environments of residential, commercial, and industrial buildings; may specialize in the decorative aspect and be called an interior decorator.

INTERNAL AUDITOR—See Auditor.

INTERNAL REVENUE AGENT—A government officer who conducts independent field audits and investigations of federal income tax returns to verify or amend tax liabilities.

INTERNIST—A medical doctor who specializes in the diagnosis, treatment, and prevention of diseases, conditions, and injuries of human internal organs and systems.

JOB ANALYST—A professional who collects, analyzes, and prepares information on various occupations; observes jobs and interviews workers; writes job descriptions and specifications; may specialize in classifying positions.

JOB SETTER—A machinist who sets up and adjusts various machine tools such as lathes, milling, and boring machines, drill and punch presses, etc.; usually works by blueprint, job order, and other specifications.

LANDSCAPE ARCHITECT—A professional who plans and designs the development of land areas for parks, airports, highways, parkways, hospitals, schools, factories, housing projects, business establishments, and other projects.

LANDSCAPE GARDENER—A worker who plans and executes small-scale landscaping operations and maintains grounds of businesses and private residences.

LATHER—A construction worker who fastens wooden, metal, or rockboard (lathe) to walls, ceilings, and partitions of buildings to provide supporting base for plaster, fireproofing, or acoustical material, using hand tools and portable power tools (not to be confused with someone who uses a tool called a lathe).

LAYOUT WORKER—A worker who lays out metal stock or work pieces such as castings, plates, or machine parts to indicate location, dimensions, and tolerances necessary for further processing; analyzes specifications and computing dimensions; and follows blueprints.

LEGAL INVESTIGATOR—A legal assistant who researches and prepares cases relating to administrative appeals of civil service members; also presents arguments and evidence to support appeals hearings.

LEGAL SECRETARY—A secretary who prepares legal papers and correspondence of a legal nature such as summonses, complaints, motions, and subpoenas.

LIBRARY TECHNICIAN—One who provides information services, including answering cataloging questions, assisting users with research tools, filing cards, answering routine inquiries, and making referrals.

LICENSED PRACTICAL NURSE—A health care worker, licensed by the state, who provides direct bedside care for those who are sick, injured, or elderly in hospitals, clinics, private homes, convalescent homes, and other institutions.

LINE INSTALLER—A worker who, using electrician's hand tools, installs and repairs telephone and telegraph lines, poles, and related equipment according to diagrams and other specifications.

LINGUIST—A professional who studies the components, structure, nature, and modification of language and speech and may help to prepare language teaching materials, dictionaries, and handbooks.

LITHOGRAPHER—A worker who transfers positive or negative images to offset printing plates using various methods.

LOBBYIST—A public relations specialist who contacts and meets with members of the legislature and other public officials to persuade them to support laws that are favorable to a client's interest.

MACHINIST—A worker who, applying knowledge of mechanics and machinery procedures, sets up and operates machine tools and fits and assembles parts to make or repair metal parts, mechanisms, tools, or machines.

MAITRE D'HOTEL—The head waiter or steward of a hotel or restaurant.

MANPOWER DIRECTOR—An administrator who directs and supervises employees and activities aimed at securing qualified temporary workers to fill job vacancies.

MANUFACTURER SALES WORKERS—A salesperson who sells single, allied, diversified, or multiline products to wholesalers or other customers for one or more manufacturers on a commission basis.

MARBLESETTER—A construction worker who cuts, tools, and sets marble slabs in the floors and walls of a building and repairs and polishes existing slabs.

MARKET RESEARCH ANALYST—A professional who researches marketing conditions and trends in a local, regional, or national area to determine the potential sales of a product or service.

MEDICAL ASSISTANT—One who serves as a secretary, receptionist, and/or bookkeeper and performs duties such as arranging for X rays and other medical procedures, billing and collecting fees, and filing insurance claims.

MEDICAL ENGINEER—An engineer who works with physicians and scientists to apply engineering principles to medical diagnosis, surgery, and rehabilitation.

MEDICAL/SCIENTIFIC ILLUSTRATOR—An artist who sketches, draws, paints, and develops diagrams and models illustrating medical and scientific findings for use in publications, exhibits, consultations, research, and teaching.

MEDICAL LAB TECHNICIAN—A health care worker who performs routine laboratory tests, such as taking blood samples, for use in the treatment and diagnosis of disease.

MEDICAL OFFICER—A public service worker who plans and participates in medical research programs in hospitals, clinics, or other public medical facilities to provide medical services to those who qualify.

MEDICAL RECORDS TECHNICIAN—An individual who specializes in compiling and maintaining medical records of hospital and clinic patients.

MEDICAL TECHNOLOGIST—A medical specialist who performs chemical, microscopic, serologic, hematologic, immunohematologic, parasitic, and bacteriologic tests to provide information for use in treatment and diagnosis of disease.

MENTAL HEALTH TECHNICIAN—A health care worker who assists, treats, works with, and directly supervises emotionally ill and mentally retarded patients.

MENTAL HEALTH WORKER—Any individual, from a secretary to a counselor or an administrator, who works in a hospital or agency that provides treatment and/or services to individuals who experience mental or emotional difficulties.

MERCHANDISE DISPLAYER—A worker who displays merchandise such as clothes, accessories, and furniture in windows, in showcases, and on sales floors of retail stores to attract the attention of prospective customers.

METALLURGIST—A person who researches the physical characteristics, properties, and processing of metals.

METEOROLOGIST—A physical scientist who analyzes and interprets meteorological data gathered by surface and upper-air stations, satellites, and radar to prepare weather reports and forecasts.

MICROBIOLOGIST—A scientist who studies the growth, structure, development, and general characteristics of bacteria and other microorganisms; may specialize in viruses, fungi, or in other areas.

MILLWRIGHT—A skilled worker who installs machinery and equipment in industrial plants, according to a layout plan, blueprint, and other drawings, using hoists, lift trucks, hand tools, and power tools.

MINERALOGIST—A geologist who examines, analyzes, and classifies minerals, gems, and precious stones.

MODEL MAKER—A skilled worker who constructs scale models of objects using clay, metal, wood, fiberglass, or other substances, depending on the industry for which the model is being constructed (e.g., automobile, boat, etc.).

MULTIMEDIA SPECIALIST/TECHNICIAN—A worker who skillfully blends audio, video, graphics, and text to communicate information, often working solely on a computer.

MUSIC THERAPIST—A health care specialist who plans, organizes, teaches, and supervises music and related activities for a more integrated and successful rehabilitation of patients.

MYCOLOGIST—A scientist who studies the life processes of edible, poisonous, and parasitic fungi to determine which are useful to medicine, agriculture, and industry.

NATURALIST—A professional who specializes in the study of plants or animals (e.g., zoologist, botanist, etc.).

NEUROLOGIST—A medical doctor who specializes in the diagnosis and treatment of organic diseases and disorders of the nervous system.

NUCLEAR ENGINEER—An engineer who engages in the design, development, monitoring, and operation of nuclear power plants to generate electricity and power navy ships; may also conduct research on nuclear energy and radiation.

NUCLEAR MEDICINE TECHNOLOGIST—A medical specialist who prepares, administers, and measures radioactive isotopes in therapeutic, diagnostic, and tracer studies, utilizing a variety of radioisotope equipment; prepares stock solutions of radioactive materials and calculates doses to be administered by a radiologist.

NURSE ANESTHETIST—A professional health care specialist who administers anesthetics or drugs (via fluid, gas, etc.) to lessen or alleviate pain during surgical, dental, or other medical procedures.

NURSE-MIDWIFE—A nurse who specializes in providing medical care to women under the care of an obstetrician; delivers babies and provides patients with health care during pregnancy as well as for a period of time following childbirth.

NURSE PRACTITIONER—A professional health care specialist who usually works with a physician to provide general medical care and treatment to assigned patients; may work independently.

NUTRITIONIST—A professional who conducts and organizes consumer education service or research programs involving food and nutrition.

OBSTETRICIAN—A medical doctor who specializes in the treatment of women during prenatal, natal, and postnatal periods; concerned with the mother's as well as the infant's health and comfort during pregnancy.

OCCUPATIONAL THERAPIST—A health care specialist who plans, organizes, and conducts a comprehensive rehabilitation program to help mentally, emotionally, or physically disabled persons to return to work and resume daily activities.

OCEANOGRAPHER—A specialist who studies oceans, seas, marine life, and related areas.

OPERATING ENGINEER—A heavy equipment operator of one or more types of power construction equipment such as compressor pumps, hoists, derricks, cranes, shovels, tractors, scrapers, or motor graders to excavate, move, and grade earth; erect and reinforce steel; or pour concrete or other hard surface material.

OPHTHALMOLOGIST—A medical doctor who specializes in the diagnosis, treatment, and prevention of diseases and injuries of the eyes.

OPTICIAN—A specialist who makes or orders and sells eyeglasses and contact lenses according to individual prescriptions.

OPTOMETRIST—One who specializes in eye examinations to determine visual efficiency, performance, diseases, and conditions, and prescribes corrective lenses or procedures.

ORTHODONTIST—A dentist who specializes in the prevention, diagnosis, and correction of abnormalities in the arrangement and growth of teeth.

ORTHOTIST—An individual who, in cooperation with a physician, fits and prepares devices for patients with disabling conditions of the limbs and spine.

OSTEOPATH—A medical doctor who specializes in the diagnosis, treatment, and prevention of diseases and injury through an integrated or holistic approach using drugs, surgery, radiation, physical and/or manipulative therapy; particular focus is on the correction of musculoskeletal disorders.

OTOLARYNGOLOGIST—A medical doctor who specializes in the diagnosis, treatment, and prevention of diseases of the ear, nose, and throat.

OUTPLACEMENT SPECIALIST—A professional who assists workers in transitions, particularly those from executive and management backgrounds who have been laid off or fired, to find other employment; may help with career planning and job hunting techniques and by providing referrals.

PALEONTOLOGIST—A professional who studies the fossilized remains of plants and animals found in geological formations to trace the evolution and development of past life and identify geological formations according to nature and chronology.

PARALEGAL—A law clerk who studies law, researches facts, and prepares documents to assist lawyers.

PARASITOLOGIST—A professional scientist who studies characteristics, habits, and life cycles of animal parasites such as protozoans, tapeworms, roundworms, and flukes to determine how they attack and affect humans and animals.

PARK RANGER—An officer who enforces laws, regulations, and policies in state or national parks.

PAROLE/PROBATION OFFICER—A professional social worker involved in the conditional release of juvenile or adult offenders from correctional institutions; establishes relationships, provides supervision, and evaluation, and performs other duties.

PATENT AGENT—A professional worker who prepares and presents patent applications to the U.S. Patent Office and in patent courts.

PATENT LAWYER—A lawyer who specializes in advising clients such as inventors, investors, and manufacturers concerning the patentability of inventions, infringements, validity, and similar items; prosecutes and defends clients.

PATHOLOGIST—A medical doctor who specializes in determining the nature, cause, and development of diseases, structural and functional changes caused by them, cause of death, and effects of treatment.

PEDIATRICIAN—A medical doctor who specializes in the general medical care of children through adolescence.

PEDODONTIST—A professional dental specialist who specializes in the treatment of children's teeth.

PENOLOGIST—A professional sociologist who specializes in research on punishment for crime, crime control and prevention, management of penal institutions (jails and prisons), and rehabilitation.

PERFUSIONIST—A health care worker who operates equipment designed to support or temporarily replace a patient's circulatory or respiratory functions.

PERSONNEL DIRECTOR—An individual who plans and carries out policies relating to all phases of personnel activity; recruits workers, interviews, fills vacancies, plans and conducts new employee orientations; keeps records of promotions, insurance, transfers, and hires; may be called a human resources manager.

PETROLOGIST—A professional who studies the composition, structure, and history of the rock masses that form the earth's crust.

PHARMACIST—A medical professional who specializes in mixing chemical compounds and dispensing medications prescribed by physicians, dentists, and other health care professionals; also makes recommendations regarding over-the-counter drugs.

PHARMACOLOGIST—A biological scientist who specializes in the study of drugs, gases, dusts, and other materials and their effect on the tissue and physiological processes of animals and human beings.

PHOTOENGRAVER—A worker who photographs copy, develops negatives, and prepares photosensitized metal plates, such as copper, zinc, aluminum, and magnesium, for use in printing using photography and developing equipment and engraver's tools.

PHOTOGRAMMETRIST—A surveyor who specializes in the preparation of maps and drawings by measuring and interpreting aerial photographs using analytical processes and mathematical formulas.

PHOTO-OPTICS TECHNICIAN—A worker who sets up and operates photo-optical instrumentation to record and photograph data for scientific and engineering projects.

PHYCOLOGIST—A life scientist who specializes in the study of seaweeds or algae.

PHYSIATRIST—A medical doctor who specializes in the clinical and diagnostic use of physical agents and exercise to provide physiotherapy for physical, mental, and occupational well-being.

PHYSICAL THERAPIST—A health care specialist who plans and administers medically prescribed treatment programs to relieve pain and treat malfunctions in the neuromuscular and other systems caused by disease, injury, or loss of body parts.

PHYSIOLOGIST—A professional scientist who conducts research on cellular structure and organ-system functions of plants and animals, studying growth, respiration, circulation, excretions, movement, reproduction, and other functions.

PIPEFITTER—A plumbing specialist who lays out, builds, assembles, installs, and maintains piping and piping systems, fixtures, and equipment for steam, hot water, heating, cooling, lubricating, sprinkling, and industrial processing systems.

PLANT BREEDER —A professional who plans and conducts breeding studies to develop and improve varieties of crops; seeks to improve size, quality, yield, maturity, and resistance to disease, frost, and pests.

PLASTERER—A construction worker who applies coats of plaster to the interior walls, ceilings, and partitions of buildings to produce a finished surface.

PLASTIC SURGEON—A medical doctor who specializes in skin grafts and bone tissue replacement and restoration and repair of lost, deformed, or injured parts of the face and body.

PLAYWRIGHT—A professional who writes original plays, such as tragedies, comedies, or dramas, or adapts themes from fictional, historical, or narrative sources for dramatic presentation.

PODIATRIST—A medical doctor who specializes in the diagnosis, treatment, and prevention of foot diseases, conditions, and deformities.

POLICE COMMISSIONER—A professional government worker who administers a municipal (city) police department.

POLYGRAPH EXAMINER—See Administrative Examiner.

PROCTOLOGIST—A medical doctor who specializes in the diagnosis and treatment of diseases and disorders of the anus, rectum, and colon; performs surgical removal of diseased or malfunctioning parts; and prescribes medication or other procedures when necessary.

PRODUCTION SUPERINTENDENT—A manager who, using knowledge of product technology, production methods and procedures, and capabilities of machines and equipment, directs and coordinates other supervisory personnel in activities concerned with the production of a company's products.

PROSTHETIST—A worker who, working with a physician, provides care to patients with partial or total absence of limbs by planning the construction and fitting of devices.

PSYCHIATRIC SOCIAL WORKER—A professional social worker who specializes in providing psychiatric social work assistance to mentally or emotionally disturbed patients at hospitals, clinics, and other medical centers, as well as to their families, collaborating with a psychiatric and allied team in providing a diagnosis and treatment plan.

PSYCHIATRIST—A medical doctor who specializes in the study, diagnosis, and treatment of mental, emotional, and behavioral disorders.

PSYCHOLOGIST—A professional who specializes in the research, collection, interpretation, and application of scientific information about human behavior and mental processes; may specialize in experimental, educational, social, clinical, counseling, school, industrial, engineering, or developmental psychology.

PSYCHOMETRIST—A professional who administers, scores, and interprets intelligence, aptitude, achievement, and other psychological tests.

PUBLIC HEALTH EDUCATOR—An individual who plans, organizes, and directs health education programs for groups and communities; prepares and distributes educational information materials; conducts surveys; and offers workshops.

PUBLIC HEALTH SERVICE OFFICER—A health care professional who administers a public-health program for a county or city; inspects public facilities for health hazards; may help establish free clinics, impose quarantines, or close establishments for safety reasons.

PUBLIC RELATIONS SPECIALIST—A professional worker who specializes in the planning and conducting of a public relations program designed to create and maintain a favorable public image for an employer or client.

PUPPETEER—An entertainer who stages puppet shows, moving controls of puppets to animate them; also may design and construct puppets.

PURCHASING AGENT—A professional worker who purchases raw materials or other unprocessed goods for processing machinery, equipment, tools, parts, produce, or other supplies, or services necessary for the operation of an organization or business.

RADIATION THERAPY TECHNOLOGIST—A health care specialist who assists radiologists in the treatment of disease by exposing the affected areas to prescribed doses of X-ray or other ionizing radiation; maintains operation controls; assists in treatment responsibilities and record keeping.

RADIOGRAPHER—A health care specialist who applies roentgen rays and radioactive substances to patients for diagnostic and therapeutic purposes; X-ray technicians may do the actual equipment operation and body positioning.

RADIOLOGIST—A medical doctor who specializes in the diagnosis and treatment of disease using X rays and radioactive substances to examine organs, make diagnoses, and administer treatments.

RECREATIONAL THERAPIST—A health care specialist who plans, organizes, and directs medically approved recreation programs for patients in hospitals and other institutions.

REGISTERED NURSE—A professional health care worker who specializes in providing those who are sick, injured, or elderly with direct personal care, support, and ongoing medical supervision.

REGISTRAR—A professional who directs and coordinates registration activities at a college or university, handling transcripts and credit evaluations, coordinating class schedules, and preparing statistical reports.

RELIGIOUS BROTHER/RELIGIOUS SISTER—In the Roman Catholic Church, a member of a religious community (e.g., Benedictines, Carmelites, etc.) living vows of poverty, chastity, and obedience in the service of God; religious brothers may or may not be priests.

RESEARCH ANALYST—A professional who analyzes management and operational problems and develops solutions using mathematics and computer simulation.

RESPIRATORY THERAPIST—A health care worker who administers respiratory therapy and life support to patients with deficiencies and abnormalities of the cardiopulmonary system under the supervision of a physician and by prescription.

RIGGER—A worker who assembles rigging (material used to hold something together) to lift and move equipment or material at a manufacturing plant, shipyard, or a construction site.

SAFETY ENGINEER—An engineer who specializes in the design, development, implementation, and evaluation of safety programs, apparatus, and other equipment to prevent or correct unsafe environmental working conditions utilizing knowledge of industrial processes, mechanics, chemistry, psychology, and industrial health and safety laws.

SANITARY ENGINEER—A public health engineer who designs and directs the construction and operation of hygienic projects such as waterworks, sewage systems, garbage and trash disposal plants, drainage systems, and insect/rodent control projects.

SCHOOL SUPERINTENDENT—An administrator who directs and coordinates the activities and administration of a state, city, or county school system in accordance with board of education standards; the highest ranking administrator in a school system.

SECURITIES ANALYST—See Financial Analyst.

SECURITIES CLERK—A worker who compiles and maintains records of a firm's securities (stock purchases) transactions.

SECURITIES SALES AGENT—One who buys and sells in a trading division of an investment and brokerage firm.

SECURITY OFFICER—A worker who plans and establishes the security procedures for a company engaged in manufacturing products or processing duty or materials for the federal government.

SEISMOLOGIST—A geologist who studies and interprets seismic (earthquake) data to locate earthquakes and earthquake faults.

SHEET METAL WORKER—A worker who fabricates, assembles, installs, and repairs sheet metal products and equipment such as control boxes, drainpipes, ventilators, and furnace casings according to a job order or blueprint.

SILVICULTURIST—A professional who establishes and cares for forest stands and manages tree nurseries and other forests to encourage natural growth of sprouts and seedlings of designated variety.

SOCIAL WORKER—A professional worker who provides assistance through counseling, activities, referrals, and other means to individuals and groups challenged by poverty, illness, family troubles, antisocial behavior, financial mismanagement, inadequate housing, and other concerns; may specialize in medical, psychiatric, industrial, school, child welfare, family, or other areas.

SOCIOLOGIST—A professional who researches the developmental, structural, cultural, and behavioral patterns of human beings and societies; may specialize in criminology, industrial, rural, social problems, gerontology, urban, medical, or other areas.

SOFTWARE SALESPERSON—A worker who sells, either wholesale or retail, computer programs and/or related materials.

SOIL CONSERVATIONIST—A professional who plans and develops coordinated practices for soil erosion control, moisture conservation, and efficient soil use.

SOIL SCIENTIST—A scientist who studies soil characteristics, maps soil types, and monitors results of soil management techniques.

SOUS CHEF—A chef who supervises and coordinates the activities of cooks and other workers in preparing and cooking foodstuffs.

SPECIAL AGENT—An investigator of alleged or suspected criminal violations of federal, state, or local laws who determines if evidence is sufficient to recommend prosecution; obtains evidence, maintains surveillance, performs undercover work, makes reports, testifies, etc.

SPECIAL EDUCATION TEACHER—A teacher who specializes in the education of students with mental, emotional, behavioral, developmental, learning, or physical disabilities.

SPEECH PATHOLOGIST—A professional who specializes in the diagnosis, treatment, and prevention of speech and language problems; may also research human communications.

SPORTS MARKETER—A public relations and advertising specialist who works to increase and/or maintain spectator patronization of a particular sporting endeavor.

STATISTICIAN—A professional mathematician who plans information collection; analyzes and interprets numerical information from experiments, studies, surveys, and other sources; and applies statistical methodology to provide for further research or statistical analysis.

STOCKBROKER—A professional who buys and sells stocks and bonds for individuals and organizations as a representative of a stock brokerage firm applying knowledge of securities, market conditions, government regulations, and financial circumstances of customers.

STONE MASON—A construction worker who sets stone to build stone structures such as piers, walls, and abutments or lays walks, curbstones, or other special types of masonry using mason's tools.

STRATIGRAPHER—A professional who studies the relative position and order of succession of deposits that contain or separate archaeological fossil or plant material.

STRUCTURAL ENGINEER—An engineer who directs or participates in developing, designing, and reviewing building plans to determine load, size, shape, strength, and material requirements necessary for structural integrity.

SURGICAL TECHNICIAN—A health care worker who performs such tasks as washing, shaving, and sterilizing before, during, and after surgical operations.

SURVEYOR—A worker who specializes in the inspection of the earth's surface by measuring angles and distances to determine location, elevation, lines, areas, and contours for purposes of construction, mapmaking, land divisions, title claims, mining, etc.

SYSTEMS ANALYST—A professional who analyzes business or operating procedures to devise the most efficient methods of accomplishing work.

SYSTEMS PROGRAMMER—A professional who develops and writes computer programs to store, locate, and retrieve documents, data, and information for science, engineering, medicine, language, law, military, library science, and other purposes.

TAILOR—A worker who applies principles of garment design, construction, and styling to the construction of new clothing or, more commonly, to the alteration of ready-made apparel.

TAXONOMIST—A plant or animal scientist who specializes in the identification and classification of species and organisms.

TECHNICAL ILLUSTRATOR—A drafter who lays out and draws illustrations for reproduction in reference works, instructions, brochures, and technical manuals showing the assembly, installation, operation, maintenance, and repair of machines, tools, and equipment.

TECHNICAL WRITER—An individual who develops, writes, and edits materials for reports, manuals, briefs, proposals, instruction books, catalogs, and other technical and administrative publications.

TECHNICIAN—A worker who, in direct support of engineers or scientists, uses theoretical knowledge of scientific, engineering, mathematical, or draft design principles to solve practical problems.

TERRAZZO WORKER—A construction worker who applies cement, sand, pigment (color), and marble chips to floors, stairways, and cabinet fixtures to create durable and decorative surfacing according to specifications and drawings.

TISSUE TECHNOLOGIST—A medical specialist who cuts, stains, mounts, and prepares tissue for examination by a pathologist; may assist in autopsies.

TITLE ATTORNEY—A lawyer who specializes in examining abstracts of titles, leases, contracts, and other legal documents to determine ownership of land, gas, oil, and mineral rights; may assist in related trials.

TOOL-AND-DIE MAKER—A skilled worker who analyzes specifications, lays out metal stock, sets up and operates machine tools, and fits and assembles parts to make and repair metal-working dies, cutting tools, jigs, fixtures, gauges, and machinist hand tools.

TOOL PROGRAMMER—A skilled worker who plans a numerical control tape program to control contour-path machining of metal parts on automatic machine tools by means of magnetic or perforated tape.

TOXICOLOGIST—A professional who studies the nature and effects of toxins (poisons) and the treatment of poisoning.

TRAFFIC MANAGER—An individual who directs and coordinates the activities of an organization, including the routing and transportation of goods and products, scheduling, and loading.

TREE SURGEON—A worker who prunes and treats ornamental and shade trees in yards and parks to improve their appearance, health, and value.

TRUST ADMINISTRATOR—A professional who directs and coordinates the creation and administration of private, corporate, probate, and guardianship trusts (safeguarding of goods or items) in accordance with a trust, will, or court order.

TUTOR—A teacher of academic subjects such as English, mathematics, and foreign language to pupils requiring private instruction, adapting the curriculum to meet their needs.

TYPESETTER—A worker who arranges type by computer or by hand in preparation for printing.

UNDERWRITER—A worker who reviews individual insurance applications to evaluate the degree of risk involved and either declines or accepts them.

UPHOLSTERER—A skilled worker who engages in spreading, marking, cutting, and sewing fabric padding, covering, and trimming to articles such as furniture, mattresses, and vehicle seats; may work on new furniture or the renovation of older items.

URBAN PLANNER—A professional who develops comprehensive plans and programs for the utilization of land and physical facilities of cities, counties, and metropolitan areas.

UROLOGIST—A medical doctor who specializes in the diagnosis, treatment, and prevention of diseases and disorders of the urinary or urogental tract..

VIROLOGIST—A microbiologist who specializes in the study of viruses and the diseases they cause.

VOCATIONAL REHABILITATION COUNSELOR—A professional counselor who specializes in counseling individuals with disabilities in job readiness, placement, preparation, and training.

WEBMASTER—A computer specialist who is responsible for overseeing all aspects of a company's or organization's Web site (includes design, development, operations, performance, and maintenance).

WELDER—A worker who is skilled in joining, surfacing, building, or repairing structures or parts of weldable materials using such processes as arc, gas, resistance, solid state, and others.

WHOLESALER—One who manages a store that sells a specific line of merchandise such as groceries, meat, liquor, apparel, jewelry, appliances, furniture, or other items to retailers, who then sell directly to consumers.

WIRELESS SPECIALIST—A technician who specializes in the design and service of small high-tech instruments such as cellular phones, fax machines, and pagers.

APPENDIX C
Definitions of Selected Skill Statements

ABSTRACT REASONING—The ability to work with and apply ideas and concepts that are difficult to understand; also, the ability to think through that which is not concrete or easily understood from a practical perspective.

AGILITY—Quality of nimbleness or being quick and light-footed; performing body movements with ease.

ANALYZE—To effectively look at an item, event, or situation to determine its nature and how to gain a better understanding.

ANALYZE OR LISTEN INTROSPECTIVELY—To examine and understand the various aspects of your own or another's behavior; to interpret feelings, thoughts, and behaviors effectively.

APPROPRIATE DECISION MAKING—The ability to make effective decisions at the right time, usually resulting in a suitable outcome.

APTITUDE FOR ACCURACY AND DETAIL—The ability to carefully perform tasks that involve much detail.

CHARISMA—The ability to draw or attract others to listen, observe, or follow.

FINGER DEXTERITY—The ability to move one's fingers rapidly or accurately when handling small items or objects.

FORM PERCEPTION—The ability to notice details in objects, pictures, or other materials and to see fine differences in shape, shading, figures, and widths and lengths of lines.

FORMULATE AND DEFEND POSITION—To effectively present and back up with factual evidence a belief, opinion, or position.

INTERPERSONAL COMMUNICATION—The ability to skillfully give, listen to, and understand messages to and from other people through the use of words, listening techniques, eye contact, body language, actions, etc.

INTERPRET—To provide a definition for something in a manner that can be more clearly understood by others.

KEEN OBSERVATION—Alertness; the ability to pick up detail and notice things others may miss.

LOGICAL THINKING—Thinking in which opinions and decisions are based on factual evidence; the ability to arrive at a decision following standard and predictable reasoning procedures.

MAINTAIN COMPOSURE IN STRESSFUL SITUATIONS OR UNDER PRESSURE—To remain rational and calm in the face of danger, frustration, fear, disaster, or unexpected events.

MAKE ANALOGIES—To make connections, often revealing similar events, situations, and problems that occurred under different circumstances.

MANUAL DEXTERITY—The ability to work skillfully with one's hands, accomplishing tasks deftly and accurately.

MOTOR COORDINATION—The ability to work one's fingers or hands in coordination with one's eyes to accomplish tasks deftly and accurately.

OBJECTIVITY—The ability to listen or react to a statement, event, or situation in a factual manner without allowing negative or positive impressions to interfere with one's reaction; the tendency to keep responses relatively free from biased emotions and feelings.

PHYSICAL STAMINA—The ability to physically endure periods of sickness, disease, fatigue, etc.

READ OR SPEAK ARTICULATELY—To read aloud or speak clearly using correct pronunciation.

SOLVE QUANTITATIVE PROBLEMS—To figure out answers to problems that involve numbers, measurements, or mathematics.

SOUND JUDGMENT—The ability to look at an event, situation, or problem from all angles, using decision-making techniques along with your education, training, and experiences to determine what is occurring and how to react to it.

SPATIAL PERCEPTION—The ability to look at blueprints, flat drawings, or diagrams and accurately visualize how the structure will appear in physical form, including height, width, and depth.

SYNTHESIZE INFORMATION—To integrate or put together parts to arrive at a solution or answer or to create a whole.

APPENDIX D
Definitions of Values and Personal Attributes

ACHIEVEMENT—Making progress; successfully completing or accomplishing a goal or task.

ADAPTABILITY—The ability to adjust to and fit into different situations; the ability to alter one's behavior or thinking in order to suit circumstances.

AESTHETIC AWARENESS—The ability to grasp and appreciate the beauty of an event, performance, situation, or physical or social environment; the ability to relate to the beauty in music, song, dance, pictures, structures, nature, and behavior.

ALERTNESS—The ability to quickly recognize details and things that others miss; tendency to observe closely and remain watchful.

ANALYTICAL AND LOGICAL THINKING—The ability to look at and understand the various aspects of an event, situation, or item and arrive at a decision using standard and predictable reasoning procedures.

COMPETITIVE DRIVE—The spirit of challenging and contesting others in order to win or gain something desired; a liking for rivalry and competition with others.

CONSCIENTIOUS—Aware of what you do and sensitive to how your behavior may be affecting another.

CURIOSITY AND ENTHUSIASM FOR GADGETRY—The tendency to handle, take apart, ask questions, and be excited about manipulating items and objects (machines, etc.).

DECISIVENESS—The ability to decide without delay; making a decision to act firmly and without doubt.

DEDICATION—Strong commitment to something to the extent that you are willing to go through much discomfort, if necessary, to achieve the end result; loyalty; giving your total effort.

DEPENDABLE—Trustworthy, reliable, and responsible; can be counted on to come through and to behave as expected.

DILIGENCE—The quality of working steadily at a task until done.

DIPLOMATIC—Careful to do what is appropriate and to consider the various sides of an issue; having the ability to manage and negotiate with others without hurting their feelings.

DISCREET—Showing good judgment; not likely to do something without thoughtful consideration; capable of keeping quiet about a private or controversial matter.

EMPATHY—The ability to genuinely relate to other people by imagining their emotions and feelings; the ability to put yourself in another person's shoes.

ENDURANCE—The ability to withstand discomfort, painful circumstances, hardship, boredom, or stress.

FRAME INQUIRY AND RESPOND OBJECTIVELY—To ask questions that can be logically and scientifically researched as well as respond to others relatively free from biased emotions and feelings.

IMAGINATION—The ability to think and form images of things, events, or ideas that do not presently exist or have never existed.

INDEPENDENCE—The desire to think or perform tasks and activities without being helped, controlled, directly supervised, or assisted; liking to do things on one's own; freedom from authority and confining rules.

INDUSTRIOUS—The ability to work hard continuously, steadily; diligent; to keep busy.

INITIATIVE—The ability to take the lead; to move ahead or take the first step.

INQUISITIVE—Curious; wanting answers; desiring to gain knowledge.

INTEGRITY—Honesty; truthfulness and desire to do what is morally right; uprightness; can be trusted to follow through without corruption.

INTELLECTUAL GROWTH—The ability and desire to continually gain knowledge, understanding, and wisdom without stagnation or hindrance.

LINGUISTIC ABILITY—The ability to analyze and understand the structure of languages, make comparisons, etc.

LOYALTY—A strong sense of commitment or unbroken support; faithfulness.

MENTAL AND EMOTIONAL WELL-BEING—The ability to remain calm, make appropriate decisions, and control one's emotions in stressful or extremely difficult circumstances; not easily shaken emotionally or mentally.

PERSEVERANCE—The quality of not quitting; never giving up; steadfastness; to persist in spite of difficulties.

PERSUASIVE—The ability to influence and draw others to think or behave in a certain way.

POISE AND COMPOSURE UNDER CLOSE PUBLIC SCRUTINY AND CRITICISM—The ability to maintain control over your thoughts and actions and calmly continue in your tasks or activities while being observed (or having something you are responsible for observed) and/or criticized by others.

PRACTICAL—The tendency to take effective action instead of theorizing or speculating; pragmatic.

REFLECTIVE NATURE—Thoughtful; making mental connections between disparate situations.

RESOURCEFULNESS—The ability to solve problems and get through difficult situations, particularly when standard resources are scarce or nonexistent.

RESPONSIBLE—Trustworthy and dependable; having the ability to adequately carry through, oversee, or supervise; can be relied on to perform as expected.

SECURITY—Safety from danger, hurt, discomfort, or instability; firmly fixed and sure; occupationally, the relative assurance of a steady income and job stability.

SELF-DISCIPLINE—The ability to control and positively direct one's emotions, feelings, thoughts, and behavior.

SENSITIVITY TO MULTIPLE PERSPECTIVES—Openness and understanding in terms of different viewpoints, techniques, methods of operation, uses, etc.

SENSITIVITY TO THE INCONSISTENCIES OF HUMAN BEHAVIORS—Understanding, helpfulness, and patience with those who demonstrate abnormal, antisocial, and/or self-defeating behaviors.

SPIRIT OF SCIENTIFIC INQUIRY—Thinking and questioning in a manner and spirit that reflect a preference for and use of scientific laws and procedures.

TACTFULNESS—The ability to say and do the appropriate things at the appropriate times; being sensitive to the feelings of others.

THOROUGHNESS—The tendency to bring an endeavor to completion with attention to detail; leaving nothing undone.

VERSATILITY—The ability to readily change or move into something different; the ability to easily adapt to many circumstances or environments.

WISDOM—Good judgment; the ability to make appropriate decisions; applying knowledge to do what is right and true; using knowledge rightly.

Index of Occupations

4-H Agent, 77

Abstractor, 239
Academic Librarian, 131
Academic Teacher, 68
Account Executive, 38, 59, 74, 134, 240
Accountant, 11-12, 38-39, 47, 74, 137
Accounting Clerk, 185, 239
Acoustical Engineer, 35, 80
Acoustical Physicist, 35
Acquisitions Librarian, 131, 239
Activities Supervisor, 105, 239
Actor/Actress, 59, 86, 92, 158
Actuary, 11, 38, 74, 137, 239
Adjudicator, 125, 239
Administrative Assistant, 185
Administrative Examiner, 128, 239, 260
Administrative Officer, 152
Administrator, 242-243, 246, 248, 254-255,
    262, 265
Admiralty Lawyer, 125, 239
Adult and Vocational Education Teacher,
    77, 240
Advertising Account Executive, 134, 240
Advertising Executive, 47
Advertising Manager, 38, 134, 173
Advertising Salesperson, 134
Advertising Worker, 59
Aerodynamist, 14, 164, 240
Aeronautical Drafters, 29
Aeronautical Engineer, 14, 80, 164, 240
Aerospace Airplane Pilot, 14
Aerospace Engineer, 14, 35, 137, 140, 164,
    240
Aerospace Engineering Technician, 35
Agricultural Engineer, 17, 50
Agricultural Extension Worker, 95
Agronomist, 17, 44, 50, 53, 95, 113
Air Traffic Controller, 152, 194
Air-Conditioning, Refrigeration, and
    Heating Mechanic, 143
Aircraft Electronics Technician, 83
Aircraft Mechanic, 143
Airplane Engineer, 152
Airplane Pilot, 14, 152, 164, 194
Airport Manager, 47, 116
Allergist, 146
Ambulance Driver, 194
Anatomist, 167
Anesthesiologist, 53, 146, 167
Animal Breeder, 197
Animal Control Officer, 197
Animal Laboratory Technician, 197
Animal Scientist, 17, 264

Announcer, 59, 92, 170
Announcer (Radio, TV), 158
Anthropologist, 26, 92, 98, 107, 161, 191
Antique Dealer, 32
Appeals Referee, 125
Appellate Court Judge, 125
Appraiser, 32, 38, 74, 137
Appraiser/Assessor, 38, 74
Arbitrator, 59
Archaeologist, 26, 107
Architect, 29, 32, 56, 98, 113, 246, 253
Architectural Drafter, 29
Architectural Engineer, 56
Architectural Technician, 29
Archivist, 26, 32, 107, 131, 240
Armed Forces Recreation Leader, 176
Art Appraiser, 32
Art Conservator, 26
Art Director, 32
Art Therapist, 32, 155, 179, 240
Assistant Buyer, 134
Assistant Housekeeper, 116
Assistant Manager, 116
Assistant Principal, 78
Assistant Restaurant Manager, 89
Astronaut, 140
Astronomer, 14, 35, 101, 137, 164
Astrophysicist, 14, 35, 164, 240
Athletic Trainer, 23, 155, 176, 179
Attorney, 68, 125, 128, 244, 246, 265
Auctioneer, 59
Audio and Sound Specialist, 83
Audiologist/Speech Pathologist, 179
Auditor, 11, 38, 62, 74, 240, 252
Author, 9, 86
Automated Equipment Technician, 83
Automotive Body Repairer, 143
Automotive Engineer, 119, 140
Automotive Mechanic, 143

Bacteriologist, 44, 240
Bailiff, 128, 240
Baker, 71, 211
Bank Economist, 38
Bank Officer, 11, 74, 137
Bank Teller, 38, 185
Bankruptcy Attorney, 125
Banquet Manager, 89
Bar Examiner, 125, 240-241
Bibliographer, 26, 86, 131, 241
Bicycle Repairer, 143
Bilingual Educator, 92
Biochemist, 17, 41, 44, 50, 53, 113, 167,
    197, 241, 243

Biologist, 17, 41, 197-198
Biomedical Engineer, 23, 80, 140, 241
Biomedical Equipment Technician, 20, 83, 211, 241
Biophysicist, 35, 164, 167, 241
Biostatistician, 23, 241
Blacksmith, 122, 241
Blood Bank Specialist, 23, 241
Boilermaker, 122, 211, 241
Book Conservator, 131
Book Store Manager, 86
Bookbinder, 241
Bookkeeper, 11, 137, 254
Border Patrol Officer, 128
Botanist, 17, 41, 44, 95, 113, 167, 241, 256
Branch Manager, 38
Bricklayer, 65, 211
Broadcast Technician, 59, 83
Broiler Cook, 71
Budget Accountant, 11, 38
Building Contractor, 29, 244
Building Engineer, 116
Building Manager, 65, 116
Bus Driver, 194
Butcher, 71, 122, 211
Buyer, 74, 110, 125, 134, 241

Cabinetmaker, 122, 211
Cable Splicer, 143, 242
CAD/CAM Operator, 122
Cafeteria Manager, 89, 116
Camp Director, 176, 182
Campaign Worker, 170
Campus Minister, 182
Campus Religious Coordinator, 182
Cardiologist, 146, 167, 242
Career Counselor, 2, 7, 9-10, 152, 203-205, 207, 216-218, 222, 234
Carpenter, 65, 211
Carpet Installer, 65
Cartographer, 29, 35, 98, 101, 137, 152, 242
Cartographic Technician, 98
Cartoonist, 32
Case Worker, 68, 110, 128, 188, 191
Cashier, 75, 90, 185
Cataloger, 131, 242
Caterer, 71, 242
Cattle Farmer, 17
Ceramic Engineer, 50, 53, 149, 242
Chamber of Commerce Manager, 170
Chamber of Commerce President, 47
Chaplain, 68, 182, 242
Chauffeur, 194
Chef, 71, 89, 91, 110, 263
Chemical Engineer, 50, 53, 149
Chemical Engineering Technician, 50
Chemical Lab Technician, 17
Chemical Research Engineer, 50
Chemist, 23, 50, 53, 101, 167, 243
Chief Dietitian, 105

Chief Executive Officer, 47, 242
Chief Information Officer, 62
Child Care Worker, 110
Child Welfare Worker, 68, 110, 188, 242
Children's Librarian, 131
Chiropractor, 146, 243
Choreographer, 158, 243
Christian Education Worker, 78
Church Camp Director, 182
Church Recreation Director, 176
CIA Agent, 68, 92, 107, 170
Cinematographer, 32, 243
Circuit Engineer, 80
Circulation Manager, 243
Circus Performer, 158, 176
City Manager, 47, 170, 191, 243
Civil Engineer, 29, 56, 149, 164, 243, 250-251
Civil Engineering Technician, 29, 56
Civil Service Worker, 92
Classifier, 131
Climatologist, 98, 243
Clinical Chemist, 23, 243
Clothing Designer, 110
Club Manager, 116
Coach, 158, 176-177
Coal Pipeline Operator, 194, 243
Coffee Maker, 71
College Administrator, 161, 243
College Dean, 48, 78, 243
College Instructor, 161
College Professor, 78
College Recreation Instructor, 176
Columnist, 59, 86, 243
Comedian, 158
Commentator, 59
Commercial Artist, 29, 243
Commercial/Industrial Electronic Equipment Repairer, 143
Communications Engineer, 80
Community Center Director, 176
Community Outreach Librarian, 131
Community Service Agency Director, 188, 243
Composer, 158
Compositor, 122, 244
Comptroller, 48, 105, 244
Computer Animator, 32, 62
Computer Applications Engineer, 62
Computer Graphics Technician, 30
Computer Mapper, 98
Computer Operator, 62
Computer Programmer, 14, 35, 38, 62, 137, 153, 164
Computer Science Engineer, 14, 50, 62, 80, 140
Computer Security Specialist, 62, 244
Computer Service Technician, 62, 143
Computer Systems Analyst, 11
Computer-Aided Designer, 62
Concert Promoter, 176

Concrete Mason, 65
Conservationist, 17, 44, 95, 98, 113, 197, 244, 263
Construction Engineer, 56, 65, 149
Consultant, 48, 179, 191, 244
Consulting Engineer, 15, 50, 56, 81, 119, 140, 149
Consumer Protection Specialist, 53
Contractor, 244
Contractor Administrator, 30
Control Engineer, 81, 119
Controller, 11, 74, 134, 152, 194, 244
Controller-Accountant, 38
Convention Manager, 48
Cook, 71
Cook/Chef, 110
Cooperative Extension Agent, 17
Cooperative Extension Worker, 44, 110, 188, 244
Coordinator of Rehabilitation Services, 105
Copy Editor, 59, 86, 92
Copywriter, 32, 60, 244
Coroner, 68, 244
Corporation Lawyer, 125
Corrections Facilities Manager, 68
Corrections Officer, 128, 244
Correspondent Banking Officer, 39
Cost Accountant, 11, 39, 74
Costumer, 158
Counselor, 19, 255
County Prosecutor, 244
Court Administrator, 68
Court Reporter, 185, 244
Credit Analyst, 39
Credit and Loan Worker, 74
Credit Manager, 12, 39, 137, 245
Criminal Investigator, 68, 128
Criminal Lawyer, 125
Criminologist, 68, 191, 245
Cultural Anthropologist, 26
Curator, 26, 32, 44, 107, 197, 245
Curriculum Supervisor, 245
Customs Inspector, 92, 245
Cytologist, 23, 44, 245
Cytotechnologist, 20, 245

Dairy Farmer, 17
Dance Instructor, 158, 176
Dance Therapist, 177, 179, 245
Dancer, 158
Data Input Operator, 185
Data Processing Manager, 62
Database Analyst, 62
Database Manager, 48, 62, 245
Data-Entry Equipment Operator, 62
Day Care Director, 110
Deep Submergence Vehicle Operator, 194
Demographer, 191
Dental Assistant, 20, 185
Dental Hygienist, 20, 23, 245
Dental Lab Technician, 20, 245

Dentist, 146, 245, 257
Department Store Manager, 48
Deputy Sheriff, 128
Dermatologist, 146, 246
Design/Building Specialist, 30, 246
Designer, 33, 250, 252
Desktop Publisher, 246
Detective, 69, 128
Diagnostic Medical Sonographer, 20, 246
Diesel Mechanic, 143
Dietetic Technician, 20, 246
Dietitian, 23, 41, 44, 53, 71, 89, 105, 110, 113, 167, 246
Dining Room Attendant, 89
Diplomat, 92, 161, 170, 246, 249
Direct Salesperson, 134
Director of Admissions, 78, 246
Director of Career Placement, 48, 78, 246
Director of Food Service, 110
Director of Guidance, 78, 246
Director of Marketing, 134
Director of Recipe, 89
Director of Religious Education, 182
Director of Sales, 116
Director of Student Affairs, 78
Director of Volunteer Services, 105
Disc Jockey, 60, 86
Dispatcher, 194, 246
District Attorney, 69, 125, 128, 244, 246
District Court Judge, 125
Diver, 153
Drafter, 29-30, 140, 211, 242, 247, 265
Drama Coach, 158
Dressmaker, 110
Driving Instructor, 194
Drug Enforcement Agent, 69
Drug Enforcement Officer, 128
Drug Rehabilitation Counselor, 188
Drywall Applicator, 65

Ecologist, 41, 44, 56, 95, 98, 197, 247
Economist, 12, 38, 74, 89, 99, 107, 110, 134, 188, 247, 251
Editor, 33, 60, 86, 92, 136, 161, 247
Education Consultant, 78
Educational Secretary, 185
Educator, 12, 17, 26, 29, 33, 35, 38, 41, 44, 53, 60, 62, 74, 86, 95, 98, 107, 113, 119, 137, 153, 158, 164, 170, 173, 179, 185, 188, 191, 194, 197, 245, 261
EEG Technologist, 20, 247
EKG Technician, 20
Electrical Appliance Repairer, 83
Electrical Engineer, 15, 50, 81, 119, 140, 149, 164
Electrical Engineering Technician, 81, 83
Electrical Technician, 84
Electrical/Electronics Engineer, 35
Electrician, 65, 80-81, 211, 254
Electronic Data Processing Auditor, 62

Electronic Equipment Salesperson, 84
Electronic Home Equipment Repairer, 143
Electronic Systems Tester, 84
Electronics Instructor, 81
Electronics Technician, 83-84, 153
Elementary School Teacher, 78
Emergency Medical Services Coordinator, 105
Emergency Medical Technician, 20, 167, 211, 247
Employee Assistance Administrator, 173, 188
Employment Counselor, 173
Employment Lawyer, 126
Endocrinologist, 146-147, 247
Engine Specialist, 143
Engineer, 140, 247
Engineering Mechanic, 140
Engineering Officer, 153
Engineering Technician, 29, 50, 140-141, 149-274
Entomologist, 17, 113, 247
Entrepreneur, 248
Environmental Engineer, 15, 51, 56, 80, 119, 149, 164, 248
Environmental Health Technician, 20, 248
Environmental Lawyer, 126
Environmental Scientist, 98, 101
Environmental Technician, 98
Environmentalist, 248
Ergonomist, 248
Escrow Officer, 125, 248
Estimator, 65, 248
Ethnologist, 26
Evangelist, 182
Executive Chef, 71
Executive Housekeeper, 89, 105, 110, 116, 248
Executive Secretary, 186
Exercise Physiologist, 177, 179

Family Services Social Worker, 188
Farm Equipment Mechanic, 18, 143
Farm/Ranch Manager, 44, 95, 197
Farmer, 17-19, 44
Fashion Designer, 110
Fashion Illustrator, 33
Fashion Model, 134, 159
Fast Food Worker, 89
FBI Agent, 68, 248
FBI/CIA Agent, 92, 107, 170
Feed Store Operator, 17
Ferryboat Operator, 194
Field Representative, 134
Field Service Engineer, 80
File Clerk, 186
Film Director, 159
Film Editor, 33, 92, 161
Film Producer, 32
Financial Aid Director, 78, 248
Financial Analyst, 12, 38, 248, 262

Financial Planner, 12, 38, 74, 137, 248
Fire Chief, 68
Fire Protection Engineer, 51, 80, 119
Firefighter, 129, 211
Fish and Game Warden, 129
Fish Farmer, 17
Fishery Biologist, 197
Fitness Instructor/Specialist, 177
Flight Attendant, 92
Floriculturist, 249
Florist, 17, 32, 41, 44, 113
Food and Beverage Director, 89, 116
Food and Beverage Inspector, 249
Food and Drug Analyst, 53
Food and Drug Inspector, 110, 249
Food Production Manager, 90, 117
Food Scientist, 17, 41, 45, 50, 53, 71, 110, 113, 249
Food Service Manager, 90, 105, 110, 117, 249
Food Service Supervisor, 71
Foreign Correspondent, 60, 92, 107, 161
Foreign Service Officer, 68, 74, 93, 107, 170, 246, 249
Foreign Service Secretary, 186
Foreign Service Worker, 191
Forensics Psychologist, 68
Forester, 41, 45, 95, 113, 197, 249
Forestry Technician, 95, 249
Freelance Artist, 32
Freelance Writer, 87, 107, 161, 220, 249
Front Office Manager, 116
Funeral Director, 41, 167, 249

Game Official, 177
Gastroenterologist, 146
Genealogist, 26, 107, 249
General Contractor, 65, 249
General Duty Nurse, 155
General Maintenance Mechanic, 143
General Manager, 116
General Practitioner, 250
General Superintendent, 65, 250
Geneticist, 41, 45, 53, 96, 113, 167, 250
Geodesist, 250
Geographer, 26, 98, 101, 170, 250
Geological Engineer, 50, 56, 149
Geologist, 35, 53, 57, 98, 101, 149, 250-251, 255, 263
Geomorphologist, 98, 250
Geophysical Engineer, 149
Geophysicist, 35, 98, 101, 150, 164, 250
Geotechnical Engineer, 57, 250
Geriatric Care Manager, 250
Geriatric Case Worker, 188
Geriatrician, 146
Gerontologist, 107, 188, 191, 250
Glazier, 66, 211, 250
Graphic Designer, 29, 32, 153, 250
Greenskeeper, 250
Grounds Manager, 113

Groundskeeper, 44, 250
Group Home Director, 188
Guard, 69, 129, 153-154
Guidance Counselor, 173
Gunsmith, 122, 143
Gynecologist, 146, 168, 251

Hand Molder, 122, 251
Hardware Salesperson, 62
Hardware Service Person, 62
Head Nurse, 155
Health Care Administrator, 24
Health Advocate, 251
Health Consultant, 105
Health Educator, 23, 105, 261
Health Information Specialist, 105
Health Microbiologist, 23, 251
Health Services Administrator, 105
Heating and Air-Conditioning Engineer,
    141
Highway Engineer, 57
Historian, 26, 93, 99, 107, 161, 191, 249
Histotechnologist, 24
Home Economist, 74, 89, 110, 188, 251
Home Health Aide, 110, 251
Horticultural Therapist, 113, 180
Horticulturist, 17, 41, 44, 113, 249, 251
Hospital Administrator, 23
Hospital Comptroller, 105
Hospital Food Service Manager, 105
Hospital Personnel Director, 105
Hospital Records Administrator, 105
Host/Hostess, 89
Hotel Information Clerk, 92
Hotel Manager, 92
Hotel/Motel Manager, 47, 89, 110, 251
Human Resource Manager, 173
Human Rights Counselor, 153
Human Services Worker, 189, 191
Humane Society Worker, 197
Hydraulics Engineer, 57, 251
Hydrographer, 101, 251
Hydrologist, 57, 101, 251

Illuminating Engineer, 80
Illustrator, 29, 32, 252, 254, 265
Immunologist, 146
Import/Export Clerk, 92
Industrial Designer, 29, 32, 252
Industrial Electronics Maintenance Worker,
    83
Industrial Engineer, 56, 119, 141
Industrial Health Engineer, 53
Industrial Hygienist, 252
Industrial Machine Repairer, 143
Industrial Psychologist, 173
Industrial Truck Operator, 194, 52
Information Scientist, 131, 252
Instrument Maker, 123
Instrument Mechanic, 143, 211
Instrument Repairer, 143, 252
Instrumentation Technician, 83, 143, 252

Insulation Worker, 66
Insurance Adjuster, 252
Insurance Agent, 12, 38, 74, 134
Insurance Attorney, 125
Intelligence Specialist, 152
Interior Decorator, 32, 110, 252
Interior Designer, 29, 252
Internal Auditor, 11, 38, 252
Internal Revenue Agent, 11, 74, 252
International Accountant, 11
International Banking Officer, 38
International Economist, 99
Internist, 53, 147, 168, 252
Interpreter/Translator, 87, 92, 152
Investment Banker, 11, 38
Ironworker, 66

Jeweler, 32, 123
Job Analyst, 173, 253
Job Setter, 253
Job Superintendent, 66
Journalist, 60, 87, 92, 152, 161
Judge, 68, 125-126, 161, 170, 246-247

Kennel Operator, 197
Kitchen Manager, 71

Labor Relations Specialist, 74, 170, 191
Laboratory Analyst, 53
Laboratory Assistant, 17
Laboratory Technician, 101, 152, 164, 197,
    242
Landscape Architect, 29, 98, 113, 253
Landscape Gardener, 17, 44, 113, 253
Lather, 253
Lawyer, 107, 125-126, 161, 171, 239, 246,
    258, 265
Layout Worker, 123, 253
Lecturer, 59, 161
Legal Investigator, 253
Legal Secretary, 185, 211, 253
Librarian, 42, 77, 87, 107, 131, 133, 161,
    239, 242
Library Assistant, 131
Library Consultant, 131
Library Director, 131
Library Technical Assistant, 86
Library Technician, 60, 131, 253
Licensed Practical Nurse, 155, 253
Lifeguard, 128, 176
Line Installer, 143, 254
Linguist, 86, 92, 254
Linguistic Anthropologist, 26
Lithographer, 123, 254
Loan Officer, 38
Lobbyist, 59, 86, 171, 254
Locksmith, 123, 143
Locomotive Engineer, 194

Machine Operator, 122
Machine Repairer, 122, 143
Machine Tool Operator, 122

Machinist, 122, 211, 253-254, 265
Magician, 158
Maitre d'Hotel, 89, 92, 254
Mall Manager, 116
Management Accountant, 11
Management Consultant, 11
Managing Director, 116
Manpower Director, 74, 254
Manufacturer Sales Workers, 135
Manufacturing Engineer, 119
Marblesetter, 65, 254
Marine Biologist, 198
Marine Electronics Specialist, 83
Marine Engineer, 14
Market Research Analyst, 11, 74, 98, 107,
    135, 137, 161, 173, 254
Market Researcher, 110
Marketing Manager, 116
Marriage Counselor, 189
Materials Handling Engineer, 50, 119, 140,
    150
Mathematician, 35, 137, 164, 264
Mayor, 171
Meatcutter, 71
Mechanical Drafter, 140
Mechanical Engineer, 14, 56, 80, 119, 140,
    248
Mechanical Engineering Technician, 140
Media Center Manager, 131
Media Specialist, 59, 86
Medical Assistant, 20, 168, 185, 254
Medical Assistant Secretary, 185
Medical Engineer, 23, 105, 254
Medical Lab Technician, 20, 42, 152, 255
Medical Librarian, 42
Medical Officer, 255
Medical Public Librarian, 131
Medical Records Administrator, 105
Medical Records Technician, 20, 255
Medical Technologist, 23, 164, 255
Medical/Scientific Illustrator, 23, 32, 42,
    254
Mental Health Technician, 20, 255
Mental Health Worker, 173, 255
Merchandise Displayer, 110, 158, 255
Merchandising Supervisor, 89
Merchant Mariner, 194
Metallurgical Engineer, 14, 35, 50, 101,
    149, 164
Metallurgical Engineering Technician, 149
Metallurgist, 50, 53, 102, 149, 164, 255
Meteorological Technician, 102
Meteorologist, 35, 98, 164, 243, 255
Microbiologist, 17, 23, 41, 168, 198, 240,
    251, 255, 266
Military Officer, 68, 128, 170
Millwright, 122, 140, 143, 211, 255
Mineralogist, 35, 101, 255
Mining Engineer, 56, 101, 149
Minister, 173, 182, 188, 191
Minister of Music, 182

Missionary, 92, 182
Model Maker, 29, 32, 255
Motion Picture Photographer, 32, 158
Motorboat Operator, 194
Motorcycle Mechanic, 143
Multimedia Specialist/Technician, 256
Municipal Recreation Director, 176
Museum Worker, 26
Museum/Zoo Worker, 197
Music Director, 59, 158
Music Teacher, 158
Music Therapist, 155, 176, 180, 256
Musical Instrument Repairer, 143
Musician, 152, 158, 160
Mycologist, 41, 44, 96, 256

Naturalist, 96, 256
Nature Photographer, 197
Neurologist, 147, 256
News Photographer, 8, 59
News Reporter, 107, 170
Nuclear Engineer, 14, 50, 80, 101, 149,
    164, 256
Nuclear Medicine Technologist, 23, 164,
    256
Nuclear Scientist, 53, 137
Nuclear Technician, 164
Nurse, 256, 261
Nurse Anesthetist, 155, 256
Nurse Clinician, 155
Nurse Instructor, 155
Nurse Practitioner, 155, 256
Nurse Supervisor, 155
Nurse-Midwife, 155, 256
Nursery Manager, 17, 44, 96
Nursing Home Director, 105
Nutritionist, 23, 41, 44, 53, 71, 89, 110,
    113, 167, 251, 256

Obstetrician, 147, 256-257
Occupational Safety and Health Inspector,
    23, 105
Occupational Therapist, 41, 155, 173, 179,
    257
Occupational Therapy Assistant, 20
Oceanographer, 35, 98, 101, 257
Office Clerk, 185-186
Office Machine Servicer, 143
Office Manager, 116, 185
Oil Pumper, 194
Online Content Developer, 59
Online Marketer, 134
Operating Engineer, 65, 119, 194, 257
Operating Room Technician, 20
Operations Manager, 62
Ophthalmic Medical Assistant, 20
Ophthalmologist, 147, 257
Optical Physicist, 35
Optical Technician, 164
Optician, 20, 257
Optometric Assistant, 20

Optometrist, 147, 257
Orchestra Conductor, 158
Orthodontist, 146, 257
Orthotics/Prosthetics Technician, 20, 179
Orthotist, 257
Osteopath, 146, 167, 257
Otolaryngologist, 257
Outplacement Specialist, 173, 257

Package Designer, 134
Packaging Engineer, 140
Painter, 32-33, 65, 211
Paleontologist, 26, 101, 258
Paperhanger, 65
Paralegal, 125, 128, 130, 185, 258
Paramedic, 41
Parasitologist, 17, 41, 258
Park Police, 96
Park Ranger, 96, 113, 176, 197, 258
Parole/Probation Officer, 125, 128, 170,
    258
Pastor, 182
Pastry Chef, 71
Patent Agent, 125, 258
Patent Examiner, 53
Patent Lawyer, 125, 258
Pathologist, 92, 146, 167, 173, 179, 197,
    258, 263, 265
Peace Corps/VISTA Volunteer, 93, 107, 188,
    191
Pediatrician, 146, 167, 258
Pedodontist, 258
Penologist, 128, 170, 173, 258
Perfusionist, 20, 258
Personnel Director, 78, 105, 116, 258
Pest Control Worker, 197
Pet Shop Manager, 197
Petroleum Engineer, 14, 50, 56, 101, 149
Petrologist, 98, 101, 259
Pharmaceutical Sales Representative, 53,
    134
Pharmacist, 23, 50, 53, 101, 167, 179, 259
Pharmacologist, 50, 53, 146, 167, 259
Photoengraver, 122, 259
Photogrammetric Technician, 98
Photogrammetrist, 56, 98, 101, 259
Photographer, 8, 30, 32-33, 59, 98, 158,
    197
Photojournalist, 33
Photo-Optics Technician, 83, 259
Phycologist, 44, 259
Physiatrist, 259
Physical Distribution Manager, 194
Physical Education Instructor, 176
Physical Therapist, 41, 155, 179, 259
Physical Therapy Assistant, 20
Physician, 20, 23, 41, 146, 167, 243, 256-
    257, 260, 262
Physician Assistant, 20, 23, 146, 167
Physicist, 14, 35, 53, 81, 101, 137, 164,
    240

Physiologist, 17, 41, 167, 177, 179, 259
Pipefitter, 65, 259
Pipeline Engineer, 56, 149
Plant Breeder, 44, 113, 260
Plant Engineer, 119
Plant Geneticist, 96, 113
Plasterer, 65, 260
Plastic Surgeon, 146, 260
Plastics Engineer, 50, 119, 140, 149
Playground Leader, 176
Playwright, 86, 260
Plumber, 65, 211
Podiatric Assistant, 20
Podiatrist, 146, 260
Police Commissioner, 128, 260
Police Officer, 128, 173
Police Supervisor, 68
Political Consultant, 170
Political Scientist, 107, 161, 170, 191
Politician, 68, 170
Polygraph Examiner, 128, 260
Preschool Teacher, 78
Priest, 182
Principal, 78
Printing Press Operator, 122
Prison Recreation Specialist, 176
Private Duty Nurse, 155
Private Investigator, 128
Probation Officer, 125, 128, 170, 173, 188,
    191, 258
Process Engineer, 119
Proctologist, 260
Producer, 32, 59, 158
Producer (Film, TV), 59
Product Manager, 134
Production Superintendent, 47, 260
Professional Athlete, 176
Programmer, 11
Project Manager, 65
Proofreader, 59, 86, 92
Psychiatric Nurse, 173
Psychiatric Social Worker, 105, 173, 188,
    260
Psychiatrist, 146, 167, 173, 260
Psychologist, 68, 78, 161, 173, 175, 188,
    191, 260
Psychometrist, 173, 261
Public Accountant, 11
Public Administrator, 107, 161, 191
Public Health Director, 41
Public Health Educator, 105, 261
Public Health Official, 170
Public Health Service Officer, 105, 261
Public Health Specialist, 197
Public Health Statistician, 105
Public Information Specialist, 152
Public Recreation Director, 170
Public Relations Manager, 191
Public Relations Specialist, 47, 59, 105,
    158, 173, 254, 261
Public Safety Captain, 128

Public Works Engineer, 56
Publisher, 0, 9, 59, 86, 161, 219, 246
Puppeteer, 158, 261
Purchasing Agent, 12, 89, 110, 116, 134, 261

Quality Control Engineer, 119
Quality Control Technician, 83

Rabbi, 182
Radar Technician, 84, 137
Radiation Therapy Technologist, 23, 261
Radio and Electrical Inspector, 84
Radio Engineer, 81
Radio Equipment Technician, 153
Radio Repairer, 84
Radiographer, 35, 261
Radiologic Health Specialist, 23
Radiological Technologist, 20
Radiologist, 146, 256, 261
Rancher, 95
Range Manager, 44, 95, 197
Reading Specialist/Consultant, 86
Real Estate Agent, 74, 134
Real Estate Buyer, 125
Receptionist, 185, 254
Records Manager, 185
Recreation Director, 47, 170, 176
Recreation Facility Manager, 176
Recreational Therapist, 155, 176, 179, 239, 261
Recruiter, 153
Reference Librarian, 131
Registered Nurse, 155, 261
Registrar, 78, 262
Religious Brother, 182, 262
Religious Education Teacher, 182
Religious Educational Administrator, 182
Religious Researcher, 182
Religious Sister, 182, 262
Religious Writer, 182
Reporter, 60, 86, 107, 170, 177, 185, 244
Reproductive Endocrinologist, 147
Research Analyst, 262
Research Assistant, 41, 98, 107, 161, 170, 191
Research Associate, 26
Research Engineer, 14, 50, 56, 119, 140, 149
Research Library Technician, 60
Research Technician, 35
Resident Manager, 116
Residential Counselor, 188
Resort Manager, 117, 176
Respiratory Therapist, 41, 155, 167, 179, 262
Respiratory Therapy Technician, 20
Restaurant Manager, 47, 89
Restaurant Owner, 71
Rigger, 65, 262
Robotics Technician, 62, 84

Roofer, 65
ROTC Instructor, 153

Safety Engineer, 14, 50, 56, 65, 81, 119, 140, 149, 262
Salad Maker, 71
Sales Manager, 48, 74, 110, 134
Sales Promotion Manager, 134
Sales Representative, 53, 74, 134, 254
Sales Supervisor, 134
Salvation Army Officer, 182
Sandwich Maker, 71
Sanitary Engineer, 57, 150, 262
Sanitation/Maintenance Worker, 89
School Administrator, 48, 170
School Counselor, 188
School Nurse, 155
School Psychologist, 78, 175, 188
School Superintendent, 78, 262
Science Technician, 53
Sculptor, 33
Secondary School Teacher, 78
Secret Service Agent, 68
Secretary, 87, 185-186, 211, 253-255
Securities Analyst, 74, 262
Securities Clerk, 38, 262
Securities Sales Agent, 134, 262
Security Officer, 129, 262
Seed Analyst, 44, 95, 113
Seismologist, 35, 98, 101, 164, 263
Service Station Worker, 194
Set Designer, 158
Set Up Worker, 122
Sheet Metal Worker, 66, 263
Sheriff, 68, 128
Ship's Pilot, 153
Shoe Repairer, 123
Sign Painter, 33
Silviculturist, 44, 95, 113, 263
Singer, 159
Ski Instructor, 177
Smoke Jumper, 95
Social Service Aide, 110, 188
Social Service Director, 188
Social Service Worker, 129
Social Worker, 26, 68, 78, 105, 110, 161, 173, 182, 188, 191, 242, 250, 258, 260, 263
Sociologist, 26, 98, 188, 191, 193, 245, 250, 258, 263
Software Engineer, 62
Software Package Developer, 62
Software Package Marketer, 62
Software Salesperson, 62, 263
Soil Conservationist, 17, 44, 95, 98, 113, 263
Soil Scientist, 18, 263
Sous Chef, 71, 263
Special Agent, 129, 248, 263
Special Collections Librarian, 131
Special Education Teacher, 78, 180, 263

Speech Pathologist, 92, 173, 179, 263
Speech Writer, 60, 87
Sports Marketer, 177, 264
Sports Reporter, 177
Sports/Special Events Executive, 134
Stage Manager, 159
Statistician, 12, 38, 62, 74, 105, 137-138,
    241, 264
Stenographer, 186
Steward/Stewardess, 89
Stockbroker, 39, 74, 264
Stone Mason, 66, 264
Store Controller, 134
Store Manager, 48, 86, 135
Storeroom Supervisor, 90
Stratigrapher, 101, 264
Structural Engineer, 29, 57, 264
Substance Abuse Counselor, 69
Surgeon, 96, 113, 146-147, 167, 260, 265
Surgical Technician, 20, 264
Surveying Technician, 171, 191
Surveyor, 29, 95, 98, 102, 137, 259, 264
Systems Analyst, 15, 35, 39, 62, 119, 131,
    137, 141, 153, 264
Systems Consultant, 62
Systems Engineer, 15, 119, 141, 150
Systems Manager, 62
Systems Programmer, 264

Tailor, 110, 264
Tax Accountant, 12
Tax Attorney, 125
Tax Preparer, 12, 39, 74
Taxi Driver, 194
Taxonomist, 42, 44, 95, 197, 264
Teacher (ESL), 78
Teacher Aide, 78
Technical Illustrator, 30, 265
Technical Photographer, 30
Technical Support Technician, 62
Technical Writer, 24, 26, 30, 53, 60, 62, 71,
    74, 81, 84, 87, 92, 102, 107, 113, 171,
    188, 197, 265
Technician, 265
Telephone Installer/ Repairer, 143
Terrazzo Worker, 66, 265
Test Engineer, 141
Textile Engineer, 51
Tilesetter, 66
Tissue Technologist, 24, 265
Title Attorney, 125, 265
Tool and Die Maker, 123, 137
Tool Programmer, 123, 265
Topographic Engineer, 153
Tour Planner, 116
Toxicologist, 51, 53, 168, 265
Traffic Court Magistrate, 126
Traffic Manager, 48, 194, 265
Train Conductor, 194
Trainer, 23, 153, 155, 176, 179
Translator, 87, 92, 152

Transmissions Engineer, 81
Transportation Engineer, 57, 194
Travel Agent, 93
Treasurer, 12, 39, 75, 138
Tree Nursery Manager, 96
Tree Surgeon, 96, 113, 265
Trial Court Judge, 126
Truck Driver, 194, 252
Trust Administrator, 39, 74, 265
Tutor, 78, 174, 189, 266
TV Director, 33, 48, 60
TV Technician, 84
Typesetter, 266
Typist, 186

Underwriter, 12, 266
Upholsterer, 123, 266
Urban Planner, 30, 57, 74, 99, 171, 191,
    266
Urologist, 147, 168, 266

Vending Machine Servicer, 143
Veterinarian, 18, 42, 147, 168, 197
Veterinary Assistant, 197
Veterinary Technician, 20
Video Engineer, 60
Video Recording Engineer, 81
Virologist, 45, 96, 266
Vocational Rehabilitation Counselor, 78,
    173, 180, 189, 266

Warden, 69, 129
Warehouse Manager, 48
Watchmaker, 143
Webmaster, 62, 266
Welder, 123, 266
Wholesaler, 48, 266
Wildlife Biologist, 197
Wildlife Manager, 96
Wireless Sales Worker, 135
Wireless Specialist, 266
Wood Scientist, 53
Wood Technologist, 45, 96
Word Processor, 62, 186

X-Ray Technician, 20

YMCA/YWCA Director, 48, 117
Youth Minister, 182

Zookeeper, 198
Zoologist, 42, 198, 256